...IES

ON

PRAGMATISM

Cornelis De Waal
Indian University-Purdue University

THOMSON

WADSWORTH

Australia • Canada • Mexico • Singapore • Spain • United Kingdom • United States

Printed in the United States of America
1 2 3 4 5 6 7   07 06 05 04

Printer: Thomson West

0-534-58404-7

For more information about our products, contact us at:
Thomson Learning Academic Resource Center
1-800-423-0563

For permission to use material from this text, contact us by:
Phone: 1-800-730-2214
Fax: 1-800-730-2215
Web: http://www.thomsonrights.com

Thomson Wadsworth
10 Davis Drive
Belmont, CA 94002-3098
USA

Asia
Thomson Learning
5 Shenton Way #01-01
UIC Building
Singapore 068808

Australia/New Zealand
Thomson Learning
102 Dodds Street
Southbank, Victoria 3006
Australia

Canada
Nelson
1120 Birchmount Road
Toronto, Ontario M1K 5G4
Canada

Europe/Middle East/South Africa
Thomson Learning
High Holborn House
50/51 Bedford Row
London WC1R 4LR
United Kingdom

Latin America
Thomson Learning
Seneca, 53
Colonia Polanco
11560 Mexico D.F.
Mexico

Spain/Portugal
Paraninfo
Calle/Magallanes, 25
28015 Madrid, Spain

For Ashley & Sophia Arisbe

Table of Contents

Preface

What I have to do is, as it were, to describe the office of a king; in doing which I must never fall into the error of explaining the kingly dignity by the king's usefulness, but I must leave neither his dignity nor his usefulness out of account.

—Ludwig Wittgenstein

This volume is a concise introduction to pragmatism. Starting point and recurrent theme is Charles Peirce's *pragmatic maxim,* which is found in his landmark 1878 "How to Make Our Ideas Clear." Next the attention shifts to William James, who made the maxim known, but also gave it a spin of his own, and to Ferdinand Schiller, who took James's interpretation even further left field. Both the Peircean and the James-Schiller line of pragmatism surface in a particularly vocal group of Italian pragmatists, the Leonardini. Among them are Papini, Prezzolini, Vailati, and Calderoni. These early pragmatists were influenced solely by the 1878 Peirce of "How to Make Our Idea Clear." Peirce's reaction to the developments to which his maxim had given rise, as well as the brand of pragmatism he developed in reply, is therefore given a separate chapter. This second chapter of Peirce is followed by an analysis of the instrumentalism of John Dewey. Next comes C. I. Lewis, who in important ways is a transitional figure, followed by a discussion of Charles Morris, Rudolph Carnap, and W. V. O. Quine, in an attempt to bring out the relation of pragmatism with logical positivism and the analytic tradition. The next two chapters are devoted to two contemporary pragmatists, who in many respects are diametrically opposed: Richard Rorty and Susan Haack. Whereas Rorty is often closest to Schiller (even though he generally allies himself with Dewey), Haack follows mostly in the footsteps of Peirce. The book concludes with some comments on the prospects of pragmatism, including an answer to the question "Why be a pragmatist?"

On Pragmatism

The philosophers treated in this volume are only the tip of the iceberg, and it is an iceberg that runs deep and wide. There are many more important figures than can with reasonable lucidity be treated here, and painful choices had to be made. Part of what motivated the choice made was to present the diversity of pragmatism, from the wild Papini to the meticulous Lewis, while staying close to its core idea, which is Peirce's 1878 pragmatic maxim. This means that pragmatism is considered first and foremost a doctrine of meaning. It should be added immediately, though, that since this is a doctrine that has deep ramifications for philosophy as a whole, it has flowered into a distinct and full-fledged philosophical framework so that one can truly speak of pragmatist philosophy and pragmatist philosophers.

Schiller once said about the diversity of pragmatism that there are as many pragmatisms as there are pragmatists. And since many pragmatists have changed their views, this estimate may even be called conservative. To make matters worse, the many strands of pragmatism are often ill at ease with each other, if not straightforwardly contradictory. Of course, that need not be something bad. As Peirce once optimistically declared, "[Pragmatism] is, so far, a house at war against itself concerning not inconsiderable questions; but perhaps this will not endanger its stability, and it certainly renders the discussions more interesting."[1] This is certainly true for the contemporary debate between Susan Haack and Richard Rorty, which is found in section 11.5.

A central theme of pragmatism is that philosophical research is a profoundly social enterprise. This is true also for the present volume, which would not have been possible without the generous support of many friends and colleagues. I would like to thank Martin Coleman, Mathias Girel, Micah Hester, Nathan Houser, Robert Lane, Rosa Mayorga, Hugh McDonald, Mark Migotti, Murray Murphey, Jaime Nubiola, Sandra Rosenthal, John Shook, and Robert Talisse for their most valuable comments on individual chapters. Special thanks go to Giovanni Maddelena and Suzanna Marietta who also helped translating several passages from Italian for chapter five, and to Luise Morton and Kelly Tully-Needler, who carefully read the entire manuscript for content, typos, and grammatical idiosyncracies. Of course, this volume would not have had the slightest chance of completion without the constant support of my wife Ashley, and the delightful distractions of our daughter Sophia Arisbe, who was born when the manuscript was about half finished. Many thanks, finally, to Tafika and Matopo, pragmatists at heart.

1

Pragmatism and Its Critics

As, to papal minds, protestantism has often seemed a mere
mess of anarchy and confusion, such, no doubt, will pragmatism often seem to ultra-rationalist minds in philosophy.

—William James[2]

Pragmatism emerged in the early 1870s when a small group of young men
from Cambridge, Massachusetts, met regularly to talk about philosophy.
The group included, among others, William James, Charles Sanders
Peirce, Oliver Wendell Holmes Jr., and Nicholas St. John Green. These
men called themselves, half-ironically and half-defiantly, "The
Metaphysical Club," since in the early 1870s metaphysics was considered
outmoded. Central to their discussions was Alexander Bain's definition of
belief as "that upon which a man is prepared to act." When that definition
is granted, Peirce later recalled, pragmatism follows almost immediately
as its natural outcome.

This is not to say that these men believed pragmatism was something
radically new, a revolutionary method that had never before been
discovered. It was rather a conscious and systematic adoption of a method
that philosophers have been practicing from antiquity onward. Peirce
boldly declared the newness of a philosophical idea as one of the surest
signs that it is false. And to show pragmatism's noble pedigree, he called
even Jesus a pragmatist, reading the latter's "ye may know them by their
fruit" as an early version of the pragmatic maxim. James sought to bring
home the same point when he subtitled his famous book *Pragmatism* as
"A New Name for Some Old Ways of Thinking." The British pragmatist
Ferdinand Schiller saw Protagoras as the first pragmatist, thereby situating
the birth of pragmatism in the fifth century B.C.

Taken broadly, pragmatism draws an intimate connection between
theory and practice, between thought and action. In its more narrow

interpretation, held most prominently by Peirce, it is solely a criterion of meaning, which stipulates that the meaning of *any* concept is nothing but the sum total of its conceivable practical consequences. On this view, concepts that have no conceivable practical consequences are meaningless, and if the conceivable practical consequences of two concepts are identical, both concepts are synonyms. In its broader interpretation, which began with James, pragmatism is not just a theory of meaning, but also, and more prominently, a theory of truth. As philosophy textbooks are fond of putting it, for the pragmatist something is true when it is advantageous to believe it.

The close connection between meaning and practical effects is not only present in the work of Peirce and James, but also in that of the other Metaphysical Club members. In an 1870 article for the *American Law Review*, Nicholas St. John Green argues that legal responsibility should not be defined abstractly as how far the individual's acts are removed from their effects (the classic doctrine of proximate and remote causes), but as whether the individual could predict that these effects would follow from his acts. In the same vein, Justice Oliver Wendell Holmes Jr. identifies the meaning of a law with how it causes the judge to rule in particular cases.

1.1 Pragmatism and America

Pragmatism is often hailed as America's contribution to world philosophy. The doctrine originated within the United States and in contrast to earlier American philosophy, is truly an American school of thought. Earlier schools, such as the New England Transcendentalists or the St. Louis Hegelians, were mostly extensions of the European philosophy that the colonists had brought with them and transplanted into the new world.

That pragmatism originated in America is not without significance. As Dewey keenly observes in *Reconstruction in Philosophy,* "The distinctive office, problems and subject matter of philosophy grow out of stresses and strains in the community life in which a given form of philosophy arises" (MW 12:256). Opinions are divided, however, on what these stresses and strains were. Suggestions include Puritanism, the pioneer mentality of the settlers, and the Civil War. In his monumental *The Protestant Ethic and the Spirit of Capitalism,* the German sociologist Max Weber sees a close connection between Calvinism and James's will-to-believe argument, adding that "James's pragmatic valuation of the significance of religious ideas according to their influence on life is . . . a true child of the world of ideas of the Puritan home of that eminent scholar."[3] Michael Novak, in *American Philosophy and the Future,* attributes pragmatism's distinctive edge to the pioneer mentality that had found its way into America's intellectual circles:

> On this at first dark continent, and now in the dark and unknown reaches of technological power, Americans have always sensed that there may not be any rules made up in advance, no finished and a priori world "out there" to operate as an absolute, secure standard by which to measure themselves.[4]

Louis Menand, in *The Metaphysical Club,* emphasizes the influence of the American Civil War (1861–65), which radically discredited the basic presuppositions and beliefs that had defined intellectual life before it.[5]

1.2 Critics of Pragmatism

Critics of pragmatism also love to point out that pragmatism originated in America. Its emphasis on "practical effects" and on the "cash value" of our ideas made it relatively easy to dismiss pragmatism offhandedly as a product of crass American capitalism and its apology.[6] Pragmatism is here seen as the reflection of a culture where the value of a painting is determined, and precisely quantified, on the auction block, and where the greatness of a movie or theater production equals its box-office revenue. What doesn't generate material benefit is meaningless. As Bertrand Russell, an early and outspoken critic of pragmatism, puts it, unwittingly confirming Novak's observation of pragmatism's pioneer mentality:

> Pragmatism appeals to the temper of mind which finds on the surface of this planet the whole of its imaginative material; which feels confident of progress, and unaware of non-human limitations to human power.[7]

In Russell's view the pragmatist's outlook is too narrow. It robs life "of all that gives it value, and [makes] Man himself smaller by depriving the universe which he contemplates of all its splendour."[8] The British author and culture critic G. K. Chesterton makes a similar observation when he observes, "Pragmatism is a matter of human needs; and one of the first human needs is to be something more than a pragmatist."[9]

Similar sentiments are expressed by Max Horkheimer, a member of the *Frankfurter Schule,* who saw in pragmatism the triumph of the means over the end, as it defines each end wholly in terms of the means by which to attain it. What cannot be reached, practically, must be wholly vacuous. It is, Horkheimer wrote in 1947, the philosophy of a society that has no

3

time to spare for reflection or meditation. For the pragmatist, Horkheimer contends, only those ideas are meaningful that produce "concrete answers to concrete questions, as posed by the interests of individuals, groups, or the community"; all other ideas are unproductive, meaningless, and a waste of time.[10] Such criticisms continue until today. The American bioethicist Leon Kass recently dismissed pragmatism as a thoughtless advance toward whatever serves expediency.[11]

John Dewey ridicules such fast-and-easy comparisons of pragmatism with certain perceived traits of the American people, stating that this sort of criticism

> is of that order of interpretation which would say that English neo-realism is a reflection of the aristocratic snobbery of the English; the tendency of French thought to dualism an expression of an alleged Gallic disposition to keep a mistress in addition to a wife. (MW 13:307)

At the same time Dewey acknowledges that pragmatism, like any intellectual enterprise, is in important ways a reflection of the social and cultural environment in which it emerged. But from there it is still a long way to the contention that pragmatism is merely "a formulated acquiescence in the immediately predominating traits of its day" (LW 3:147). In a criticism of Julien Benda's "The Attack on Western Morality," Dewey went straight in the counterattack:

> It is absolutism, not pragmatism, which rationalizes the success of the status quo by identifying the real with the rational and existence with the real. It is still absolutism, and not pragmatism, which makes success in accomplishing a specially devised result its ultimate and all-sanctifying goal at the price of any means. (LW 15:25)

Because of his repeated reference to the cash value of our ideas, James bears the brunt of the criticism. Ironically, the chief motivation that drove James was precisely the opposite. He hoped to restore a place for religious faith in an age that, in his view, had become overly materialistic and scientistic. Peirce makes similar observations when he calls capitalism "the gospel of greed."

1.3 Method, Not Theory

Pragmatism is a method for doing philosophy rather than a philosophical theory. In this sense it differs from, say, materialism. What makes someone a materialist is the belief, in some form or other, that matter is the primordial or fundamental constituent of the universe. Materialism is thus a theory about what the universe is like. Pragmatism makes no such claims, but rather concerns how we should do our business as philosophers, scientists, homicide detectives, accountants, etc., whenever we engage in inquiry. This is not to imply that method can be neatly separated from content, but the emphasis is clearly on method.

Pragmatism was originally devised as a method for determining the meaning of words, most significantly philosophical and scientific terms. Its initial impetus was polemic. The aim was to show that numerous philosophical terms had no meaning and that certain key philosophical problems were caused by terminological unclearness. In this sense the main objective of pragmatism was not different from that of the nineteenth-century positivists, who also sought to eradicate meaningless philosophical verbiage, in their case by replacing metaphysical speculations by what they considered solid empirical science.

For some, pragmatism is also a theory of truth. Even the pragmatists themselves are divided on the question whether the principle that defines pragmatism is merely a criterion of meaning or whether it is also a criterion of truth. Peirce maintained that they are altogether different issues and that pragmatism, as expressed in his principle, is strictly a criterion of meaning. What is often referred to as the pragmatist theory of truth results then from applying the pragmatist criterion of meaning to the concept of truth. For Peirce, "truth," like "hardness," "identity," "simultaneity," etc., is just one of those concepts that one should have a pragmatist conception of. What is called the pragmatist theory of truth is thus an outgrowth of the desire to clean up philosophical discourse. Hence it is a *consequence* of pragmatism, and certainly a very important one, but not a defining characteristic.

Much of the criticism of pragmatism is directed specifically against their conception of truth. Broadly speaking the criticism is that pragmatists have exchanged truth for gratification. In the pages that follow, we will look into this accusation, because, if justified, it undermines all forms of pragmatism, as even those that see pragmatism as merely a doctrine of meaning hold that "truth" is one concept to which this doctrine applies. Incidentally, the pragmatists were not the only ones to associate truth with tangible results. The same sentiment resonates firmly in Goethe's *was fruchtbar ist, allein ist wahr,* and Nietzsche famously identified knowledge with power.

2

Peirce and the
Principle of Pragmatism

Obstinate disputes in philosophy are maintained by *life*
presenting itself under diverse aspects. . . . My great word is
that the thing to go your bottom dollar on should not be a
doctrine but a method. For a vital method will correct itself
and doctrines too. Doctrines are crystals, methods are fer-
ments.

—Charles Sanders Peirce[12]

Peirce's pragmatism can be divided roughly into two periods. The first is
that of its initial formulation and is the subject of the current chapter. This
period culminates in Peirce's second "Illustrations of the Logic of
Science" paper entitled "How to Make Our Ideas Clear." In this paper,
which appeared in 1878, Peirce develops a method for determining the
meaning of a concept, which he summarizes in the form of a maxim. It is
this maxim that William James makes famous twenty years later in his
1898 Berkeley Union address, where he called it "the principle of
pragmatism."

   The second period, which is treated in chapter 6, begins around the
turn of the century. Motivated by the popularity pragmatism had gained,
but disappointed with the interpretation given to it by most of its
proponents, Peirce sought to show how his own version of pragmatism
differed from those that had become mainstream. In 1903, Peirce delivered
six lectures on pragmatism at Harvard, and two years later he published
three articles in the *Monist* outlining his views: "What Pragmatism Is,"
"Issues of Pragmaticism," and "Prolegomena to an Apology for

Pragmaticism." However, living in relative isolation in the small town of Milford, Pennsylvania, and without any students of his own to carry his views forward, Peirce's later attempts had little effect on the development of pragmatism for most of the twentieth century.

It is important to emphasize that this division into two parts is inspired by the *reception* of Peirce's pragmatism, not by a change in his own thought (as was the case, for instance, with the early and the late Wittgenstein). Peirce's views did change over time, but the changes were more gradual and multifaceted, and were only tangentially related to his criticisms of the other pragmatists. What motivates the division into an early and a late Peirce, devoting separate chapters to each, is historical circumstance: Peirce's influence on the early stages of pragmatism was almost exclusively confined to his 1878 "How to Make Our Ideas Clear."

2.1 The Limits of Thought

In 1851, when he was only twelve years old, Peirce discovered in his brother's bedroom a copy of Richard Whately's *Elements of Logic*. He immediately stretched himself out on the floor and began to read. The young Peirce quickly devoured the book, and from then on, logic would remain his passion. Peirce was not a dry, bookish logician, however. As he liked to remind his readers, he developed his views on logic and philosophy in the laboratory. The scope of this laboratory work is staggering. Far from being an armchair scientist, Peirce made important contributions to gravimetry, geodesy, astrophysics, and spectroscopy. Because of his scientific background, Peirce's approach to philosophy, and to pragmatism in particular, was most of all that of a scientist at work. It is no accident that his first statement of pragmatism—even though the term itself does not occur there—appeared in a series of articles called "Illustrations of the Logic of Science."

Peirce opens his "Illustrations of the Logic of Science" series with a paper entitled "The Fixation of Belief." Peirce continued there the criticism of Cartesian philosophy which he had begun almost a decade earlier in a series of articles for the *Journal of Speculative Philosophy*. In these articles, Peirce had argued that we have no power of intuition, we have no power of introspection, we cannot think otherwise than in signs, and we have no conception of the absolutely incognizable (EP1:30). By taking this position, Peirce went radically against the grain of established opinion. Philosophy, he maintained, was in need of a serious overhauling. Because Peirce's pragmatism developed largely from these four denials, I will discuss them each briefly.

7

Peirce's first objection is to the claim that we possess any intuitive knowledge. The notion of intuitive knowledge goes back at least to Plato and draws heavily on a comparison with the faculty of vision. Just as we see sensory objects when light shines upon them, so do we "see" intelligible objects when they are "illuminated" by what some have called the "light of reason." On this view, one has intuitive knowledge when one immediately "sees" that something is true. Classic examples are the claim that the whole is always greater than any of its parts, that whenever we think we must also exist, etc. This notion of intuitive knowledge is intimately tied to Descartes's conception of clear and distinct ideas, which proved to be at once a criterion of meaning and a criterion of truth. In the *Meditations on First Philosophy,* Descartes had derived the general rule that whatever is clearly and distinctly perceived is true.[13]

It would lead us too far astray to examine in detail Peirce's objections against this notion, but Peirce's objections are empirical, not a priori. He points to a number of circumstances where claims of intuitive knowledge are shown to be wrong or at least compromised beyond repair. Peirce argues, for instance, that our direct perception is seriously compromised by the ease with which magicians make us "see" things that do not happen. It also happens quite frequently that what seems absolutely clear and true at the outset later turns out to be deceptive and wrong. Take the thesis that the whole is always greater than any of its parts. This thesis is constantly confirmed in simple and convincing ways. Just try to cut up a birthday cake in a way that defies the maxim. In fact, this thesis is so deeply ingrained in our understanding of the world that it seems altogether impossible to conceive of anything for which this thesis would not hold, suggesting that it is a self-evident, universal truth.

Not quite. Take, instead of a birthday cake, the set of natural numbers and divide it into two equal parts: the set of odd numbers and the set of even numbers. Are these two sets really smaller than the set of natural numbers, as is required by the thesis? Let's first look at the set of even numbers. First, it can be established that this is truly a subset of the set of natural numbers. In fact, even numbers seem to make up exactly half of the natural numbers, with odd numbers making up the other half. This follows from the simple circumstance that there is an odd number in between any two subsequent even numbers. But although the set of even numbers is thus truly a part of the set of natural numbers, and one that is equal in size to the set of numbers not included (the set of odd numbers), the set of even numbers, far from being smaller than the set of natural numbers, turns out be exactly the same size: there are precisely as many even numbers as there are natural numbers. For this we only have to multiply each natural number by two. This will give us a set of numbers that has just as many members as the set of natural numbers (as for each natural number there is exactly one number that is its double), but which is also identical to the set of even numbers, as the double of each natural number (whether the original is odd or even) is always an even number. Consequently, the thesis that the whole is always greater than any of its parts, which was believed to be a self-evident truth for over two millennia, cannot be considered intuitive knowledge. In fact, the thesis is false as we have here a case where cutting something in equal parts gives two halves that each have the very same size as what they are halves of.[14]

Peirce's rejection of intuitive knowledge, and of the Cartesian notion of clear and distinct ideas that comes with it, forced him to develop a new criterion of meaning. The pragmatic maxim, or as James calls it, "the principle of pragmatism," gives him such a criterion.

Peirce's second denial is that we have no power of introspection. This again puts Peirce on a direct collision course with Descartes. Descartes's argument in the *Meditations* not only demands that we have such a power, but it also privileged it. According to Descartes, we are much more familiar with our own mind than we are with the world in which we live. Peirce turns Descartes's approach literally inside-out. According to Peirce, we *first* learn about the so-called external world, and *then* derive from our interaction with this external world that we have a self and what this self entails. Hence, for Peirce, our knowledge does not progress, as with Descartes, from the inside out, but from the outside in. Peirce's rejection of the power of introspection follows from his earlier denial of intuitive knowledge.

Peirce's third denial is that we cannot think without signs. This third objection follows straight from the previous denial of introspection. If we have no direct access to our own thoughts, then we can only access our own thoughts indirectly through their external aspects, that is, through how they present themselves to us, as signs. But this is as much as to say that the *only* thought we can *cognize* is thought in signs, and since it belongs to the essence of thought that it can be cognized (incognizable thoughts being a contradiction in terms), all thought must be in signs. This has important ramifications, because the meaning of a sign lies in what it points at. Consequently, if all thought is in signs, the meaning of any thought lies in the thoughts it calls up. As we will see, this future-directed aspect of thought is central to pragmatism.

Finally, Peirce argues that the absolutely incognizable is absolutely inconceivable. Peirce is here directing his criticism to those who believe that there are (or may be) certain things that are utterly beyond our reach,

9

so that they cannot possibly be known.[15] It is in his critique of this line of thought that Peirce first introduces his *pragmatic maxim:*

> There can be no conception of the absolutely incognizable, since nothing of that sort occurs in experience. But *the meaning of a term is the conception which it conveys.* Hence, a term can have no such meaning. (EP1:24; emphasis added)

Although this is Peirce's first published formulation of the maxim (albeit not the one that James later referred to), the idea behind it was entertained already a few years before in a notebook entry that is dated 20 November 1866. On that day Peirce concludes, "What is not a question of a possible experience is not a question of fact" (W1:9).

Peirce's four claims concerning the limits of our thought (that we have no power of intuition, that we have no power of introspection, that we can think only in signs, and that we have no conception of the absolutely incognizable) pave the way for Peirce's own philosophy.

2.2 The Purpose of Thought

Returning to Peirce's "Illustrations of the Logic of Science" papers, we can see that his starting point differs dramatically from the earlier approaches of Descartes and Locke. Descartes began by doubting everything in an almost desperate attempt to see whether anything was beyond doubt. What he found was that when he is doubting he cannot possibly doubt that he is doubting, which led him to his famous conclusion, "I think, therefore I am," which he then made the unshakable foundation of his philosophical system.

Locke rejected this kind of reasoning, arguing instead that we can analyze all our thoughts and perceptions and break them down into their most basic components, which he called "simple ideas." These simple ideas, analogous to the atoms of classical physics in that they are discrete and cannot be further divided, Locke considered the basic building blocks of all our ideas, ranging all the way from our ideas of gold and lithium to those of honesty and life insurance. Locke called the latter "complex ideas." According to Locke, we cannot doubt the simple ideas we have. We either have a simple idea or we don't. We can only raise doubts about what the simple ideas we have represent. For instance, we can have all the simple ideas that are commonly associated with gold, but doubt whether the object that is in front of us is really made of gold. To put it very briefly, Locke made "simple ideas" the unshakable foundation of all our knowledge.

Peirce breaks radically from both traditions. Instead of singling out specific ideas as absolutely certain and building his philosophy upon them, he begins with the beliefs we possess when we begin our inquiry. Inquiry always takes place against a backdrop of beliefs that are taken for granted. The archeologist who wants to know who built the pyramid of Cheops not only takes it for granted that there is an external world and that the pyramid is part of it, but also that most of our knowledge about ancient Egypt is more or less correct (our translations of the hieroglyphic script, the dating of the pyramid in relation to other ancient structures, the assumption that the pyramids were built as tombs for pharaohs, how they were built, etc.).

As with Descartes, Peirce begins by contrasting doubt with belief. According to Peirce, these are two states of mind that are relatively easy to distinguish. The state of doubt, Peirce observes, is "an uneasy and dissatisfied state from which we struggle to free ourselves" (EP1:114). In contrast, the state of belief is "a calm and satisfactory state" (ibid.). Not only do we feel a strong desire to change doubt into belief, but we even do our very best to maintain the beliefs we have to avoid lapsing back into doubt. As Peirce puts it, "We cling tenaciously, not merely to believing, but to believing just what we do believe" (EP1:114).

There is another important difference between states of doubt and belief, and this has to do with action. Doubt and belief each lead to action, but they do so differently. Doubting is very much like having an itch. It requires immediate action directed to its relief. Doubt is thus a direct stimulus to inquiry, and we stop inquiring as soon as the doubt is gone, just as we stop scratching when the itch disappears.

Belief, Peirce observes, does not make us act with the same immediacy. Instead, it puts us into "such a condition that we shall behave in some certain way, when the occasion arises" (EP1:114). That is to say, for Peirce, belief is the establishment of a certain *habit* that will determine how we will act when appropriately stimulated. As is shown later, this notion of beliefs as habits is crucial to Peirce's pragmatism and marks a major difference between Peirce's view and the pragmatisms of James and Schiller, who focus rather on the particular *consequences* of a belief, or the particular sensations we should expect if the belief were true.

Since, for Peirce, the very motive of inquiry is to rid ourselves from the discomfort of doubt, the ultimate aim of all inquiry is nothing other than to regain a state of belief. The belief arrived at is not necessarily *true* belief. *Any* belief that satisfies us will work, no matter whether it happens to be true or false. By taking this course, Peirce makes the attainment of belief, or the settlement of one's opinion, the sole purpose of inquiry.

11

Peirce's doubt-belief theory fits nicely with the views expressed by Darwin more than two decades earlier in *The Origin of Species*. Inquiry, or the exercise of reason, is no longer the godlike feature that separates man from beast, but is a mechanism by which certain organisms adapt themselves to concrete changes in their environment so as to regain their homeostatic equilibrium.

2.3 The Fixation of Belief

Given the previous account of inquiry and belief, the central question becomes, How can we fix our beliefs in such a way that we are unlikely to fall back to a state of doubt? In "The Fixation of Belief" Peirce discussed four methods: the method of tenacity, the method of authority, the a priori method, and what he called "the scientific method." For each of these methods, Peirce examined how well it succeeds in fixing our belief.

The first and most primitive method is the method of tenacity. On this method, opinion is settled purely by obstinately holding on to one's beliefs with all one's might. One could choose to actively avoid interacting with people with different opinions, or one could develop a habit of despising and offhandedly rejecting everything that challenges one's own beliefs. Conspiracy theorists often think in this manner. They fully embrace all evidence in support of their view (say, that an alien spaceship crashed near Roswell) and reject or 'reinterpret' everything that counts against it.

In Peirce's view this first method only works up to a point. Our confidence in our own beliefs is too easily shaken when interacting with others, or when we are confronted with brute facts. As Peirce put it, "The social impulse is against it. The man who adopts it will find that other men think differently from him, and it will be apt to occur to him, in some saner moment, that their opinions are quite as good as his own, and this will shake his confidence in his belief" (EP1:116). As Mark Twain once captured it brilliantly for religious beliefs, "The easy confidence with which I know another man's religion is folly teaches me to suspect that my own is also."

The second method aims to solve this problem by raising the method of tenacity to the social level. This results in what Peirce names the method of authority. On this second method, belief is not fixed by the individual itself, but is enforced by a social institution, such as the church or state. The individual no longer needs to shield itself from contrary evidence, as with the method of tenacity, but contrary evidence is here purposely withheld from people by a regulating institution through censorship and the oppression, or even elimination, of so-called subversive elements.

The method of authority has a far better chance of success than the method of tenacity. The history of organized religion testifies to this. As Peirce remarks, "Except the geological epochs, there are no periods of time so vast as those which are measured by some of these organized faiths" (EP1:118). However, as no institution can undertake to regulate opinion on *every* subject, this method too is unlikely to fix belief in the long run. For instance, Galileo's fascination with a swinging lamp in the cathedral of Pisa when he attended mass as a young boy stimulated his interest in physics, which led eventually to the destruction of the long held and authoritatively fixed belief that the sun revolved around a stationary earth that is positioned at the very center of the universe.

The third method of fixing belief Peirce names the a priori method. On this method, belief is fixed by seeking out those beliefs that are agreeable to reason. With this Peirce is not thinking of beliefs that agree with empirical facts, but beliefs that we find ourselves inclined to believe because they, so to say, "sound good." Although Peirce found this method superior to the first two, he still denied that this method is likely to result in stable belief. He observes, "The opinions which today seem most unshakable are found tomorrow to be out of fashion" (CP 5.382n). This means that, like the methods of tenacity and authority, the a priori method is unlikely to result in a stable belief. It is rather to be expected, Peirce remarks, that the pendulum of taste will endlessly swing back and forth between a number of alternatives (EP1:119).

Part of what lies behind Peirce's criticism of the a priori method is his earlier dismissal of intuitive knowledge, discussed above. If we have no intuitive knowledge, then a mere inclination to believe, however strong, can never become sufficient grounds for knowledge. The whole notion of intuitive knowledge trades on the very idea that if something is agreeable to reason, to the extent that we cannot possibly see anything wrong with it, then it must be true. However, the history of thought shows ample examples of such beliefs that were later found to be incorrect or at least disputable. They include the already mentioned belief that the whole is always greater than any of its parts, the longheld conviction that the stars and the planets move in circles, the belief that the earth is the center of the universe (with the entire universe revolving around it), and the belief that the order in the universe can be explained only in terms of a rational Designer.

Peirce's dismissal of the a priori method, with the notion of intuitive knowledge that lies behind it, is also closely related to Peirce's criticism of those who confound logic (the study of how people should think) with psychology (the study of how people do think). Although Peirce raises this criticism well before "The Fixation of Belief," I will postpone a discussion of this aspect of Peirce's thought until chapter 6, where it is examined within the context of Peirce's mature views on pragmatism.

This third method differs from the first two in an important respect. Not only does this third method provide us with an impulse to believe, as did the others, but it also determines *what* is to be believed, namely, one should believe what is agreeable to reason. Consequently, this time there is an intrinsic relation between the belief and how adherence to the belief is secured. Such a relation is absent in the previous two methods, where the content of the belief is wholly immaterial to how the belief is attained. What secures the belief in the first two methods is not the content of the belief, but the willpower and the ability of individuals (or with the second method, of the authorities), to entrench existing beliefs and suppress dissenting opinions. Alternatively, one could argue that whereas the method of authority involves censorship and indoctrination, the a priori method involves something similar, namely self-censorship and self-indoctrination, thus reducing the a priori method to a more refined version of the method of tenacity.

The fourth and final method Peirce distinguished is the scientific method. This method differs from the first three in that the fixation of the belief is no longer a purely human endeavor, in the sense that what ideas are fixed is ultimately determined by what we wish to believe. In its stead our beliefs are determined "by something upon which our thinking has no effect" (EP1:120). The scientific method, Peirce observes, proceeds from the hypothesis that

> there are real things, whose characters are entirely independent of our opinions about them; those realities affect our senses according to regular laws, and, though our sensations are as different as our relations to the objects, yet, by taking advantage of the laws of perception, we can ascertain by reasoning how things really are; and any man, if he have sufficient experience and he reason enough about it, will be led to the one true conclusion. (EP1:120)

About fifteen years later, when preparing these articles for a book, Peirce further explicates this method by contrasting it with the a priori method discussed above. Within the scientific method, Peirce explains,

14

changes of opinion are brought about by events beyond human control. All mankind were so firmly of opinion that heavy bodies must fall faster than light ones, that any other view was scouted as absurd, eccentric, and probably insincere. Yet as soon as some of the absurd and eccentric men could succeed in inducing some of the adherents of common sense to look at their experiments—no easy task—it became apparent that nature would not follow human opinion, however unanimous. So there was nothing for it but human opinion must move to nature's position. (CP 5.384n)

As opposed to the first three methods, where human understanding sets the terms, the scientific method proceeds from the recognition that nature does not accommodate itself to our beliefs, but that our beliefs must accommodate themselves to nature. True, nature does accommodate itself to some extent to human *action*—we can even change the course of entire rivers—but it does so only up to a point and only on its own terms. Hence, by the fourth method, we fix our beliefs by having external realities guide our thoughts, as opposed to having our thoughts guide themselves. This process only results in a fixed belief, however, when these external realities do not pull us in many directions at once, but exert a truly centripetal force upon our thoughts. That there is such a permanent externality that exhibits a centripetal force upon our thought, Peirce sees confirmed in the enormous progress that was being made by science:

Who would have said, a few years ago, that we could ever know of what substances stars are made whose light may have been longer in reaching us than the human race has existed? Who can be sure of what we shall not know in a few hundred years? Who can guess what would be the result of continuing the pursuit of science for ten thousand years, with the activity of the last hundred? And if it were to go on for a million, or a billion, or any number of years you please, how is it possible to say that there is any question which might not ultimately be solved? (EP1:140)

Later, Peirce acknowledged that there might be important questions that remain, in the end, unanswered. But that does not take away the need that we should always proceed on "[the] *hope* that the particular question into which we are inquiring is susceptible of an approximate answer in a reasonable time" (R 422:16). That is to say, for Peirce, the idea that there is a reality becomes a practical postulate of reason.

15

Peirce not only believed that inquiry would eventually lead to the right answers, he also maintained that in many cases we have already found the right answer, even though we cannot say for any *particular* question that we have found it. In this way, Peirce sought to wedge a third option between skepticism and dogmatism, which he named fallibilism. The skeptics insist that we can never know anything for sure and that we should therefore suspend our judgment. The dogmatists, in turn, believe that some truths are self-evident, and they found their philosophic edifices thereon. Peirce rejects the dogmatist's claim that we know with certainty that some particular beliefs are true, while at the same time dismissing the skeptic's conclusion that it follows from this that all our beliefs must be regarded untrustworthy. Instead, Peirce argues that overall we can trust our beliefs, but we should not bet our lives on any single one of them; a view he later referred to as critical common-sensism (section 6.4). In Peirce's eyes, the skeptic makes the basic mistake of concluding from the fact that *each* belief can be doubted, that therefore *all* beliefs can be doubted. But these are different things. If at an intersection you can go in any direction, this does not mean that you can go in all of them at once.

To conclude, these are the four ways Peirce thinks belief can be fixed. We have seen that Peirce sees fixing belief as the sole purpose of inquiry, and that for a belief to be fixed it is not necessary that the belief be true (it suffices that it is *believed* to be true). Now it may be objected that the purpose of inquiry is not belief, but action. For instance, when we inquire into the cause of a fever, the aim of the inquiry is not to fix our belief (or to alleviate ourselves from the discomfort of doubt), but to act, which is, in this case, to cure the disease that causes the fever. However, this objection rests upon a misconception. The purpose of inquiry is a belief which, being a *disposition* to act, will cause the inquirer to act when he or she is properly stimulated.

Peirce's argument in "The Fixation of Belief" is often criticized. Not only are there many instances where the first three methods have a distinct edge above the scientific method, but the scientific method itself also seems to generate more doubt than belief. It is not uncommon that in utilizing the scientific method we uncover whole new areas we had never even dreamt of before and which introduce all sorts of new doubts. One only has to think of the discovery of subatomic particles or the use of radio telescopes to listen for extraterrestrial intelligence.

Others protest that Peirce's list of four ways of fixing belief is arbitrary and incomplete. One possible defect is that he pays no attention to positive reinforcement as a method for fixing belief. On this method, people are *rewarded* when they hold certain beliefs, rather than being punished when they make certain transgressions. Positive reinforcement can be developed into a far more refined tool for social and psychological control than is attainable through the old-fashioned method of fear and punishment. Consider, for instance, Rousseau's remarkable advice for teachers, in *Émile ou de l'éducation*:

> Let [the child] believe that he is always in control, though it is always you who really controls. There is no subjugation so perfect as that which keeps the appearance of freedom, for in that way one captures volition itself. The poor baby, knowing nothing, able to do nothing, having learned nothing, is he not at your mercy? Can you not influence him as you wish? . . . Doubtless he ought only to do what he wants; but he ought to want to do only what you want him to do.[16]

This method is far more subtle than that of authority, as you do not just control what people can—or dare to—believe, but you can also control what they *want* to believe.

There is no doubt that in Peirce's mind the scientific method was the most advanced. At the same time, however, he maintains that in their own special way, each of the four methods is legitimate and could even be preferred over the scientific method as the best way of fixing belief. Hence, Peirce does not hold that the scientific method should replace the others.

2.4 The Fixation of Meaning

In the second of his "Illustrations of the Logic of Science" papers, called "How to Make Our Ideas Clear," Peirce developed what is best described as a theory of meaning. In this paper, Peirce argues that there are three different grades of clearness that our ideas can reach. Peirce's conception of meaning follows directly from the doubt-belief theory of inquiry he developed in "The Fixation of Belief." If the sole purpose of inquiry is to establish belief, and if belief is a habit or a disposition to act, then the meaning of a word, sentence, or road sign must naturally be understood in terms of the habits connected with it; that is to say, in terms of how it leads us to act. I know what words such as "chair" and "cauliflower" mean when I associate with them certain reasonably well-defined habitual responses or attitudes. Peirce goes even further. For him, those responses or attitudes actually determine what those words mean; that is to say, they constitute their *entire* meaning. There is nothing else that is required, such as an intuition of chairness or of cauliflowerhood. As Peirce puts it

17

concisely, "What a thing means is simply what habits it involves" (EP1:131).

The first and lowest grade of clearness that Peirce distinguishes is obtained when an idea is "so apprehended that it will be recognized wherever it is met with, and so that no other will be mistaken for it" (EP1:124). Our idea of "chair" is of this kind. We recognize a chair the moment we see one. Similarly, the pawnbroker who can see instantly whether a piece of jewelry is made of gold has a clear idea of gold. Of course he could be mistaken and call something gold when it is not. But, even then, we would acknowledge at least that it looked like gold. To know what a word means does not entail that one is infallible when applying it.

For many of our conceptions, the clearness with which we apprehend them does not extend beyond this first level. In Peirce's view, however, this first grade of clearness is not substantial enough to act as a *criterion* of meaning. What this first grade in the end comes down to, he argues, is only "a subjective feeling of mastery which may be entirely mistaken" (EP1:125).

The second grade of clearness is obtained when the idea does not merely seem clear at the outset, as with the first method, but can also be demarcated with enough precision to sustain the test of dialectical examination, meaning that subsequent discussions will not bring to light any points of obscurity connected with it (EP1:125). This second grade of clearness is traditionally obtained by developing abstract criteria that unambiguously determine what falls under the conception and what does not. The scientific definition of gold is an example of an idea that has reached this second grade of clearness. By this definition, gold is defined as the element that has atomic number 79, meaning that it has exactly 79 protons in its nucleus. This definition uniquely determines gold, since no other element has this atomic number. Peirce's second grade of clearness comes close to the traditional notion of clear and distinct ideas that is found in Descartes, Leibniz, and others.[17]

A problem with definitions like these is that they are made entirely in the abstract. Consequently, they do not provide any guidelines on how to determine whether an object we encounter actually falls under it; they do not even reveal whether they apply to anything to begin with. There are excellent definitions of centaurs, but that does not mean that centaurs exist. Similarly, the definition of gold given above only stipulates that *if* something fits the criteria of the definition, then it is by definition gold. In other words, to say that something is made of gold *means* that the definition of gold applies to it.

18

In a sense, it is misleading to say that ideas of the second grade of clearness are the product of definitions that are made entirely in the abstract, since this second grade is generally built upon the first. Talking about gold in terms of its atomic number is in essence an attempt to speak in more precise terms about the stuff the pawnbroker calls gold. This is not to deny that sometimes we come to know something first through its abstract definition. For instance, when Dmitry Mendeleyev published his periodic table, it defined several elements in terms of their atomic number that were only later discovered to exist.

Peirce aims to overcome the deficiency of traditional definitions by introducing what became later known as the pragmatic maxim:

> Consider what effects, that might conceivably have practical bearings, we conceive the object of our conception to have. Then, our conception of these effects is the whole of our conception of the object. (EP1:132)

Application of this maxim to a conception of the second grade of clearness gives us what Peirce calls the third grade of clearness. A crucial advantage of this third grade of clearness is that it relates meaning directly to the process of inquiry, instead of imposing it upon inquiry from without as an abstract definition.

In short, pragmatism is, for Peirce, a method for ascertaining the meaning of concepts, ideas, beliefs, claims, propositions, etc., of anything that can act as a sign. This view Peirce would maintain his whole life. As he told the audience of his "Harvard Lectures on Pragmatism" in 1903, "One of the faults that I think [the new pragmatists] might find with me is that I make pragmatism to be a mere maxim of logic instead of a sublime principle of speculative philosophy" (EP2:134). What pragmatism boils down to, Peirce explains not much later in the same lecture, is the ability to say "here is a definition and it does not differ at all from your confusedly apprehended conception because there is no *practical* difference" (EP2.141). As will appear in chapter 5, this is a far cry from the views of someone like Giovanni Papini, who sought to mold his pragmatism into a tool that would enable us to become nothing less than gods.

2.5 Applications of the Pragmatic Maxim

Immediately after introducing the pragmatic maxim, Peirce sought to explicate the maxim further by applying it to a number of concepts. One of them is the concept of weight: "To say that a body is heavy means simply that, in the absence of opposing force, it will fall," adding that this is "evidently the whole conception of weight" (EP1:133). Similarly, when the physicist speaks of a "natural force," what is meant with this notion "is completely involved in its effects" (ibid.). Applying the pragmatic maxim to scientific concepts, such as weight or force, results in more well-defined conceptions than we would have otherwise.

In contrast, the notion of transubstantiation—the change of bread and wine into the body and blood of Christ during the Eucharist—fails the pragmatic test. According to Catholic dogma, the bread and wine literally change into the body and blood of Christ, but they do so without changing any of their perceptible qualities. That is to say, after the transubstantiation, the two still look, taste, and smell like ordinary bread and wine.

It is quite easy to obtain an idea of transubstantiation that reaches the second grade of clearness, as such a notion fits in very well with the classic substance-attribute view. On this view, the object, or substance, is distinguished from its qualities, or attributes. This distinction was introduced, in part, to allow for accidental change. When we say "Socrates is bearded," "Socrates" is the substance, and "being bearded" is the attribute. Now, were Socrates to shave his beard, he would no longer be bearded, but he would still be Socrates.

The substance-attribute view has given us the widely accepted notion of transformation. What happens in a transformation, say from caterpillar to butterfly, is that the attributes change, while the substance—i.e., that which *has* the attributes—remains the same. The exact same animal that had the attributes of a caterpillar now has the attributes of a butterfly.

What happens in transubstantiation can easily be explained along the same lines. As opposed to a change of attributes that leaves the substance unaffected—as with the change from caterpillar to butterfly—transubstantiation involves a change of substance that leaves the attributes unaffected. This is precisely what Catholics claim happens to the bread and wine during the Eucharist. However, when we apply Peirce's pragmatic maxim to the concept of transubstantiation, the idea is directly shown to be devoid of meaning because, by its very definition, transubstantiation can have no conceivable practical bearings.

Peirce's criticism of transubstantiation is part of a deeper criticism based on the view, referred to earlier, that what is absolutely incognizable is absolutely inconceivable. This view does away with the philosophical notion of an incognizable substance (known only through its attributes), on which the idea of transubstantiation trades. The same argument can be brought against Descartes's malicious demon, who makes him believe that he has hands, and eyes, and feet, etc., and that there are trees, lakes, and mountains, and so on, while in fact there is nothing of the kind.[18] The concept of such a deceiving demon fails the pragmatic maxim, for the very same reason that transubstantiation does; namely, whether there is such a demon or not makes no conceivable practical difference. For us, everything remains just as it is.[19]

Interestingly, William James reached the opposite conclusion, arguing that transubstantiation does have practical effects and is thus pragmatically meaningful, even though the underlying philosophical concept of substance has none and must be dismissed as meaningless. However, there is an important difference between the views of Peirce and James, and one that is best laid immediately on the table. Whereas Peirce is thinking of the practical effects caused by *the belief being true,* James is thinking of the practical effects of *the belief being believed to be true.* We return to this in the following chapter.

The application that raised the most dust, however, is not the one on transubstantiation, but the one on the concept of hardness. What do we mean when we say that a diamond is hard, Peirce asks, and he replies with confidence:

> Evidently that it will not be scratched by many other
> substances. The whole conception of this quality, as of every
> other, lies in its conceived effects. There is absolutely no
> difference between a hard thing and a soft thing so long as
> they are not brought to the test. (EP1:132)

In this passage Peirce not only reduces the meaning of "hardness" to the practical effects we associate with certain objects (for instance, that we cannot scratch them with a knife), but he reduces it still further by strictly limiting it to the *actual* effects experienced. Only when objects are *brought to the test,* for instance by trying to scratch them with a knife, can we say that they are hard or soft, depending on whether the knife leaves a mark. As long as the object has *not* been brought to the test, Peirce continues, we cannot truly say that the object is hard. For all we know all untouched objects are soft, with some of them hardening when they are touched, their hardness increasing with pressure until they are scratched. This leads Peirce to conclude "that the question *of what would occur* under circumstances which do not actually arise is not a question of fact, but only of the most perspicuous arrangement of [these facts]" (EP1:132; emphasis added).

Peirce's view at this point differs from the one he held in the early 1870s, and to which he would later return. In one of his numerous attempts to write a logic book, Peirce concludes with respect to the hardness of a diamond,

> But though the hardness is entirely constituted by the fact of another stone rubbing against the diamond yet we do not conceive of it as beginning to be hard when the other stone is rubbed against it; on the contrary, we say that it is really hard the whole time, and has been hard since it began to be a diamond. And yet there was no fact, no event, nothing whatever, which made it different from any other thing which is not so hard, until the other stone was rubbed against it. (W3:30)[20]

What happens in "How to make Our Ideas Clear," however, is not a mere slip of the pen. Around that time, Peirce had come to reject the view that is tacitly implied in his earlier account, namely, that what would occur when certain circumstances were to take place is a real fact. Because of this, Peirce came to reject subjunctive and counterfactual conditionals as proper tools for clarifying our ideas.

A *subjunctive conditional* is a claim like the following: "Were I to fly to Rome, I would land in Italy." This statement is generally thought to be true, independent of whether I would ever fly to Rome. Were I never to fly to Rome, the statement would still be considered true. What suffices is that the antecedent *can* be materialized. That is, we *can* make the antecedent true by taking a plane to Rome.

With *counterfactual conditionals*—counterfactuals for short—the situation is different. Take the following example: "Had I flown to Rome last Fall, I would have landed in Italy." This claim also rings true; however, whereas with subjunctive conditionals the antecedent could be made true, with a counterfactual the antecedent cannot be materialized. Calling the *objects* of counterfactuals real facts seems to be especially problematic, as counterfactuals are by their very nature *counter* the facts; it is a real fact that I *did not* fly to Rome last fall.

Accepting subjunctive conditionals would allow us to say that certain objects that have not yet been brought to the test can still be called hard on the grounds that *if* they were to be brought to the test, they *would* not get scratched.

Allowing for counterfactual conditionals would even enable us to call something hard that has not been tested and can no longer be tested, for instance, because it no longer exists or because it has changed considerably in a way that is irreversible. Accepting counterfactual conditionals would allow us to call certain objects hard on the grounds that *had* they been brought to the test, they *would not have been* scratched.

Later, Peirce came to repudiate this radical dismissal of subjunctive and counterfactual conditionals. The step to remedy this, however, is by no means a small one. It involves the acceptance of real possibilities and real habits; or as Peirce puts it, of real can-bes and real would-bes. It may even involve the acceptance of certain real would-have-beens, real might-have-beens, etc. According to Peirce, the denial of real possibilities results from the in his eyes erroneous view that the potential, or possible, "is nothing but what the actual makes it to be" (CP 1.422). Peirce denies that possibilities can be thus reduced, remarking that "it is sheer insanity to deny the reality of the possibility of my raising my arm, even if, when the time comes, I do *not* raise it" (CP 4.579). Around the same time, Peirce describes the quality of hardness as "a capacity or a habit, the possibility that its subject should sustain the moderate pressure of a knife edge drawn over it without being scratched" (R 283:157).

To accept that some possibilities are real Peirce later comes to regard as indispensable for pragmatism. For this reason, Peirce holds that one can only be a pragmatist if one is also a realist, meaning that one accepts that there is more to reality than existing individuals alone. We will return to this in chapter 6. It is important, though, to keep this later view in mind when examining the views of James and Schiller, as both reject this type of realism.

The application of the pragmatic maxim is by no means confined to scientific or religious concepts, such as hardness, weight, transubstantiation, and force. It should be applied equally to the most basic philosophical conceptions. The philosophical conception Peirce chooses as an example in "How to Make Our Ideas Clear" is that of reality. As it turns out, however, this conception is closely related to that of truth. Since the pragmatists' conception of truth has come to play such a dominant role in the development of pragmatism, the application of Peirce's pragmatic maxim to the conception of truth is discussed instead.

2.6 The Pragmatic Conception of Truth

As shown in the previous sections, the pragmatic maxim is for Peirce a criterion of meaning, *not* a criterion of truth. Having said that, it should be added that the maxim can, and even should, be applied to the existing notion of truth, which we may assume to have reached the second grade of clearness. Applying the pragmatic maxim to the existing notion of truth is what is often referred to as the pragmatic conception of truth. It is important, though, to realize that this new conception of truth does not stand all by itself, as if philosophy could be saved simply by furnishing it with a pragmatic conception of truth. The pragmatic maxim should be applied not just to the concept of truth, but to all core philosophical conceptions, such as identity, reality, leading principle, equality, personhood, autonomy, necessity, freedom, infinity, etc.

In "How to Make Our Ideas Clear," Peirce does not directly apply the pragmatic maxim to the concept of truth. Instead he applies it to the concept of reality, which is intimately connected with that of truth. About the relation between the two, Peirce writes later, when replying to a criticism by *Monist* editor Paul Carus, "My view is that the real is nothing but the immediate object in a true cognition"; it is that which a true cognition (whether it's an idea, belief, statement, etc.) is about (R 958:205).

According to Peirce, our conceptions of truth and reality do attain the first grade of clearness. We use both terms with perfect confidence not doubting even for a moment that we know their meaning. Our concept of reality reaches the second grade of clearness with a definition that can be traced back to the medieval philosopher Johannes Duns Scotus. By Scotus's definition, something is real when it is independent of what you or I or anyone in particular thinks it to be.[21] This definition furnishes a precise demarcation by delineating clearly and unambiguously the difference between reality and its opposite, fiction. In this manner we obtain a clear-cut rule for distinguishing what is real from what isn't.

As noted before, the third grade of clearness is obtained by applying the pragmatic maxim to the definition that makes up the second grade, as the latter gives the most precise rendition of the concept. If we apply the pragmatic maxim to Scotus's definition, our conception of reality becomes the conceivable practical bearings we conceive real objects—that is, those objects that are independent of what you or I or anyone in particular thinks them to be—to have. Now the *only* effect such objects *can* have upon us, Peirce claims, is to produce belief. Therefore, *if* our conception of these effects is the whole of our conception of "real object," as the pragmatic maxim asserts that it is, then the *belief* these real objects *can* effect upon us is our whole conception of those real objects.[22] To put it briefly, "reality" can mean nothing *other* than the object of permanently settled belief or opinion.

Returning to the claim that a cognition is true when its immediate object is real, the above derivation can be used to derive a pragmatic definition of truth which is that truth is nothing more, and also nothing less, than permanently settled opinion. In "How to Make Our Ideas Clear,

Peirce states that, "the opinion which is fated to be ultimately agreed to by all who investigate, is what we mean by the truth, and the object represented in this opinion is the real" (EP1:139).

The above account, however, should not be taken as the prediction of a future empirical fact—i.e., the reaching of a final agreement among those who investigate the matter—but as the claim that the terms "truth" and "final opinion" are in fact synonyms. To say, for instance, that a proposition P is true, means nothing other than that if P were inquired into long enough this will eventually result in the settled belief that P. For example,

> The truth of the proposition that Caesar crossed the Rubicon consists in the fact that the further we push our archeological and other studies, the more strongly will that conclusion force itself on our minds forever—or would do so, if study were to go on forever. (CP 5.565)

Similarly, to say that it is true that there was once life on Mars is to say that anybody who examines the planet long enough will come to agree with that statement.

Application of the pragmatic maxim to Peirce's conceptions of truth and reality gives the following pragmatic definition of truth when applied to propositions:

> Proposition P is true if and only if, if inquiry into P (by an indefinite community of inquirers) continues long enough, this inquiry will ultimately result in a permanently settled belief that P (within an indefinite community of inquirers).

The underlying idea is that this ultimate belief is reached when all that can be inquired into is inquired into, so that no future inquiry can possibly reveal anything new of it. Therefore, the ultimate belief, or as Peirce also phrases it, the final opinion, is a permanently settled belief. The phrase "permanently settled belief" refers in this context to a belief that no future inquiry can undermine; that is, no future inquiry can show it to be false or cast any doubt on it. The locution "by an indefinite community of inquirers" is further added to filter out any distorting elements that may result from the peculiarities which individual inquirers may bring with them, such as a propensity for conspiracy theories, a general distrust of mathematics, or a desire to interpret everything as part of the overall plan of an all-powerful and benevolent God.

The pragmatic conception of truth, thus arrived at, does not commit Peirce to maintain that there is one mammoth super story, "the truth," which contains the last word on all there is to know about life, the

25

universe, and everything. Peirce's aim is much more modest, as the following analogy of his makes clear:

> The fact that I try to get well of each given bodily malady I may suffer from, is no argument that I am cherishing any hope to escape from *every* malady that I may ever suffer from. So the fact that I try to find the truth in respect to each doubt that presents itself involves no assumption on my part that there is any real truth about *all* questions. (R 787:11)

Peirce's conception of truth (as the final opinion) and of reality (as the object of this final opinion) has received much criticism. It has been argued, for instance, that we will never reach such final opinion; that we will never be in a position to know that we have reached it; and that the definition of truth as the final opinion does not adequately reflect what we generally mean with "truth."[23] An argument in this last category is the so-called buried-secrets objection. What about the truth of facts that are long forgotten? It is surely conceivable that Cleopatra sneezed five times on the morning of her fifth birthday, making the claim that she did true on most accounts. At the same time, however, it is almost certain that if we were to begin investigating this issue today, and assuming she did sneeze, we would never reach the permanently settled opinion that she did so, as it is most likely (and if not likely, at least possible) that we will never have sufficient data to establish this fact beyond doubt. On Peirce's theory, on which the final opinion is the truth and its object reality, the sneezes would then have to be classified as not real and the claim that she sneezed as not true, even though as a matter of fact she did sneeze.

In sum, the pragmatic maxim is for Peirce a method for determining, or fixing, the meaning of our concepts. In his 1898 "Philosophical Conceptions and Practical Results," William James would reintroduce Peirce's maxim to the public, calling it "the principle of pragmatism." In the process of this, however, the maxim underwent a shift in emphasis that pushed pragmatism in a different direction than was envisioned by Peirce, so much even that Peirce found himself obliged to publicly distance himself from the term "pragmatism," choosing for the far less appealing "pragmaticism" to describe his view. The term pragmaticism never caught on and Peirce's later views remained long neglected. These later views are the subject of chapter 6. But first, the pragmatisms of James, Schiller, and the Italian Leonardini.

3

James: Pragmatism and the Will to Believe

In this real world of sweat and dirt, it seems to me that when a view of things is 'noble,' that ought to count as a presumption against its truth, and as a philosophic disqualification.

—William James[24]

William James (1842–1910) studied medicine at Harvard, after which he slowly drifted from physiology, to psychology, to philosophy. He made a name for himself with his monumental two-volume *Principles of Psychology,* which appeared in 1890. However, his philosophical interests date from much earlier. With Peirce, James was a member of the Metaphysical Club and he developed an alternative strand of pragmatism that was well beyond its infancy when he began working on *Psychology.* In this work James drew a tight connection between mind and purpose-directed behavior, arguing for the principle that "no actions but such are done for an end, and show a choice of means, can be called indubitable expressions of Mind."[25] Especially in the early years James's *Psychology* is cited often as a key text in pragmatism.

3.1 Birth of the Term "Pragmatism"

James was the first to use the word "pragmatism" in print. He used it in a lecture on 26 August 1898 before the Philosophical Union of Berkeley University. Shortly afterward the lecture appeared in *The University Chronicle* under the title "Philosophical Conceptions and Practical Results."[26] In this lecture James tries to show his audience "the most likely

27

direction in which to start upon the trail of truth," in the course of which he introduces the "principle of pragmatism" as his compass, and he explicitly attributes this principle to Peirce (WJ:347).

The principle is nothing other than James's interpretation of the maxim that Peirce had formulated twenty years earlier in "How to make Our Ideas Clear," and which is discussed in section 2.4 above. In his lecture, James paraphrases Peirce's maxim as follows:

> To attain perfect clearness in our thoughts of an object . . . we
> need only consider what effects of a conceivably practical kind
> the object may involve—what sensations we are to expect
> from it, and what reactions we must prepare. Our conception
> of these effects, then, is for us the whole of our conception of
> the object, so far as that conception has positive significance at
> all. (WJ:348)

James's rendition of the maxim differs in several respects from Peirce's 1878 original, which runs like this:

> Consider what effects, that might conceivably have practical
> bearings, we conceive the object of our conception to have.
> Then, our conception of these effects is the whole of our
> conception of the object. (EP1:132)

The idea Peirce sought to convey in this maxim was that our conception of an object (that is, its meaning, or the *idea* we have of it) cannot be anything other than the *effects* we conceive the object to have, adding that those effects must be such that they might conceivably have practical bearings.

In his own rendition, James widened Peirce's maxim by identifying our conception of an object with the effects that the object "may involve." However, objects of our conception often "involve" many effects that we would not consider to be part of our conception of those objects. For example, the act of snatching someone's purse may involve the effect of tripping and getting a bloody nose, but that does not make getting a bloody nose part of our *conception* of purse snatching.

With respect to what precisely he had in mind with these "effects," James's rendition of the maxim is more explicit than Peirce's original. The effects are the *sensations* we are to expect and the *reactions* we must prepare. Here too, however, there is a crucial difference between Peirce and James. Whereas Peirce aims to relate the meaning of an idea with the habits to which the idea gives rise (which are *generals*, not particulars), James relates the meaning of an idea strictly to *particulars;* i.e., sensations and reactions. As shown in the previous chapter, this reading of the maxim

28

agrees with Peirce's own reading in 1878, as is clear from Peirce's discussion of "hardness," but it does not agree with Peirce's later reading in which he explicitly rejects such an interpretation, dismissing it as nominalistic. Peirce rejects *nominalism,* which is the view that only particulars are real, in favor of *realism,* which is the view that some generals are real also. In fact, Peirce's realist interpretation of the pragmatic maxim marks a crucial difference between his pragmatism and that of James.

In his treatment of the maxim, James further seeks to draw a much closer connection to our practical lives than does Peirce. For James, the pragmatist is interested primarily in those effects that can be conceived to make a *practical* difference, opposing this to those effects that are of mere theoretical value. For this reason James prefers to call Peirce's maxim the "principle of practicalism" rather than the "principle of pragmatism" (WJ:348).

Most of the changes brought about by James's reformulation of the maxim return in an influential criticism by Arthur Lovejoy, written a decade later on pragmatism's tenth anniversary. Apparently unfamiliar with Peirce's original maxim, Lovejoy paraphrases James's paraphrase as follows:

> The meaning of any proposition whatever is reducible to the
> future consequences in experience to which that proposition
> points, consequences which those who accept the proposition
> *ipso facto* anticipate as experiences that someone is
> subsequently to have.[27]

By reducing meaning to anticipated experiences—thereby reducing the meaning of any proposition to a group of particulars—James's nominalistic interpretation returns here in full force. James's version of pragmatism had become mainstream.

The 1898 Berkeley address, however, was not James's first reference to Peirce's maxim. James had referred to the maxim before, drawing similar conclusions. There is an explicit reference to Peirce's maxim in "Reflex Action and Theism" of 1881, which was reprinted in *The Will to Believe* (WB:99), and in "The Function of Cognition" of 1885 (WJ:151).

It is unlikely that James's pragmatism is an outgrowth of the doctrine set forth by Peirce in "How to Make Our Ideas Clear" and James's (mis)interpretation of it, as is often argued. James uses a principle that is very similar to Peirce's in a paper that appeared in the very same month as "How to Make Our Ideas Clear." In this paper, *"Quelques considérations sur la méthode subjective,"* which originally appeared in

French, James discusses what he calls the "subjective method." In this method James's own brand of pragmatism is already clearly discernable.[28] James observes, for instance,

> that every question is significant and is propounded with propriety, from which an obvious practical alternative results in such sort that accordingly as it be answered in the one way or the other, one, or the other line of conduct should be followed. (EPh:335)

In the same paper, while reflecting upon two rival hypotheses on the nature of the universe, James calls the distinction between the two hypotheses a significant one, precisely because "it admits of conclusions so opposite in the conduct of life" (EPh:336).

Also around this time, we find James's first use of the phrase "the principle of pragmatism." In manuscript notes for his 1879 "The Sentiment of Rationality" James writes, "The general principle of pragmatism proves every thing by its result," and a little later, "the principle of 'pragmatism' . . . allows all assumptions to be of identical value so long as they equally *save the appearances"* (EPh:352, 364). The term "pragmatism" is omitted in the published essay. In contrast, no instances of the term are found in Peirce's writings preceding James's 1898 Berkeley address.

James's early use of the term "pragmatism" and the similarity of the approaches of Peirce and James in "How to Make Our Ideas Clear" and in *"Quelques considérations sur la méthode subjective, "* cast doubt on the thesis, advocated most notably by Ralph Barton Perry in *The Thought and Character of William James,* which claims that "the modern movement known as pragmatism is largely the result of James's misunderstanding of Peirce."[29] It seems more likely that by the time Peirce published his famous maxim, James's emphasis on conduct and practicalness was already firmly in place. Hence, James did not take Peirce's pragmatism for a ride; rather, their views are two different strands of pragmatism, that each have their separate origin in the discussions that took place within the Metaphysical Club in the early 1870s.[30]

Before discussing James's pragmatism, however, some attention should be given to his 1896 "The Will to Believe." In the previous chapter it was shown that Peirce's "The Fixation of Belief" formed a prelude to his pragmatism. To a large extent the same is true for James's "The Will to Believe."

3.2 The Will to Believe

In his famous but often misunderstood "The Will to Believe," James argues that in certain circumstances one has the right to believe something even when there is no sufficient evidence of its truth.[31] James is in part reacting to the view of the British mathematician William Kingdom Clifford who concludes in an 1877 essay entitled "The Ethics of Belief" that "it is wrong always, everywhere, and for anyone, to believe anything upon insufficient evidence."[32]

Clifford opens his essay with the example of a shipowner who manages to convince himself that an old ship that is about to sail is seaworthy:

> Doubts had been suggested to him that possibly she was not
> seaworthy. These doubts preyed upon his mind and made him
> unhappy; he thought that perhaps he ought to have her
> thoroughly overhauled and refitted, even though this should
> put him to great expense. Before the ship sailed, however, he
> succeeded in overcoming these melancholy reflections. . . . He
> would put his trust in Providence, which could hardly fail to
> protect all these unhappy families that were leaving their
> fatherland to seek for better times elsewhere. He would
> dismiss from his mind all ungenerous suspicions about the
> honesty of builders and contractors. In such ways he acquired
> a sincere and comfortable conviction that his vessel was
> thoroughly safe and seaworthy.[33]

The ship sinks, of course, mid-ocean. Clifford concludes that although the shipowner managed to make himself *genuinely believe* that the ship is safe, he *has no right* to believe this on the evidence he has before him.

It is unlikely that James would disagree with Clifford on this point. What James did disagree with is Clifford's extrapolation that this holds for *all* situations; i.e., that no one is ever allowed to believe anything on insufficient ground. According to James, in certain situations, one not only has the right to believe when there is no conclusive evidence, but it would even be wrong not to do so.[34]

James begins his argument with a number of technical distinctions. First, he reserves the term "hypothesis" for anything that may become an object of our belief. Such a hypothesis is either a living hypothesis or a dead one. The hypothesis that humans will someday land on Mars, or that we will find a cure for AIDS, is for many a living hypothesis. In contrast, the hypothesis that centaurs really roamed the countryside of ancient

31

Greece is, for most of us, a dead one. We do not consider it seriously or have anything at stake in it. Next, James calls the decision between two rival hypotheses an "option." Such options, he continues, are either living or dead, depending on whether the hypotheses one has to choose from are living hypotheses or not. In addition, options can be forced or avoidable, and they can be momentous or trivial.

Momentous options, in James's view, are those that deeply affect one's life. Some of them will be once-in-a-lifetime affairs, whereas others, such as breaking from one's professional career to return to graduate school, can be postponed. However, to postpone one's choice (say until one is absolutely certain it is the right one), is itself a choice. For the once-in-a-lifetime opportunity, it comes down to flatout rejecting it. In a sense, momentous options are thus always forced. By insisting that some options are momentous, James shows that we cannot always simply suspend our belief until we are better informed, which is basically what Clifford asks us to do. For James, he who suspends his belief also makes a choice, and that choice might very well not be the best one.

A living option that is both forced and momentous, James calls a *genuine option.* For genuine options *that cannot be decided on intellectual grounds,* James accepts that we may or even must make up our mind even when there is not enough evidence to support our choice. According to James, we must be willing to take the risk and prepared to face the consequences. In the words of Fitz James Stephen, whom James quoted by way of conclusion, "In all important transactions of life we have to take a leap in the dark. . . . Each must act as he thinks best; and if he is wrong, so much the worse for him" (WJ:735).

James explicitly rejects the idea, however, that such leaps in the dark are permitted in science:

> But in our dealings with objective nature we obviously are recorders, not makers, of the truth; and decisions for the mere sake of deciding promptly and getting on to the next business would be wholly out of place. (WJ:728)

Such leaps are also not really needed in science, James continues, as the options faced by scientists are not genuine options (i.e., options that are living, forced, and momentous). What difference does it make to us to know how the dinosaurs became extinct, whether black holes exist, or precisely how many varieties of butterflies there are? Because the questions raised by scientists are generally trivial options involving hypotheses that are barely living and for which the choice between

32

believing their truth or falsehood is seldom forced, a disinterested quest into their truth is not only possible but even requisite.

Notice that James appears to be advocating two different and independent arguments at this point. The first proceeds from the premise that science deals with "objective nature," and that in such matters we are "obviously" only the "recorders, not the makers, of truth," to the conclusion that "deciding promptly" is "wholly out of place." Put differently, for issues relating to objective nature, James concedes that Clifford is right, and, relating it to Peirce's views discussed in the previous chapter, Peirce's "scientific method" would be the appropriate way to deal with them.

The second argument is based on the altogether different premise that scientific options are not truly genuine options. This raises the immediate objection that such a view leaves us at a complete loss when confronted with pressing issues in the applied sciences, such as finding a cure for AIDS or reducing the greenhouse effect.

James seeks to avoid this type of objection by further restricting the "freedom to believe" to only those genuine options that cannot be resolved by the intellect. The genuine options faced by scientists are, almost by definition, such that they can be resolved by the intellect, as it is precisely this aspect of them that allows them to be *scientific* problems in the first place.

James's strongest argument for why we should sometimes believe something even when there is insufficient evidence is that *some things become true precisely because we believe them.* James gave the following example to illustrate his point: suppose that I am grappling with the question whether you like me or not. Many times, James argues, the answer to this question will depend on what we believe the answer to be. If I am *willing* to believe that you must like me, I am much more likely to be nice to you myself, thereby increasing the chance that you will like me. In contrast, when I decide to wait until I have objective evidence that clearly points in one way or the other, I am much more likely to cause your dislike by my aloof attitude. In general, James observes, "The desire for a certain kind of truth here brings about that special truth's existence; and so it is in innumerable cases of other sorts" (WJ:730). Note that James is not implying here that evidence is irrelevant for determining the truth of such beliefs. What he rejects is merely that evidence must always precede the belief in time.

We might call this argument the argument from self-fulfilling prophecies. Not all living, momentous, and forced options, however, are self-fulfilling prophecies. In "The Will to Believe," James mentions three areas where genuine options are numerous, without taking the form of a self-fulfilling prophecy: law, morality, and religion.

First, in a court of law the options are often momentous, and it is generally imperative that decisions are made expediently. As James puts it somewhat uneasily, "Few cases are worth spending much time over: the great thing is to have them decided on *any* acceptable principle, and get them out of the way" (WJ:728). James holds a similar view for moral issues: "*Moral questions* immediately present themselves as questions whose solution cannot wait for sensible proof' (WJ:729). However, James's discussion of moral issues in "The Will to Believe" remains brief and unsatisfactory. He moves too soon to his argument from self-fulfilling prophecies, and leaves it at that.

James's discussion of religious faith, the third area, is more thorough. He begins by reaffirming that he is limiting his discussion specifically to genuine options. Hence, he does not concern himself with dusty dogmas, or with metaphysical proofs for the existence of God that are so complicated and removed from life that they are of no use to anyone. The affirmation of faith must be part of an option that is at once living, momentous, and forced.

Next, James cut short the skeptic by arguing that skepticism is only the expression of a certain conservative epistemic temperament, namely that it is always better to risk a loss of truth than to chance an error (WJ:732). The issue is, therefore, not that of the intellect against the passions, but that of one passion against another. For James, the religious believer is just more adventuresome than the skeptic.

James continues his argument with a variant on Pascal's wager. In his *Pensees,* Pascal had argued that it is better to accept what Scripture tells us because this is our best bet. A belief in the Scripture carries the promise of an infinite gain (to be included in the Kingdom of Heaven), at only a minimal cost (like going to church and saying our prayers). Thus, should we be mistaken, the worst that can happen to us is that we have wasted some of our time. On the other hand, if we *refuse* to believe what Scripture tells us, we get only minimal gains (like having our Sunday mornings free) while running the risk of eternal damnation. Pascal directed his wager against the skeptic who would not be convinced otherwise. The wager aimed, moreover, to provide a *rational* argument for why the skeptic should accept what the Scripture says. Genuine belief in the Scripture would come later, Pascal envisioned, as the natural outcome of practicing the religion.

Pascal's argument fails, James argues, because the option he presents is not a live one for those to whom it is addressed. It is unlikely to convince the staunch skeptic, and it is even less likely to convince the Hindu or the Buddhist. However, James continues, if the option is a truly genuine one—that is, a forced, living, and momentous one—such an argument would work. The skeptic "who should shut himself up in snarling logicality and try to make the gods extort his recognition willy-nilly, or not get it at all," James argues, "might cut himself off forever from his only opportunity of making the gods' acquaintance" (WJ:733).

In his discussion of Pascal's wager, James puts a creative spin on the self-fulfilling prophecy argument that he has used before. Instead of the belief contributing to *its* truth, as with the self-fulfilling prophecy, the belief contributes to the future well-being of the believer. That is to say, one is better off by believing that it is true. That one is better off holding a certain belief, James considers sufficient ground for believing it, even when there is insufficient evidence. James even goes a step further and argues that it would be absurd to make someone accept the skeptic's temperament when she has a strong will to believe.

It is important, though, to recall the restrictions James has placed on his argument. The freedom to believe is far from absolute. It concerns only genuine options, and of these it may concern only those "which the intellect *of the individual* cannot by itself resolve" (WJ:734; emphasis added).

The reference to the individual in the last statement is at once important and problematic. It is important, because it emphasizes that beliefs are always the beliefs of a *particular* individual, and because it relates those beliefs directly to the individual's motives for holding them. It is problematic, because it gives individuals with lesser intellectual capabilities a greater freedom to believe. However, since even the most private beliefs may result in overt action, or affect one's attitude to other, nonprivate beliefs, each individual can be said to have a duty to avoid as much as he can that his beliefs are unfounded, even when this means the acknowledgment that others know better (meaning that others *can* resolve it intellectually). This might suggest that a better way of limiting the freedom of belief is by restricting it to those living options that *society* cannot resolve intellectually, thereby bringing James's position somewhat closer to Peirce's community of inquirers and his acceptance of testimony as a genuine source of knowledge for individuals. However, such a social theory of knowledge has little appeal to the individualistic James.

3.3 The "Principle of Pragmatism"

As noted before, the central purpose of James's 1898 Pragmatism lecture was to lead the audience upon the "trail of truth," using Peirce's principle as their compass. In his explanation of Peirce's principle, James acknowledges that Peirce considers it a method for determining the *meaning* of our thought, but he thinks that the principle "should be expressed more broadly than Mr. Peirce expresses it." James continues by giving *his own* version of the pragmatic maxim:

> The ultimate test for us of what a truth means is indeed *the conduct it dictates or inspires*. But it inspires that conduct because it first foretells some *particular* turn to our *experience* which shall call for us just that conduct for us. (WJ:348; emphasis added)

James departs from Peirce's maxim at several points, and for the purpose of comparing the two it may be helpful to repeat Peirce's original maxim:

> Consider what effects, that might conceivably have practical bearings, we conceive the object of our conception to have. Then, our conception of these effects is the whole of our conception of the object. (EP1:132)

It is interesting to note that James replaces Peirce's "object of our conception" with "truth"—a term James seems to use as an equivalent to "thought" and "philosophical proposition." The result, as we will see, becomes a volatile mixture of truth and meaning.

James restricts Peirce's maxim in at least two respects. First, he explicitly confines the meaning of a thought, truth, or philosophical proposition to its *particular* effects. This is James's nominalist interpretation of pragmatism, mentioned before. James is fully aware of his nominalism and thinks it a good thing. The requirement that meaning is to be related to particular experiences, James considers an important safeguard for avoiding the abuses of the old metaphysicians. The second restriction is James's demand that these particular effects be *experiential*. There is no such demand in Peirce's maxim, and Peirce later emphasized repeatedly that what he had in mind was the establishment of habits, and these are not experiential effects.

At the same time, James radically broadens the maxim. For James, the effects in question are not, as with Peirce, related to the *object* of our conception, but are related to the *individual* who believes that the thought

36

or philosophical proposition is true. As James explains, "The whole function of philosophy ought to be to find out what definite difference it will make to you and me, at definite instants of our life, if this world-formula or that world-formula be the one which is true" (WJ:349).

Take, for instance, the notion of transubstantiation discussed in chapter 2. As is shown there, Peirce's maxim showed this notion to be meaningless because there are no conceivable practical differences between ordinary bread and wine, and bread and wine that have been transubstantiated into the body and blood of Christ.

James's conclusion is the exact opposite. He agrees with Peirce that the scholastic notion of substance, on which the notion of transubstantiation trades, is void, writing that, "few things would seem to have fewer pragmatic consequences for us than substances, cut off as we are from every contact with them" (WJ:391). But James immediately proceeds to say that it is precisely in the mystery of the Eucharist that this otherwise useless notion comes to life. Within the Eucharist, James contends, the notion of substance accrues "momentous pragmatic value." Granted, it does not have such a value for everyone, but it does have it for those to whom Christ is a live option. The transubstantiation, James adds, "will only be treated seriously by those who already believe in the 'real presence' on independent grounds" (WJ:392).

Thus, for James, the "pragmatic value" of the notion of transubstantiation is not, as with Peirce, related to the conceivable practical consequences related to the process of transubstantiation itself, but to the practical consequences that belief in it has for the *person* who believes it. (Note that, for James, these practical consequences must eventually reduce to particular experiences.) If believing that transubstantiation occurs during the Eucharist has practical consequences for the *believer,* then the belief has pragmatic value. In this manner, James ties his pragmatism in with the course he set out two years before in "The Will to Believe."

It is important to realize that James does not reach his contrary conclusion because he rejects Peirce's argument, but because he gives a different interpretation to the maxim and how it should be applied. Peirce argues that we should use only terms, etc., whose meaning can be cast entirely in terms of conceivable practical consequences. Thus, for Peirce, "hardness" is meaningful because we can say that an object is hard when it will not be scratched by a knife edge. For Peirce, no such conceivable practical consequences can be connected with "transubstantiation." For James, a philosophical proposition or theory is pragmatically meaningful if it has conceivable practical consequences *in the lives of those who believe in it.* Many propositions that are meaningless on Peirce's maxim will make a difference in some people's lives, making them meaningful in the eyes of James. For James, "The effective meaning of any philosophical proposition can always be brought down *to some particular consequence, in our future practical experience,* whether active or passive" (WJ:349; emphasis added). Thus, instead of making the meaning of a concept depend on the conceivable practical consequences we conceive *that concept* to have, which is what Peirce argues for, James makes the meaning of a concept (or a philosophical proposition, as James calls it here) depend on "some particular consequence in our future practical experience." This is indeed much broader than what Peirce intends the principle to convey.

3.4 Applications of the Principle

Like Peirce, James gives a number of examples to illustrate how the principle of pragmatism works. James's examples, however, are of a grander scale than those of Peirce. Whereas Peirce uses his maxim to clarify concepts such as "hardness" or "truth," James illustrated his version of the maxim by evaluating entire metaphysical systems. James's first example concerns the choice between materialism and theism as alternative and incompatible hypotheses on the origin and nature of the universe. Should we believe that the universe is the chance product of the random motion of bits of matter *(materialism),* or should we believe that the universe is created by a God *(theism)?*

James denies that one could settle the issue with a purely retrospective approach. With such an approach, one would examine which of the two hypotheses would best account for the world as it currently is. Were the two alternatives to be thus examined, James argues, the choice would cease to be a live option and the problem would become an altogether idle and insignificant one. As James puts it,

> If no future detail of experience or conduct is to be deducted
> from our hypothesis, the debate between materialism and
> theism becomes quite idle and insignificant. Matter and God in
> that event *mean exactly the same thing*—the power, namely,
> neither more nor less, that can make just this mixed, imperfect,
> yet uncompleted world. (WJ:351; emphasis added)

In other words, when the examination is purely retrospective, there will be no pragmatic difference between both hypotheses, since there will be no practical differences but only alternative interpretations of the very same facts. What matters for James is not how these rival hypotheses explain the past, but how they direct us to the future. We live in a universe that is still evolving, James argues, and in the face of such an unfinished universe the choice between materialism and theism becomes, as he put it, an "intensely practical" one because both alternatives give us a radically different outlook on life (WJ:352). As for the materialist outlook, James quotes a somber passage from James Balfour:

> The energies of our system will decay, the glory of the sun will be dimmed, and the earth, tideless and inert, will no longer tolerate the race which has for a moment disturbed its solitude. Man will go down into the pit, and all his thoughts will perish.[35]

Compared with this dismal prospect, theism has what James called a "practical superiority"; it "guarantees an ideal order that shall be permanently preserved." And he continued,

> A world with a God in it to say the last word, may indeed burn up or freeze, but we then think of Him as still mindful of the old ideals and sure to bring them elsewhere to fruition; so that, where He is, tragedy is only provisional and partial, and shipwreck and dissolution not the absolutely final things. (WJ:354)

Therefore, whereas materialism cuts off all ultimate hope, "theism means the affirmation of an eternal moral order and the letting loose of hope" (ibid.). By doing so, theism makes our world a much more hospitable place.

In this manner James uses the principle of pragmatism to transform a rather abstruse metaphysical dispute between dogmatic theologians and transcendent materialists into a genuine option. By doing so he secures for us, in accordance with the argument he presented earlier in "The Will to Believe," the *right* to believe in theism even though there is no sufficient evidence that the universe is the product of a God. Having obtained that right, it is then up to us to gather the *will*-power to believe it.

The example also shows that the consequences James has in mind are not just any practical consequences. They must be *good* practical consequences. Believing in a godless universe with no hope whatsoever surely has practical consequences when it throws the believer into a deep depression, but that is not what James has in mind. James's second example is an equally abstruse metaphysical dispute, namely, whether the world is in essence one *(monism)* or many *(pluralism)*.

Later, in his 1906–1907 Lowell lectures, James added a few examples, including the question whether the universe is designed, and the longstanding controversy between determinists and followers of the free will thesis. Physics, with its insistence that every event must have a sufficient cause, generally sides with the determinist; whereas ethics, with its insistence on accountability, tends to hold that we have a free will. Pragmatism, James argues, not only points us to the freewill alternative, but also tells us how to interpret this. This leads to James's doctrine of *meliorism*, in which the doctrine of free will has developed into a general cosmological theory that allows for novelty and improvement in the universe. This doctrine has pragmatic value because we seek to position ourselves in an imperfect world:

> Our interest in religious metaphysics arises in the fact that our empirical future feels to us unsafe, and needs some higher guarantee. If the past and present were purely good, who could wish that the future might possibly not resemble them? . . . 'Freedom' in a world already perfect could only mean freedom to *be worse,* and who could be so insane as to wish that? (WJ:403)

3.5 Rationalism, Empiricism, Pragmatism

James's *Pragmatism* appears in 1907, well after Peirce's 1903 Harvard Lectures on pragmatism (which James not only attended but also helped organize) and Peirce's 1905–1906 *Monist* papers on pragmatism. In contrast to *The Will to Believe,* which James had dedicated to Peirce, *Pragmatism* is dedicated to someone Peirce was most critical of, the late John Stuart Mill. Moreover, when positioning himself within the pragmatic tradition, James seeks no longer the company of Peirce, but rather that of Schiller, Papini, and Dewey.[36]

In *Pragmatism,* James develops his own views largely as a criticism of what he considers the two dominant tendencies within philosophy: rationalism and empiricism. James sees this opposition foremost as a clash of two different temperaments, which he calls the tough-minded and the tender-minded. James's criticism of rationalism is the most severe. His main criticism of empiricism is that it fails to sufficiently free itself from rationalist influences.

James accuses the rationalists of escapism. Rationalists, James argues, create a beautiful and self-contained system, and then they fall in love with it, turning their backs on the world they experience, and which this system is supposed to represent. In their carefully designed systems, in which everything has its place and there is a place for everything, there is no room for the messy and dirty details, the cruelties, the unfinishedness, and the bewildering surprises of the world of experience. Still prevalent in James's day, the rationalist attitude dates at least back to ancient Greece. It can be detected clearly in Plato, who, insisting that the object of true knowledge must be unchanging, radically denied that we can obtain true knowledge through the senses. For Plato, the horses we see competing at the Kentucky Derby are but imperfect imitations, or shadows, of the ideal horse, a horse that is never felt, heard, or seen, but that is somehow grasped intellectually.

The empiricists, on the other hand, take experience seriously and explicitly seek to develop their system of thought from it. But for James the empiricists do not go far enough. They tend to cling dogmatically to materialism, causing them to dismiss offhand everything that cannot be accounted for in terms of senseless matter. Most significantly, for James, this includes all religious beliefs. In a letter to his former student Arthur Lovejoy, James explains that he had written *Pragmatism* specifically "to make air and room for an empirical philosophy that might not necessarily be irreligious, to breathe in."[37]

To the traditional, materialistic form of empiricism, James contrasts his own brand, which he called "radical empiricism." James's empiricism is radical in the sense that he does not want to take anything for granted, but only accepts the experienced, finite facts as given. He even leaves open the question whether those facts are all part of a single *uni*verse. Pragmatism comes close to this radical empiricism, although James stops short of equating the two. He does so largely because he wants to keep the possibility open that someone who rejects his radical empiricism can still be a pragmatist.

For James, pragmatism thus continues to be largely a method for choosing between rival hypotheses, and the arguments he presents in his 1906 Lowell lectures are largely the same as those he gave in his 1898 Berkeley address. But it is more than just a method. It is the expression of a philosophical temperament—a way of looking at the universe and our place within it.

In part James is envisioning a change of temperament as to what is important in philosophy. The traditional enterprise of making our thoughts mimic reality and then saying with glee that we have "discovered the truth," James believes to be misguided. In *The Meaning of Truth,* he addresses the issue succinctly, posing the following question: "Why may not thought's mission be to increase and elevate, rather than simply to

41

imitate and reduplicate, existence?"[38] The result is a radical reinter-pretation of the notion of truth. Partly due to the influence of Schiller and Dewey, James widens his pragmatism by associating it explicitly with an instrumentalist theory of truth. It is to this that we now turn.[39]

Especially in the sixth lecture of *Pragmatism,* James seeks to give pragmatic meaning to the notion of truth. He does so, as did Peirce before him, by applying the principle of pragmatism to the existing notion of truth. Although there are strong similarities between how James and Peirce understand the notion of truth, there are also important differences. James begins by accepting the traditional dictionary definition of truth, on which an idea, belief, or statement is true when it agrees with reality and false when it disagrees with reality. The point where pragmatists, in James's view, depart from the rationalist and the empiricist is in their interpretation of the notion of agreement. To both the rationalists and the empiricists James ascribes a notion of agreement on which our thoughts, etc., *agree* with reality when they are faithful copies of reality. That is to say, James first attributes to them a copy theory of knowledge (or a correspondence theory of truth), and then continues by arguing that such a copy theory of knowledge is far too restrictive.

Close to the beginning of his sixth lecture, James draws a distinction between those ideas or beliefs that *can* copy their object in thought and those that *cannot*—a distinction that is given center stage in his preface to *The Meaning of Truth.* The next section contains a discussion of James's conception of truth for those ideas that can copy their object, where it will be shown that he is arguing for a wider notion of agreement. The section thereafter, will be devoted to James's discussion of those ideas that cannot copy their object.

3.6 Truth as the Agreement with Reality

According to James, the rationalist proceeds from the set opinion that there is a fixed reality that is "complete and ready-made from all eternity" (WJ:439). This conception of reality subsequently becomes the basis for the rationalist's conception of truth. The rationalist, James argues, sees the truth as the full and correct representation in thought of this ready-made and eternal reality. Science has long been looked upon as an attempt at obtaining such a true description of the world. Galileo, for instance, believed that God had written the "great book of nature" in the language of mathematics. Consequently, a scientific treatise, like a treatise in celestial mechanics, can be seen as an accurate copy of certain passages in this "book of nature," written in the very same language in which God had written the heavens themselves. In this language the heavenly phenomena are grasped intellectually instead of merely being perceived through the senses.

A similar stance was taken by the empiricists. The early members of the Royal Society, for instance, whose practice Locke sought to justify in his *Essay Concerning Human Understanding,* came to reject scientific speculation and limited scientific inquiry strictly to presenting what they called *natural histories*—detailed descriptions of groups of phenomena that, ideally, would be entirely devoid of any thoughts on how these phenomena came into being, what they are for, etc.

By the nineteenth century, however, scientists had come to reject this notion of science as a correct description of reality, moving to a more instrumental conception of scientific theories. As James observes, they have come to the position that "no theory is absolutely a transcript of reality, but that any one of them may from some point of view be useful. . . . They are only man-made language, a conceptual shorthand, as someone calls them, in which we write our reports of nature" (WJ:381).

The downfall of Euclidean geometry—the mathematical language Galileo had ascribed to God—as the obvious and true language for describing physical space relations, surely contributed to this change in attitude. Naturally, we can still employ Euclidean geometry in physics and astronomy, but we must no longer consider this as an attempt to give a true description of reality (say, a true description of the orbit of the planet Mars), but as a tool by which we can handle certain facts in thought. As James writes, "You must bring out of each word its practical cash-value, set it at work within the stream of your experience. . . . *Theories thus become instruments, not answers to enigmas, in which we can rest.*" (WJ:380).

If scientific theories are tools rather than efforts to describe reality, the copy theory of knowledge is no longer tenable as a full-fledged theory of knowledge. Truth can no longer be seen as a detached reflection upon an already ready-made world, but is now related to action. As James puts it, "Ideas (which themselves are but part of our experience) become true just in so far as they help us to get into satisfactory relations with other parts of our experience" (WJ:382). In short, we get an instrumental theory of truth.

This instrumental theory of truth holds not only for abstruse scientific topics that are far removed from our daily lives, but it holds equally for the most commonsense ways in which we think about things. Basic conceptions, such as "space," "time," "cause," "mind," and "body," were once created by our remote ancestors as tools for dealing with

43

concrete problems they faced. In James's words, "The common-sense categories . . . are but sublime tricks of human thought, our ways of escaping bewilderment in the midst of sensation's irremediable flow" (WJ:425).

Despite his adherence to an instrumental theory of truth, James does not give up on the notion that a belief, statement, or theory is true *when it agrees with reality*. What he does give up is the notion that the *only* way in which our thoughts can agree with reality is by making some sort of copy of this reality in thought:

> To copy a reality is, indeed, one very important way of agreeing with it, but it is far from being essential. The essential thing is the process of being guided. Any idea that helps us deal, whether practically or intellectually, with either the reality or its belongings, that doesn't entangle our progress in frustrations, that fits, in fact, and adapts our life to the reality's whole setting, will agree sufficiently to meet the requirement. It will hold true of that reality. (WJ:434f)

So the crucial aspect of our thoughts or beliefs agreeing with reality is not that they *copy* reality, but that they *fit within* reality—that is to say, that they lead us in the right way. As James puts it,

> To 'agree' in the widest sense with a reality *can only mean to be guided either straight up to it or into its surroundings, or to be put into such working touch with it as to handle either with it or something connected with it better than if we disagreed.* (WJ:434)

Hence, James does not at all deny that there is a reality that is independent of our thought and with which we are forced to reckon. He fully acknowledges that there are things that are beyond our control, and for which, to the extent that we can control them, we can only do so on their terms, not on ours. We can surely enrich reality with a new suspension bridge, a skyscraper, or spacecraft that can send a crew of astronauts to Venus, but we can do so only when we carefully observe the laws of nature. What James denies is that this reality is something that lies hidden behind our experiences, like the sort of reality he thinks Plato and Galileo believed in. For James, reality is the reality we experience. It is the "total push and pressure of the cosmos" that brought us to philosophize in the first place (WJ:362), and that also sets the limits upon our thought. As James puts it, "the only *real* guarantee we have against licentious thinking is the circumpressure of experience itself . . . whether there be a transempirical reality or not" (MT:47).

A key element of James's theory of truth is that when we say that something is true, we introduce a new fact into the world just as much as when we erect a new bridge, knock over a glass of lemonade, or open our hand. Taken by themselves, facts are never true. It is only when we say something *about* them that truth and falsity come in. As James puts it: "The 'facts' themselves . . . are not *true*. They simply *are*. Truth is the function of the beliefs that start and terminate among them" (WJ:439). Truth is neither a property of certain ideas, nor a property of facts, but involves the *agreement* of our ideas with facts. Consequently, James argues, when we say that a certain fact is true, we have *added* something to that fact. As he puts it elsewhere,

> Truth we conceive to mean everywhere, not duplication, but
> addition; not the constructing of inner copies of already
> complete realities, but rather the collaborating with realities so
> as to bring about a clearer result. (MT:41)

James specifically acknowledges, though, that we cannot add just about anything. In fact, he is quite conservative at this point, explaining that a "new truth" is always "a go-between, a smoother-over of transitions. It marries old opinion to new fact so as ever to show a minimum jolt, a maximum of continuity" (WJ:383). Scientific theories may be man-made systems, yet

> in the choice of these man-made formulas we can not be
> capricious with impunity any more than we can be capricious
> on the common-sense practical level. We must find a theory
> that will *work;* and that means something extremely difficult;
> for our theory must mediate between all previous truths and
> certain new experiences. It must derange common sense and
> previous belief as little as possible, and it must lead to some
> sensible terminus or other that can be verified exactly. To
> 'work' means both these things; and the squeeze is so tight
> that there is little loose play for any hypothesis. (WJ:436)

In this process of smoothing-over, truth is fluid. New experiences, James argues, lead to changes, often very minute, in the truths we already have. The result of this process is, as James explains, "the new equilibrium in which each step forward in the process of learning terminates" (WJ:419). In short, the old truths are not permanent, as the rationalists claim, but they change over time in the face of new experiences. Truths are temporary equilibria in the process of learning.

Now why does James insist on calling them truths, instead of beliefs? Nobody will deny that our beliefs change. We may, for instance, change our belief about whether Julius Caesar crossed the river Rubicon, but why imply that this means that, although it used to be *true* that Caesar crossed the Rubicon, it is now *false* that he did? Intuitively, the truth of the belief that Caesar crossed the Rubicon seems to be determined, not by what we believe, but by whether he actually crossed the river. The same holds for nonempirical truths, such as whether, in a Euclidean plane, the angles of a triangle always add up to the sum of two right angles.

The answer to this question is related to James's radical empiricism. As noted before, James was critical of the metaphysical prejudices of the empiricists. One of these prejudices is that of a single, fixed reality that lies behind our experiences. This prejudice is found, for instance, in Locke's "the real being and existence of things" and Berkeley's "Spirit." James contrasts this type of empiricism with what he called "pluralistic pragmatism," in which "truth grows up inside of all the finite experiences," where those experiences "lean on each other, but the whole of them, if such a whole there be, leans on nothing" (WJ:457).[40] Such a "bundle theory of experiences" was entertained also by the classical empiricists, but they quickly came to reject such a theory, and it might be claimed, as James does, that in doing so they slipped back into old presuppositions on what lies beyond the "veil of ideas." As James puts it, with an oblique reference to Locke, rationalists and empiricists regard such a world of experiences that lean on nothing but each other as "a tramp and vagrant world, adrift in space, with neither elephant nor tortoise to plant the sole of its foot upon" (WJ:457f).

In James's pluralistic pragmatism, the only meaning that can be given to a statement or belief being true is that it fits within our experience. In this manner, James's pragmatism leads to some sort of coherence theory of truth, albeit one that does not focus on the ivory-tower professor who, in his brown study, merely reflects upon human experiences, but on the *acting* individual who is situated in the midst of a world of experience, and for whom true ideas are those that lead to successful action (the latter being cast in terms of experience).

In short, James's notion of coherence is not a matter of looking backward and trying to fit together the pieces of a preexisting puzzle (like the jigsaw puzzles one buys in the store), but is the fitting together of the pieces of a puzzle that is still in the making, that is evolving without any preconceived plan and without the requirement that the puzzle is supposed to represent anything (as opposed to, say, a jigsaw puzzle of the Kremlin). Moreover, within this process one is to some degree in control of what the

46

new pieces will look like, and, in contrast to store-bought jigsaw puzzles, the new pieces may force changes upon what is already on the table.

By opposing the notion of an unchanging truth, James takes a stance against the fixedness of the rationalists' reality. James seeks to emphasize instead that the world we live in is in a profound sense unfinished. With this James does not mean to refer to the still evolving cosmos, but that the world, as we experience it in our daily lives, is still in important ways a work in progress. Our future is an open future. More than merely reflecting upon reality, we are required to act in it: we are forced to help shape it. By taking this course, James moves toward the humanist view of reality "as something resisting, yet malleable, which controls our thinking as an energy that must be taken 'account' of incessantly (tho not necessarily merely *copied)*" (WJ:456f).

At the same time, however, James remains well aware that our maneuvering room is limited and that many of our truths are by now pretty much fixed:

> Truth independent; *truth* that we find merely; truth no longer
> malleable to human need; truth incorrigible, in a word; such
> truth exists indeed superabundantly—or is supposed to exist
> by rationalistically minded thinkers; but then it means only the
> dead heart of the living tree, and its being there means only
> that truth also has its paleontology. (WJ:384)

This fixedness, however, does not indicate that there must be an independent world out there, and that we have found the truth when our ideas adequately *mirror* this world, but it indicates that we are very well entrenched within the world of our experiences, so that certain opinions invariably lead us to the desired results.

James not only opposes the fixedness of truth, but also its singularity. For rationalists and empiricists, to whom truth is the perfect copy of reality in thought, there is just one truth. Presumably, there is only one way that our ideas can *copy* reality. In contrast, if agreement means that our beliefs "fit in," the requirement that there is only one truth quickly loses its force. Multiple, altogether different beliefs may equally fit in, especially since the universe is yet unfinished and malleable. As James explains: "Our account of truth is an account of truths in the plural, of processes of leading, realized *in rebus,* and having only this quality in common, that they *pay*" (WJ:436).

So far, we have concentrated mainly on ideas that can somehow copy their object, such as Socrates drinking the hemlock, the orbit of the planet Mars, Newton's law of gravity, etc., and we saw that, for James, the notion of truth as the perfect copy of an independent and unchanging reality is too restrictive. The notion of agreement should be taken in a much wider sense. On one occasion, James goes even so far as to suggest that *any* idea that does not clash with reality agrees with reality, and thus must thus be called true (WJ:429). This claim is less radical than it sounds if we take into account also that James's view of reality does not allow for all that much room to maneuver. As he puts it above, "The squeeze is so tight that there is little loose play for any hypothesis." Hence, we can ascribe to James the view that those beliefs agree with reality—thus making them true—that lead us in the right way in the face of a still open future in which we are an active player with a limited playing field. In the next section we will examine those ideas that cannot copy their object.

3.7 Taking Truth Further

For the empiricist James, not all our ideas *can* copy their object (WJ:430). The question becomes then whether any of those ideas could be true. To answer this question we need to ask whether ideas that cannot copy an object can still *agree* with that object, and if so, what agreement means in those cases. Much of the groundwork for answering this question has already been laid in the preceding section, in which we were led to the view that the notion of agreement must be understood more broadly than that of being a copy of something. Ideas are true when they "fit in."

Neither in the sixth lecture, nor in the preface to the *Meaning of Truth,* where this is made a central issue, are there any clear examples of what sorts of ideas James has in mind. It is quite evident, though, that they are primarily moral and religious ideas. Moral ideas, expressing how things *should be*, for instance, may differ widely from how things *are.* However, when we see that a certain moral imperative fails to copy its object, we generally do not conclude from this that the imperative must thus be false. This point was expressed quite succinctly by John Locke about two centuries earlier. The moral rules laid out by Cicero in *On Moral Obligation*, Locke observed, are not any less true, "because there is no Body in the World that exactly practices his Rules, and lives up to that pattern of a vertuous Man, which he has given us, and which existed no where, when he writ, but in *Idea.*"[41]

With regard to ideas that cannot copy their object, James explains, "pragmatism asks its usual question. 'Grant an idea or belief to be true,' it says, 'what concrete difference will its being true make in any one's practical life?' . . . What, in short, is the truth's cash value?" (WJ:430). Put differently, ideas that cannot copy their object can still be true depending on what the consequences of believing it are for the believer. This notion leads James to his famous and often misinterpreted conclusion:

> *'The true,' to put it very briefly, is only the expedient in the way of our thinking, just as 'the right' is only the expedient in the way of our behaving.* Expedient in almost any fashion; and expedient in the long run and on the whole of course.
> (WJ:438)

James takes this to mean that "on pragmatic principles we can not reject any hypothesis if consequences useful to life flow from it" (WJ:461). In short, whatever works is true. For example, "if the hypothesis of God works satisfactorily in the widest sense of the word," then it will be a true hypothesis (WJ:471). James is quite aware of the skepticism this view is likely to encounter: "I am well aware how odd it must seem to some of you to hear me say that an idea is 'true' so long as to believe it is profitable to our lives. That it is *good*, for as much as it profits, you will gladly admit" (WJ:388).

At this point, it is almost impossible to avoid seeing a close connection with James's earlier approach in "The Will to Believe." In that paper James had argued that, under certain circumstances, one has the right to believe something even if there is no sufficient ground for doing so. Recall, however, that in "The Will to Believe" James was quite careful to specify in what sort of circumstances such a move is permissible. One is not entitled to believe just anything that is expedient, but James specifically restricted himself to only those situations where one is faced with a choice that is forced, living, and momentous, and that cannot be decided on intellectual grounds. In *The Meaning of Truth,* James makes a claim that is very similar by requiring that the truth satisfies "some vital human need" (MT:5). Recall, further, that in "The Will to Believe" James also presented moral and religious beliefs as prime examples where one would have such a right to believe. Critics point out that James slides here, perhaps unconsciously, from the view that one sometimes has a right to believe something because one is better off believing it, to the view that such beliefs are actually *true.*

Right off the bat there seems to be at least one case where such a step is defensible: when we are dealing with self-fulfilling prophecies, where believing that something is true actually makes it true, or contributes to making it true. As is noted before, however, it is hard to defend that this can be maintained for all choices that are forced, living, and momentous, or for all beliefs that are expedient.

Continuing the line of thought from the previous section, it seems that expediency can be interpreted as one way of "fitting within reality," and should be treated as such. As James observes,

> If theological ideas prove to have a value for concrete life, they will be true, for pragmatism, in the sense of being good for so much. For how much more they are true, will depend entirely on their relations to the other truths that also have to be acknowledged. (WJ:387)

Restricting ourselves to those beliefs that cannot copy their object, this would make the *truth* of such beliefs dependent on whether the consequences of my believing it fit within reality. This agrees entirely with the general notion of truth James ascribes to the pragmatist, "as something essentially bound up with the way in which one moment in our experience may lead us toward other moments which it will be worth while to have been led to" (WJ:431f). To put it somewhat differently, beliefs that originate within ourselves, but that do not copy anything without us, will still count as true when they lead us in directions that are worthwhile. What this comes down to is that they begin a process of *veri*-fication, in which they are *made true* by the events or by coming to completion within experience. James makes much of the etymology of "verification." Just as we make something pure when we purify it, or liquid when we liquify it, so we make something true when we verify it (*veritas* being Latin for truth). Thus, if my believing in God leads to good consequences (on the whole and in the long run), then we can say that this belief agrees with reality, and consequently, it can be said to be true (as truth is an agreement of our beliefs with reality).

James insists, however, that such beliefs must come to completion in particular experiences. True beliefs are beliefs that are veri-*fied,* not beliefs that are merely veri-*fiable.* Although James admits that truth lives "for the most part on a credit system," he immediately adds that "beliefs verified concretely by *somebody* are the posts of the whole superstructure" (WJ:433). We believe that there are tigers in India without bothering to *veri*-fy this ourselves, but it can only be true if someone or other has actually veri-fied it (i.e., *made* it true). Recall that being true, for James, is neither a property of facts, nor a property of beliefs, but a certain connection of beliefs to facts.

4

The Pragmatic Humanism of F. C. S. Schiller

Does it not argue an abysmal conceit and stupendous
ignorance of the history of thought to cherish the delusion that
of all philosophies one's own alone was destined to win
general acceptance *ipsissimis verbis,* or even to be reflected,
undimmed and unmodified, in any other soul?

—F. C. S. Schiller.[42]

Ferdinand Canning Scott Schiller (1864–1937) was pragmatism's main
ambassador in England. His fierce opposition against the absolute
idealism of the British Hegelians, no doubt stemming from his own
student days, made him the *enfant terrible* of the Oxford establishment.
Schiller was born in the Danish part of Schleswig-Holstein. His father, a
Calcutta merchant of German origin, sent his sons to school in England.
Schiller attended Rugby school and continued his education at Balliol
College, Oxford, which was then heavily dominated by British idealism.
From 1893 until 1897, he lived in the United States where he was an
instructor in logic and metaphysics at another bastion of idealism, Cornell
University. At that time, Schiller first came into contact with James. In
1897, Schiller returned to England where he became Assistant Tutor at
Oxford's Corpus Christi College. Upon his retirement, in 1926, he spent
part of the year at the University of Southern California, first as a visiting
lecturer and later as professor. In 1935, after marrying for the first time at
the venerable age of 71, Schiller made California his permanent home. He
died two years later.

51

On Pragmatism

Although Schiller was heavily influenced by James, and frequently paid tribute to him, he maintains that he had arrived at his own pragmatic stance independently. And indeed, the basic elements of his pragmatism can be found already in his first book, *Riddles of the Sphinx,* which appeared in 1891 under the pseudonym "a Troglodyte," or cave dweller (refering to Plato's famous allegory of the cave). In this book Schiller defends a non-skeptical relativism, arguing that knowledge is always a product of specific human interests. For Schiller, all thoughts and actions are unavoidably the product of individual human beings who are guided by human needs and desires, from which they cannot be abstracted. Schiller considers himself the modern equivalent to Protagoras, the famous Sophist who said that "man is the measure of all things."[43]

Schiller's campaign for humanism—which is how he refers to his own brand of pragmatism—begins with the 1902 essay "Axioms as Postulates," which contains a vigorous attack on the notion of a priori knowledge. It is followed by *Humanism,* in 1903, and *Studies in Humanism,* in 1907. In the following year, Schiller published *Plato or Protagoras,* in which he examined Protagoras's speech in Plato's *Theaetetus.* In 1924, Schiller published *Problems in Belief* in which he traced the epistemological implications of different varieties of belief.

In the area of logic, Schiller's first major contribution is his 1912 *Formal Logic: A Scientific and Social Problem.* In this polemical work Schiller presents a humanist critique of traditional logic, arguing that the material of logic cannot be meaningfully abstracted from actual use and interest. Seventeen years later, in 1929, Schiller published a second volume on logic, entitled *Logic for Use: An Introduction to the Voluntarist Theory of Knowledge,* which was intended as a constructive sequel to *Formal Logic.*

Schiller also published three books on eugenics, the science that seeks to improve the genetic qualities of the human race by selective breeding: *Tantalus or the Future of Man* (1924), *Eugenics and Politics* (1926), and *Social Decay and Eugenic Reform* (1932). Schiller's defense of eugenics as the savior of society, with its accompanying antidemocratic sentiments, sets him wide apart from the American pragmatists (but less so from the Italian pragmatists discussed in chapter 5). It could be argued, however, that Schiller's proactive stance toward eugenics is at least in part a logical outcome of his humanism.

4.1 The Will to Believe

The essay that most influenced Schiller, and which remained a guiding force in the development of his own brand of pragmatism, is James's "The Will to Believe." Schiller sees this essay as a clear denouncement of "the cramping rules and regulations by which the Brahmins of the academic caste are tempted to impede the free expansion of human life."[44] According to Schiller, James's approach opens up philosophy by showing that "there are not really any external and non-human truths to prohibit us from adopting the beliefs we need to live by, nor any infallible a priori test of truth to screen us from the consequences of our choice."[45] Schiller's own "Axioms as Postulates" is largely an attempt to vindicate James's "Will to Believe," by showing how it universally applies to *all* knowledge, including the so-called self-evident axioms of logic. In this essay, Schiller goes to great lengths to prove that all a priori knowledge ultimately boils down to a set of *postulates,* that is, claims that we hope, desire, or wish to be true. What subsequently makes us stick to these postulates is *that we exercise the will to believe them.*

One of the axioms Schiller discusses is the principle of identity—the claim that everything is identical with itself, or that A equals A. In his discussion of the "axiom of identity," Schiller begins by observing that, with the exception of the felt self-identity of consciousness, identity is not a product of sensory impressions. The most that the senses can give us is what Schiller calls a "feeling of likeness." Schiller then gives a different account of the origin of what we call identity: "To obtain identity we must first desire it and demand it" (AP:98). Thus, for Schiller, it is the purpose-directedness of our thought that guides us in the establishment of identities, and it is the felt self-identity of consciousness that makes this possible. Take the following example of Schiller's:

> Edwin meets Angelina in her winter furs whom he admired last summer in fig leaves; he recognizes her identity in the differences of her primitive attire. That such things as the persistence of identity through change should be, and what they mean, he could learn only from the immediate experience of his own identity. That they are *is his postulate,* a postulate that fills his heart with the delicious hope that Angelina will smile on him as bewitchingly as before. (AP:98)

The identity of Angelina is thus a postulate, and it is evidently *Edwin's* postulate: "In recognizing Angelina he had of course (although he realized it not) construed her identity upon the model of his own" (AP:99). At the same time Angelina herself changes over time: one day she is glutted, the next day she is hungry; now she likes her steak well-done, a few years later she prefers it rare; and many years down the line she will be grey, stooped, and wrinkled.

From this living notion of identity, Schiller argues, logicians have abstracted the notion of an identity that *excludes* all differences. However, such an abstract notion of identity, he observes,

> is never found, but has always to be made. It is made . . . in whatever way and to whatever extent it is needed, and remains subservient to the purpose of its maker. It is a postulated ideal which works, though nature never quite conforms to it.
> (AP:103)

Hence, although never fully realized, the abstract notion of identity may be adhered to insofar as it is useful, as it is precisely its usefulness that brings it into being. This makes Schiller conclude that "It may therefore blandly be admitted that *A* is *A* is an impotent truism, so long as it is vividly realized that *A shall be A* is an active truth that remoulds the world" (ibid.). In this manner, one of the most fundamental axioms of logic, one that is often proclaimed to be a self-evident truth, is exposed as merely a postulate in disguise. It is something we *hope* to be true, making it distinctly a product of our will to believe.

Schiller provides similar arguments for other classic axioms, such as the principle of non-contradiction, the principle of excluded middle, the principle of causation, the principle of sufficient reason, etc. By thus expanding James's will-to-believe argument, Schiller develops a *voluntaristic epistemology* in which knowledge is always directly related to the particular wills of concrete individuals. Thus, logical and scientific principles are *not* extracted from reality, as self-evident propositions or necessary presuppositions, but they are distinctly human products that are imposed upon reality to serve certain practical ends:

> For the pragmatic theory of knowledge, initial principles are literally ἀρχαί, mere starting points, variously, arbitrarily, casually selected, from which we hope and try to advance to something better. . . . truth and reality in the fullest sense are not fixed foundations, but ends to be achieved. (HP:133)

For Schiller, we are not mere spectators of reality. We are participants who are caught right in the middle. This brings us to Schiller's pragmatism, and his view that we *make* truth and *make* reality.

4.2 Pragmatism

On the exact relation between pragmatism and humanism, Schiller's signals are mixed. At times he views them as equivalent, arguing that problems associated with the *term* "pragmatism" are the main reason why he prefers "humanism."[46] As Schiller later explains, he quickly realized "that pragmatism was a very bad name and apt to hang any dog that bore it," and should therefore be avoided as much as possible.[47]

On other occasions, as in the preface to *Humanism,* Schiller describes humanism as "a greater and more sovereign principle" than pragmatism, adding that pragmatism is "only the application of Humanism to the theory of knowledge" (HP:24). Schiller's motives for separating the two are quite similar to James's: he separates pragmatism from his radical empiricism to keep open the option that one can be a pragmatist without committing oneself to the more comprehensive doctrine of humanism. As Schiller observes,

> There will . . . be many pragmatists who cannot rise to
> Humanism; nor indeed is there any logical necessity why they
> should do so. It is quite possible to accept pragmatism as an
> *epistemological method* and analysis, without expanding it
> into a general philosophic principle. No man can be compelled
> to have a metaphysic . . . or at least be conscious of it. Anyone
> can, if he chooses, stop short on the epistemological plane, as
> he can on that of science or that of ordinary life. If, on the
> other hand, he proceeds to become a Humanist, he will no
> doubt regard his pragmatism as merely a special application of
> a principle which he applies all round to ethics, aesthetics, and
> theology, as well as to the theory of knowledge.[48]

Although one can be a pragmatist without being a humanist, one cannot be a humanist (at least not in Schiller's sense) without also being a pragmatist. Hence, it is to pragmatism that we first turn.

For Schiller, pragmatism originated as an opposition movement that provided a much-needed antidote against the atrophied intellectualism that, in his eyes, reigned philosophy. Pragmatism arose, Schiller contends, from the recognition that the developments in psychology and biology, in particular the theory of evolution, have profound effects on epistemology (EB:246). The result is that pragmatism is driven by a "thoroughgoing recognition of the influence of the purposiveness of thought on all our cognitive activities."[49] We are not mere spectators, Schiller argues, but we are actors for whom all thought is always related to some purpose we seek to achieve.

In his interpretation of pragmatism, Schiller follows James's lead in "Philosophical Conceptions and Practical Results" that pragmatism cannot be seen merely as a device for determining the meaning of a statement or belief, but that it must also determine what makes that statement or belief true. As Schiller remarks in his review of the fourth volume of Peirce's *Collected Papers*, "[Peirce's] principle was ostensibly a rule for determining *meaning* and *eliminating* the unmeaning. But it was impossible to overlook its bearing on all attempts to determine *truth*."[50]

It would not be too much to say that Schiller's own view of pragmatism is entirely overshadowed by his views on truth. In his *Encyclopaedia Britannica* article on pragmatism, he gives the following rendition of Peirce's pragmatic maxim:

> The real difference between two conceptions lies in their application, in the different consequences for the purposes of life which their acceptance carries. When no such "practical" difference can be found, conceptions are identical; when they will not "work," i.e., when they thwart the purpose which demanded them, they are false; when they are inapplicable they are unmeaning (A. Sidgwick). Hence, the "principle of Peirce" may be formulated as being that "every truth has practical consequences, and these are the test of its truth." (EB:247)

One can see a marked shift in the meaning of "pragmatism." Whereas for Peirce, the maxim is a principle to determine the meaning of the terms we use, the term "truth" being one of them, Schiller makes the maxim a principle to distinguish true conceptions (or beliefs) from false ones. True beliefs are those that work, and false beliefs are those that don't.

This view of truth immediately raises the crucial question of what it means for a belief to work. In addressing this question, it is important to keep in mind that, for Schiller, all our thoughts, and hence all our concepts, are always purpose-directed. In fact, the main reason Schiller embraced pragmatism was its insistence "that the purposive character of mental life must influence and pervade our most remotely cognitive activities" (HP:15). All our conceptions, no matter how abstract and how far removed from our daily lives they might be, are ultimately purpose-directed. This purpose-directedness of all our thought led Schiller to conclude that the truth of any conception is a function of its use or application. What makes a belief or an assertion true is its effect on "any human interest," and more specifically on "the interest with which it is directly concerned" (HP:58). Hence Schiller concludes,

> Pragmatism, then, in its wider sense, refers to the way in which our attributions of 'truth' and our recognitions of 'reality' are established and verified by their working, and sooner or later brought to the definite test of experiments which *succeed* or *fail,* i.e., give or deny satisfaction to some human interest, and are valued accordingly.[51]

This brings us to Schiller's humanism.

4.3 Humanism

Schiller's humanism is best understood as a reaction against the attempts to "de-humanize" knowledge. *Humanism,* for Schiller, is a "systematic protest against the artificial elimination of the human aspects of knowing";[52] or, as he puts it elsewhere, it is "the perception that the philosophic problem concerns human beings striving to comprehend a world of human experience by the resources of human minds" (HP:65). Not only are human minds limited, they are also intrinsically intertwined with the whole person, including all its desires, fears, hopes, plans, purposes, etc. By dehumanizing thought, philosophers inadvertently severed the link between thought and reality. Schiller insists repeatedly that we should never lose sight of Protagoras's maxim that "man is the measure of all things." Philosophical conceptions such as truth, reality, determinism, etc., must always be kept within our own human perspective and may not be "dehumanized." As he vividly describes in *Studies in Humanism,*

> It is only as a concrete human being that we know thought to be a real process at all. . . . thought per se, however, "absolute" and "ideal" and "eternal" we may call it, is wafted away from earth into the immense inanity of abstractions which have lost the touch with a reality to which they can never again be applied. (HP:125)

When we abstract in actual thinking, this abstraction is not absolute, as something that can be separated wholly from the purposes and conditions that gave rise to it, but it is an instrument of thought, designed to help us cope with the world wherein we live (HP:127). Without a context, abstraction is devoid of meaning.

On Pragmatism

In Schiller's view, Western philosophy took a wrong turn with Plato. In Plato's time, philosophy was in a dilemma. On the one side, there were the followers of Heraclitus, who believed that everything was in a constant flux—a view that was captured famously in the aphorism that you cannot step in the same river twice. On the other side, there were the Eleatics who believed that everything was absolutely static, so that nothing could ever move and, *ipso facto,* you could not even step in a river once. Both views made knowledge impossible. For the followers of Heraclitus, it was impossible to assert anything about anything, since everything keeps changing; nothing is stable enough for an assertion to refer to it. For the Eleatics, the problem was a different one. Because of their fundamental commitment to the unity of being, the only assertion they could make was to declare the being of being: "What is, is." According to Schiller, Plato found a way out of this when he discovered the function of concepts in the organization of experience. By using a concept, an idea could be predicated of the Heraclitan flux. Whereas the *object* of the idea would continue to change, the *concept* through which the object is lifted out of the flux of experience, would remain constant. For instance, my car has changed significantly in the many years I have driven it, but it is still "my car." Using concepts, allowed Plato to attach permanence to the flux of experience in a way that avoided the problem of the undifferentiated unity of the Eleatic "one." In its place we get "a well-knit system of knowable ideas."[53] The central problem that Plato subsequently ran into was that of the *interface* between the Heraclitan flux of experience and this stable system of "knowable ideas." Plato's allegory of the cave in the *Republic* was one attempt to bridge this gap between the eternal world of ideas and the perpetual flux of experience.

For Schiller, it was Protagoras who gave Plato the answer to this problem, albeit Plato failed to recognize this. As Schiller sees it, what connected, for Protagoras, the ideas with the flux of sensory impressions is that they are useful for us humans in our dealings with the world within which we live. This is the true meaning of the claim that man is the measure of all things. The idea of a snow shovel is constituted, not by something otherworldly within the realm of ideas, but simply by the fact that it enables *us* to scoop snow. It is this usefulness that gives the idea of the snow shovel its stability.

The requirement of making ourselves the measure of all things holds not only for philosophy, Schiller contends, but for the sciences as well. All scientific knowledge is intimately related to human needs and desires, and the world shaped by science is ultimately a human world. As Schiller puts it, "Pure science in short is pure bosh, if by purity be meant abstraction from all human purposes and freedom from all emotional interest."[54] As Schiller expounds a few pages later, this should not be considered as derogatory to science. Quite the opposite. The conception of humanized science leads to "a much-needed vindication of the rights of man, the maker of all sciences."[55]

The above discussion brings to light the following difference between pragmatism and humanism, assuming that we follow the strategy of distinguishing the two (section 4.2). Pragmatism focuses specifically on the idea that all beliefs must have practical consequences to be meaningful and that if those practical consequences come to be, the belief is not just meaningful but also true. Humanism, is broader in that it focuses on the *whole* individual who is holding the belief, with all his fears, frailties, desires, etc., and emphasizes that in determining the meaning or the truth of a belief we may never abstract from this. According to humanism, philosophers should always keep the whole person in mind. Pragmatists do not need to go this far. They may still dehumanize truth as long as they keep sight of the fact that truth is an inherently practical affair.

4.4 The Making of Truth

Before discussing Schiller's views on the making of truth and reality, we should reflect briefly on what he means by the word "making." Three different verbs come into play in Schiller's discussions of truth and reality: to discover, to make, and to create. In "The Making of Reality," Schiller draws a pragmatic distinction between the processes of discovering and making:

> A reality is said to be discovered, and not made, when its
> behavior is such that it is practically inconvenient or
> impossible to ascribe its reality for us entirely to our subjective
> activity. And as a rule the criteria of this distinction are plain
> and unmistakable. To wish for a chair and find one, and to
> wish for a chair and make one, are experiences which it is not
> easy to confuse. (HP:131)

What is more, when we say that a carpenter *makes* a chair, we do not mean that he is creating the chair *ex nihilo,* that is, out of nothing. Rather, the carpenter makes the chair out of material that is already at hand, such as wood, fabric, and nails. Thus, making the chair is not a creation "out of nothing," but a transformation of things that already exist (meaning that they are either found or made at an earlier stage). Similarly, when speaking of the *making* of truth and reality, Schiller is not suggesting that

59

we are *creating* truth and reality "out of nothing." Our making of truth and reality is more like how the carpenter makes a chair. As Schiller puts it, "We do not make reality out of nothing . . . we are not 'creators,' and our powers are limited" (HP:146). In short, we *make* truths just as we *make* mistakes.

Schiller observes that in practice the distinction between making and finding is not as sharp as is suggested here, and he is quick to point out that finding "often involves a good deal of 'making'" (HP:132), thereby suggesting that finding is rather a limiting case of making. This raises the question as to whether it is even possible to purely find anything.

Let us now turn to Schiller's view on truth-making. Schiller insists on the *making* of truth for several reasons. Most importantly, he seeks to ensure that the notion of truth remains within the realm of human capability. With his theory of truth, Schiller opposes especially the nineteenth-century idealists who deny that truth is ever made, holding instead that truth is eternal. On this view, that the earth is round is not something that was "made true" by those who first discovered it, but it is something that was true all along, and something that would also be true were it never discovered. According to the idealists, the best we humans can aim for is to approximate this eternal truth insofar as our easily distracted and finite minds allow us to do. In Schiller's opinion, this is an odd sort of view. First, the idealists alienate "the truth" from us by abstracting it from all that is important to us (so that we would not be biased); then they set up this alien notion of truth as an ideal, calling our ideas true only when they conform to that ideal, thereby concluding that our ideas must always fall short of this ideal and that hence the truth cannot be known.

4.5 Three Pragmatic Views on Truth

Within pragmatism, Schiller distinguishes three different views on truth, which he attributes respectively to Peirce, James, and himself. Not quite grasping the purport of Peirce's pragmatic maxim, which he seems to have known only vicariously through James, Schiller attributes to Peirce the view that "the difference between the truth and the falsehood of an assertion must show itself in some visible way."[56] Schiller dismisses this view as philosophically uninteresting and lamented that Peirce was unable to keep up with the development of pragmatism. Peirce may have originated the doctrine, Schiller observes, but "also exhibited extensive inability to follow the later developments, and now calls his own specific form of Pragmatism 'pragmaticism'" (HP:59). Consequently, Schiller argues, the greater majority of Peirce's work remains on a "pre-pragmatic" level.[57]

The second pragmatic view of truth is James's. On this view, which Schiller considers an improvement upon the former, truths not only *have* consequences, but the truth of an assertion actually *consists* in the purported consequences of the assertion, adding that these consequences must be "good" (HP:59). For Schiller, this second view follows naturally from the first

> for to say that a truth has consequences and that what has none is meaningless, must surely mean that it has a bearing upon some human interest; they must be consequences *to* someone *for* some purpose. But now, we may ask, *how are these 'consequences' to test the 'truth' claimed by the assertion?* Only by satisfying or thwarting that purpose, by forwarding or baffling that interest. If they do the one, the assertion is 'good' and *pro tanto* 'true'; if they do the other, 'bad' and 'false.' Its 'consequences,' therefore, when investigated, always turn out to involve the 'practical' predicates 'good' or 'bad,' and to contain a reference to 'practice' in the sense in which we have used that term.[58]

In an article for *Mind* called "Humanism and Truth," James explicitly denies that Schiller correctly represented his view. For James, the view that the truth of any claim *consists* in its consequences goes well beyond pragmatism, and he advised that Schiller's proposal to call this wider view "humanism" be adopted.[59]

Schiller's own view, which he considers the logical outcome of the view he ascribes to James, rests on the idea that there is *nothing more* to the truth of an assertion than the consequences that are claimed by it. Consequently, Schiller argues,

> We may effect a transition from the original assertion that the truth expresses itself in the 'consequences' to the more advanced conclusion that it so expresses itself *fully, i.e.,* 'consists' in them, and that if it is really 'true' those consequences are 'good.'[60]

In short, for Schiller, an assertion is true when it has good consequences, meaning that the assertion satisfies the purpose that was (tacitly) expressed by it (recall that, for Schiller, all thought is purpose-directed). In contrast, an assertion is false when it has bad consequences, meaning that the purpose that is (tacitly) expressed by the assertion is not satisfied. For example, a man who has just spent the evening drinking concludes he is still sober enough to drive home. For Schiller, whether this man's belief is true consists entirely in the consequences of that belief, thus making the belief true if he manages to arrive home without problems and false when he ends up dead. Schiller's theory of truth can thus be called a consequentialist theory of truth.

When Schiller speaks of "success" in validating a truth, this must be understood as a relative term; it is success *"relative to the purpose* with which the truth was claimed" (HP:245). For instance, when I am looking for a place to sit, the belief that a certain object is a chair is true if I can sit in it. However, were I to be a collector of seventeenth-century Baroque furniture, that same judgment—I can sit in it, thus it is a chair—may not even be applicable. More in general, truth depends, for Schiller, "very essentially upon context, on who says what, to whom, why, and under what circumstances" (HP:62). This is true even for our most abstract claims. If we want to know whether it is true whether $2 + 2 = 4$, Schiller points out, we first need to know what the "twos" and the "fours" stand for. As Schiller observes, "It would not be true of lions and lambs, nor of drops of water, nor of pleasures and pains" (HP:62). In short, for Schiller, truth always depends upon context, even the truth of $2 + 2 = 4$.

Because Schiller relates the truth of an assertion strictly to its consequences, which must be *good* consequences, truth is, for Schiller, a value. To say that an assertion is true is to say that believing it leads to good consequences, and this is nothing other than making a value judgment about that assertion. Hence, to say that a particular assertion is true is not a statement of fact, but a normative claim. As will be shown more explicitly in chapter 6, Peirce sees pragmatism as a normative doctrine also.

Given Schiller's insistence that all thought, no matter how abstract, is purposive, it follows that even our most basic notions, such as "reality" and "fact," are not disinterested descriptions of a world of which we are merely a spectator, but are expressions of value. To call something real is to give it a value. There are no objective facts in the sense of being value-neutral. As Schiller puts it elsewhere, pragmatism is "the doctrine that 'truths' are values and that 'realities' are arrived at by a process of valuation, and that consequently our 'facts' are not independent of our 'truths,' nor our 'truths' of our 'goods.'"[61]

Schiller dismisses any attempt to develop the pragmatist theory of truth along Peircean lines, in which meaning and truth could be cast in subjunctive or even counterfactual conditionals (section 2.5). For Schiller, truth claims must be actually verified to be true:

> All 'truths' must be verified to be properly true. . . . On its
> entry into the world of existence, a truth claim has merely
> commended itself (perhaps provisionally) to its maker. To
> become really true it has to be tested, and it is tested by being
> *applied.* Only when this is done, only, that is, when it is *used,*
> can it be determined what it really means, and what conditions
> it must fulfill to be really true. (HP:61)

When trying to come to grips with Schiller's conception of truth, it
is important not to slide back into the old notion of a fixed, eternal truth.
For Schiller, truths are relative and truths are temporal. New discoveries
reveal that certain existing truths are no longer tenable, which means
literally that a new truth was made. This making of new truth is
accompanied by a re-valuation of old truths. The old truths are now called
"false," and the new truth is generally "antedated" and said to have been
"true all along" (EB:247).

Although Schiller firmly rejects the notion of a rigid, static, and
incorrigible truth, his process of truth-making and the revaluation of old
truths does allow for something like an ideal, or absolute, truth. Such an
absolute truth, and Schiller remains at this point very close to Peirce and
James, would be a truth that is adequate to every purpose and can
accommodate every contingency, so that it would no longer change.
Schiller explains,

> We can, however, conceive an ideal completion of the making
> of truth, in the achievement of a situation which would
> provoke no questions and so would inspire no one with a
> purpose to remake it, and on this ideal the name absolute truth
> may be bestowed. (HP:247)

However, whereas this conception of absolute truth was central to Peirce's
notion of truth, it plays little or no role in Schiller's humanistic outlook.
Schiller did recognize it as an implication of his pragmatism, but he did
not consider it a particularly interesting one, as it remains too far removed
from concrete individuals and their dealings with reality. In his personal
copy of Hartley Grattan's *The Three Jameses*, published in 1932, Schiller
writes in the margin of Grattan's explanation of Peirce's view of truth as
the opinion with which all who investigate are ultimately fated to agree
(cf. section 2.8), that such a state would be realized only in heaven, when
all those who disagree have been damned.[62]

4.6 The Making of Reality

Although Schiller maintains what he called a "voluntaristic metaphysic," he does not deny that there is an external world that is to a large degree independent from what we think or want it to be. As Schiller explains,

> Humanism has no quarrel with the assumptions of common-sense realism; it does not deny what is popularly described as the "external" world. . . . It insists only that the "external world" of realism is still dependent on human experience, and perhaps ventures to add that the data of human experience are not completely used up in the construction of a real external world. (HP:66)

In other words, for Schiller, the external world—or reality—is plastic, incomplete, and thoroughly anthropomorphic. What the physical scientist calls "real" is largely a product of the questions she is interested in and the experiments she performs.

How, then, is reality made? To this question Schiller gives one answer that is not so controversial and another one that is. The not-so-controversial answer is that making a new truth, or gaining new knowledge, alters our *subjective* reality; it changes how we see reality (HP:139). Gaining a new truth thus *ipso facto* changes the knower, and since the knower is herself part of reality, it changes reality itself. Since, in Schiller's terminology, changing reality comes down to making reality, this means that a new reality is made (recall that making reality is not the same as creating it).

The second and more controversial answer, is that gaining a new truth alters not only the knower but also the object known. The paradigm case is the self-fulfilling prophecy, already discussed in chapter 3. For example, my belief that I can jump over a stream may give me the strength to do this, and thereby makes the *object* of the belief (my ability to jump over the stream) real. Schiller is aware that this is a special case, but in his view it is much less of a special case than it appears at first sight. Schiller agrees that pure perception, or mere knowing, would not at all affect its object, and would thus not make any reality apart from the changes it establishes in the knower. But Schiller denies that there is such a thing as *pure* perception or *mere* knowing:

> Mere knowing does not seem capable of altering reality, merely because it is an intellectualistic abstraction, which, strictly speaking, does not exist. In the pragmatic conception, however, knowing is a prelude of doing. . . . Hence to

establish the bearing on reality of the making of truth, we must not confine ourselves to this fragmentary "mere knowing," but must consider the whole process as completed, i.e., as issuing in action, and as sooner or later altering reality. (HP:141)

For Schiller, there is no such thing as *mere* knowing. Knowing always has an active component. The mind is not wholly passive, as if sensations were to leave their impressions in us like a signet ring imprints its seal in a piece of wax, but we actively contribute to all we perceive. To experience is either to experiment or to react, and in the process we affect what we experience. For Schiller, this holds even for the most passive perceptions. Referring to the history of thought, he observes, "Our most passive receptivity of sensations can, and should, be constructed as the effortless fruition of what was once acquired by strenuous effort, rather than as the primal type to which all experience should be reduced" (AP:56). Passive perception is perception in which the active component has become almost entirely habitual or reflex-like. What is true of perception, Schiller argues, equally applies to knowledge in general. With a pun at Hegel's expense, Schiller concludes that the true method of philosophy is not dia-lectic but *trial*-ectic; our knowledge advances not by an inner dynamic of thought, as with Hegel's dialectic, but by *trying* things (AP:58). Were there even to be a pure knower, or mere spectator, Schiller concludes, it "would be the most negligible thing in the universe" (HP:141). An invisible movie camera that fails to record anything because no one has put any film in it, comes closest.

Schiller's account of the making of reality steers him in a perspectivist direction. For Schiller, reality is always the reality of some knower, and it makes little sense to speak of a knower-independent reality. For Schiller, absolute reality, if there even is such a thing, would be a bundle of different perspectives encroaching upon one another. In *Studies in Humanism,* Schiller discusses three such perspectives, that of Newton, his dog, and a stone. Although Newton's dog no doubt loved his master, the latter's theory of gravitation would not have entered into the dog's world. Newton, in turn, was most likely oblivious of many of the finer delights of canine rabbit hunting. Now, in contrast to the dog, a stone cannot even apprehend us as spiritual beings, but does that mean, Schiller asks, that the stone cannot apprehend us at all? Not so. He continues, "It is aware of us and affected by us on the plane on which its own existence is passed, and quite capable of making us effectively aware of its existence in our transactions with it" (HP:142). The plane at which the perspectives of Newton and the stone intersect, the "world" they have in common, is the physical realm of bodies. The initial reality from which all these perspectives ultimately emerged, Schiller characterizes as "sheer potentiality" with an explicit reference to Aristotle's *hyle,* the primary substratum or yet fully undifferentiated primeval matter within which all that is took shape (HP:134).

Based on his perspectivist interpretation, Schiller comes to the following conception of what is generally called "the external world":

> It seems clear that we are not the sole agents in the world, and that herein lies the best explanation of those aspects of the world which we, the present agents, i.e., our empirical selves, cannot claim to have made. (HP:146)

Thus, for Schiller, I make my own reality, but I am apparently not the only one to do so, and the work of others enters into my reality where my perspective intersects with theirs. At those intersection points, I am confronted with things for which I cannot really claim any substantial authorship. For instance, when I trip on a stone, this is because my perspective intersects with that of the stone, so that the stone becomes present to me. Schiller's perspectivist view of reality bears close similarities with James's radical empiricism, mentioned in chapter 3, and George Herbert Mead's principle of sociability.[63]

5

The Wild Years:
Pragmatism in Florence

A group of young men desirous of freedom, eager for
universality, anxious for a superior intellectual life, have
gathered in Florence under the symbolic and augural name of
"Leonardo," in order to intensify their own existence, to
elevate their own thought, to exalt their own art.

—Leonardo[64]

Schiller may have been the most vocal and long-lasting pragmatist in
Europe, but he was by no means the only one. In France, James's views
found ready acceptance among a number of philosophers, most of whom
were already developing their own thoughts along similar lines. They
included Henri Bergson, Maurice Blondel, Émile Boutroux, Pierre
Duhem, Édouard Le Roy, Henri Poincaré, and Georges Sorel. Blondel
actually used the term *"Pragmatisme"* as early as 1888, but abandoned
the term after discovering its use by the American pragmatists.

In his 1921 *De l'Utilité du pragmatisme*, the political and social
philosopher Georges Sorel reformulated James's pragmatism into a
doctrine of social criticism. In this book, Sorel complains that James's
pragmatism is "provincial, impregnated with the atmosphere of an
American, Protestant, and academic environment," and needed to be
rethought "by a European brain."[65] Earlier, in his *Réflexions sur la
violence* (1906), Sorel had developed a theory of myths that is in effect a
social version of James's individualistic will-to-believe argument. Myths,
like the myth of the general strike of all workers, give guidance to political

and social life, and they are "made true" when people come to believe in them.

In 1908, James's *Pragmatism* was translated into German by the Viennese schoolteacher Wilhelm Jerusalem. The book led to a storm of protests in Germany and was hotly debated during the World Congress of Philosophy that was held in Heidelberg later that year. James's views were seen as a clear sign that American philosophy had degraded itself to an unabashed commercialism in which truth was identified with how much your dollar can buy. German proponents of pragmatism were few and far between, and before they could set up a proper defense against the barrage of ill-informed criticism, the First World War broke out, which further deepened the divide between Germany and the U.S. Between the two World Wars, pragmatism was taken up by some philosophers with national socialist leanings, such as Eduard Baumgarten, who saw in it a philosophy of the deed. In general, however, anticapitalist sentiments resulted in an offhand rejection of pragmatism by most German intellectuals. At the same time, the views of Dewey and Mead seeped into German thought and had a profound impact on a pivotal branch of German twentieth-century philosophy—philosophical anthropology—especially through the work of Arnold Gehlen.[66]

The early influence of pragmatism was particularly striking in Italy. In an interview with the London newspaper *Sunday Times*, the Italian dictator Benito Mussolini listed James and Sorel among his three principal philosophic mentors. In the same interview Mussolini explained that he had found in James "that faith in action, that ardent will to live and fight, to which fascism owes a great part of its success."[67] Mussolini's allegiance to pragmatism, however, did not prevent him from ordering the beating of another pragmatist, Giovanni Amendola, who had become a central figure in the political opposition.[68] Amendola died from medical complications caused by his injuries shortly before Mussolini's interview with the *Sunday Times*.

A particularly vocal group of Italian pragmatists emerged in Florence, and it is to them that this chapter is devoted. It was argued in chapter 1 that pragmatism, as it developed in the United States, was in important respects a product of its time. The same is true for the development of pragmatism in Italy. Although the Italian pragmatists, especially Giovanni Papini and Giuseppe Prezzolini, depended heavily on James and Schiller, Italian pragmatism originated and flourished as a criticism of the Italian political scene that was dominated by strong displays of oratorical skills and a distinct lack of action. As Papini phrases it in his signature combative style,

In this classic land of abundant phrases we do not wish to add another formula to all those which gladden the hearts of the councils, the congresses, and the meetings in the Kingdom of Italy. All the formulas and all the ideas of which we have need are already at hand, they have already been stated, and they have often been repeated. We wish only to live to see these formulas and these ideas acted upon.[69]

When James visited Rome in April of 1905 to attend the Fifth International Congress of Psychology, he was overwhelmed by the attention that was given to his philosophy by the Italian avant-garde. From Rome he writes to his wife Alice:

I have been having this afternoon a very good and rather intimate talk with the little band of pragmatists, Papini, Vailati, Calderoni, Amendola, etc. most of whom inhabit Florence, publish the monthly journal *Leonardo* at their own expense, and carry on a very serious philosophical movement, apparently *really* inspired by Schiller and myself . . . and show an enthusiasm, and also a literary swing and activity that I know nothing of in our own land.[70]

The Florentine pragmatists, or the *Leonardini,* as they were also called, may have formed a "serious philosophical movement," but they did little to systematize their pragmatism or to define its limits. In a short essay entitled "What Pragmatism is Like," Papini simply concludes, that "there *is no such thing as pragmatism,* but that there are only *pragmatic theories,* and *thinkers who are more or less pragmatic.*" And he continues by saying that, "Pragmatism is a *coalition* of theories coming from various sources and temperaments rather than a handsome system sprung from the brain of a single philosopher, or from a homogeneous and well-organized school."[71]

This attitude toward pragmatism, which is found in Papini as well as Prezzolini, followed directly from their attitude toward philosophy in general. For Papini, as for Prezzolini, pragmatism was first and foremost a proclamation that thought should be free, and that it should not be restrained within a rigid philosophical system, like that of a Hegel or Spinoza. If philosophy is to genuinely reflect the complexity of life, we should expect a corresponding diversity of theories.

Interestingly, the Florentine pragmatists were divided roughly along Peircean and Jamesian lines. Papini and Prezzolini were staunch supporters of James and Schiller. They showed a strong literary inclination and felt particularly attracted to James's doctrine of the will to believe. On the other hand, the more scientifically minded Giovanni Vailati and Mario Calderoni felt more affinity with Peirce. In fact, James's meeting with the Florentine pragmatists coincided with the culmination of a debate that was being fought out within the pages of *Leonardo* between Prezzolini and Calderoni.

The current chapter contains a brief synopsis of the main views of the Florentine pragmatists. After a brief introduction to the movement's main mouthpiece, the review *Leonardo,* its two main currents are discussed. These are the James-Schiller inspired *magical pragmatism* of Papini and Prezzolini, and the *logical pragmatism* of Vailati and Calderoni, which has a distinctly Peircean slant. Having thus staked out the territory, the chapter concludes with an account of the Prezzolini-Calderoni debate.

5.1 The *Leonardo* Movement

Under the leadership of Giovanni Papini, *Leonardo* was founded in 1903 as a militant review for young Italian intellectuals.[72] Its founders were young indeed. Papini was twenty-two and Prezzolini twenty-one. As Papini testifies later, the journal was meant to "reveal to the masters of the present (to men no longer young, to men of thirty and forty), that the real youngsters, the new youngsters of twenty have also come of age and at last acquired the right to speak" (F:103).

The review was named after one of Florence's most illustrious natives, Leonardo da Vinci. The choice of name reflected the desire of its founders to restore the combination of science, art, and the great personality that had characterized the great Renaissance master. In contrast to university philosophy professors, Da Vinci did not approach nature in a bookish way, but sought to *live* it. "The divine Leonardo," Papini writes,

> did not compose treatises methodically divided into sections,
> in the manner of pedants who study only ancient books, but he
> takes his stand before the universe as a new man, as an
> explorer of unknown lands, and above all as an artist who
> knows better than the pure scientists themselves, how to
> penetrate to the depths and grasp the aspects and secrets of
> things.[73]

On the fourth of January, 1903, *Leonardo*'s first issue appeared. Its eight folio size pages were printed on handmade paper, and detailed attention was given to its artistic appearance. In a programmatic statement, its editors explain that "in thought they are idealists and individualists, superior to any system and to any limits; they are convinced that any philosophy is nothing but a personal mode of living—and deny any other form of existence outside of thought."[74] In their individual contributions, Papini and Prezzolini embrace the radical voluntarism of the Italian idealist Benedetto Croce, who claimed in his 1902 *Estetica* that the creative powers of humanity are so vast we can create our own history like an artist creates a piece of art. Moreover, Papini and Prezzolini rejected all organized social ideas, believing that each individual is capable of developing his or her own theory of life.

The Leonardini were iconoclasts. As Papini later remembers in his autobiography, *The Failure,* "we demolished, destroyed, dismembered, striking to right and left, sometimes with perfect holy justice, then again, as our maturer judgment admitted, too precipitously, but always in good faith and in the name of a greater love" (F:119). The ferocious beardless conquistadores, as Papini once characterized the group, radically opposed the philosophic establishment. In Papini's words,

> Philosophy hitherto had always been rational: we set out to
> combat intellectualism with might and main. Philosophy had
> always been speculative and contemplative: we decided it
> should become something active, creative, taking its part in a
> necessary reformation of the world. (F:119)

In their break with tradition, positivism, which had reigned Italian philosophy for over thirty years, was the Leonardini's main target. The review's main mission was to stir people up rather than to give them a new ideology. As Papini puts it in 1906,

> I want to awaken the drowsy ones, but I do not, at least right
> now, want to say what they must do when they awaken. It is
> enough for me that they no longer lie about on the beds of
> habit and the grass of mediocrity.[75]

5.2 Papini's Magical Pragmatism

The Florentine pragmatist movement began roughly with Giovanni Papini's 1903 "Death and Resurrection of Philosophy."[76] In this essay, Papini argues that philosophical principles are valuable only insofar as they enable us to transform or master reality. It is the distinct aim of philosophy, he claims, to set man to action. Action leads to power, which for Papini means the satisfaction of our desires. For Papini, in the attainment of power we attain a state of divinity, in essence making his pragmatism a doctrine that shows us how to become God. A few years later, he wrote a celebrated essay entitled *"Dall'uomo a Dio"* (from man to God). In the views of both Papini and Prezzolini, James's will to believe is in effect replaced by Nietzsche's will to power, making it no surprise that the early fascists felt attracted to it.[77]

James felt a strong attraction to Papini (James's "G. Papini and the Pragmatist Movement in Italy" is all about Papini and mentions the others only in passing). As James later confesses in a letter to Papini, "It is your *temper of carelessness,* quite as much as your particular formulas, that has had such an emancipating effect on my intelligence. You will be accused of extravagance, and *correctly* accused; you will be called the Cyrano de Bergerac of Pragmatism, etc., but the abstract program of it *must* be sketched extravagantly."[78]

Papini's pragmatism is extravagant indeed. It is an exuberant embracing of the will to believe, while intoxicated by the creative spirit. It is a philosophy of action. Dismissing the rational and detached contemplation of traditional philosophers, Papini advocates a total and unconditional immersion. If we want to know reality, he writes in *The Failure,*

> We must come in contact with all its aspects (even the most recondite, the most transitory, the least perceptible), blend ourselves with its fullness, abandon ourselves to its flow, lose ourselves in its immensity, become living realities in a living reality. We should not just stand in its presence like so many thinking machines, so many microscopes, so many rubber stamps, so many tape measures; rather we should dive into it headlong, penetrate into it and be penetrated by it, feel within our own selves the external multicolor, multisound, and multisavor of its flux, putting its pulse in rhythm with the pulsation of our blood, with our own heartbeat, so completely identifying ourselves with reality that it becomes wholly of us, all of us within it. (F: 201)

This magical pragmatism (*pragmatismo magico*), as Papini calls it, has close affinities with the pragmatism of Schiller. As with Schiller, it is a philosophy of the whole individual, and not just that part which we call reason; and like Schiller, it is hostile to positivism, which considers reality as something to be measured rather than lived. Pragmatism, Papini writes in *The Failure,* is a philosophy of action, a philosophy of doing, of rebuilding, transforming, creating! . . . No more wild goose chasing down roads leading nowhere save into the snares and traps of visionary logicians. The *true* is the *useful*. To *know* is to *do*. Among many uncertain truths, choose the one best calculated to raise the tone of life and promising the most lasting rewards. If something is not true but we wish it were true, we will *make* it true: by *faith*. (F:204)

Pragmatism, Papini explains, is a "tool-philosophy, a hammer-and-anvil idea, a theory that produces, a practical promotion and exploitation of the spirit!" However, declaring philosophy an instrument for action does not go far enough for him and he seeks to elevate his pragmatism even further:

I adopted therefore that part of pragmatism which promised most—the part which taught how through faith, beliefs not corresponding with reality could be made *true*. But why limit this action to beliefs? Why create the truth of a few particular faiths only? The spirit should be master of everything. The power of the will should have no limitations whatever! Just as scientific knowledge in a sense creates *facts,* and just as the will to believe creates *truth,* even so the spirit must dominate the all, create and transform at pleasure, without intermediaries. So far, to control external things, we had to use other external things: our minds control our muscles, and these in turn set other parts of material reality in motion. . . . I wanted spirit to do everything all by itself, by its own fiat, without any go-betweens. (F:205f)

In a nutshell, Papini's pragmatism was a program for men to become Gods. This is far from a humble undertaking, and Papini acknowledges this: "Great in very deed, my dream; but I did not despair of realizing it. Had men ever before set out deliberately to become God?" (F:206). Papini, however, does not try to become *like* God, or, like the mystics, seeks to lose himself *in* God, since that would already presuppose the existence of God, and Papini did not at the time believe (nor was he willing to accept) that God existed. Instead, he seeks to *create* God by first returning "to complete nudity, to the terrifying freedom of the absolute universal atheist," and, having thus rid himself of "all kinds of trumpery," by transforming himself, "a poor, weak, wretched man" into "a supreme and sovereign Being, all-rich and all powerful" (F:130, 207). A few years

73

later Papini's megalomaniacal pragmatism would convert into a devout Catholicism.

It is difficult to deny that Papini carried pragmatism too far. But his criticism of the detached view held by the positivists, who saw reality as an object that is somewhere out there, and that it is the philosopher's task to measure it precisely, is well taken. In "G. Papini and the Pragmatist Movement in Italy," James gives a somewhat toned down account of Papini's pragmatism:

> Tristan and Isolde, Paradise, Atoms, Substance, neither of them copies anything real; all are creations placed above reality, to transform, build out and interpret it in the interest of human need or passion. Instead of affirming with the positivists that we must render the idea world as similar as possible to the actual, Sig. Papini emphasizes our duty of turning the actual world into as close a copy of the idea as it will let us. (EPh:147)

Papini's message is clear. We must not resign ourselves to accept reality "as is." Our responsibility is not to *describe* reality, but to shape it according to our ideals. It is not we who must bend to reality, but reality must make way for us. We should treat our desires "as *ideal limits* towards which reality must ever more be approximated" (ibid.). In action our ideals are real-ized. For James, Papini simply carried the trend that was set by his own claim that truth is veri-fication (section 3.7), and by Schiller's conceptions of the making of truth and the making of reality (sections 4.4 and 4.6), to another level.

One final note. Mussolini's credit to James's pragmatism in the *Sunday Times* interview is often cited. However, earlier in the same interview, Mussolini remarked that "to fight for the establishment of that social order that *at a given moment* best corresponds to our *personal* ideal is one of the worthiest of human activities."[79] Mussolini does not name anyone here, but it is tempting to read into this statement a Papini-Prezzolini style pragmatism, making Mussolini's rise to power perhaps the fullest, even if diabolical, incarnation of the Man-God. The antidemocratic sentiments of Papini and Prezzolini (both favored an intellectual aristocracy),[80] and Prezzolini's later associations with Mussolini, support such a reading. One year after the demise of *Leonardo,* Prezzolini founded a new review, *La Voce,* with a strong accent on politics and social issues. In 1914, Prezzolini also helped the future dictator found *Il Popolo d'Italia,* which became the central mouthpiece for the fascists. Not long afterward, Arcangelo di Staso credited Prezzolini with having discovered Mussolini, and concluded that without *La Voce* Italy would have "fewer men of action."[81]

5.3 Vailati's Logical Pragmatism

Papini's magical pragmatism, with its focus on man's divinely-creative functions, stands in a stark contrast to the more subdued logical pragmatism of Giovanni Vailati and Mario Calderoni. Vailati and Calderoni sought their inspiration in Peirce, rather than in James and Schiller, and they joined Peirce in limiting pragmatism largely to a doctrine of meaning.

Giovanni Vailati's background and interests were markedly different from those of the more literary and artistically inclined Papini. In 1892, having completed his degree in engineering at the University of Turin, Vailati became an assistant to Giuseppe Peano, a pioneer in mathematical logic and the axiomatization of mathematics, and he contributed to the latter's ambitious *Formulario Mathematico* (Mathematical Formulary). The aim of the *Formulario* was to collect all known mathematical theorems and formulas, and express them in Peano's logic notation. The last edition, which appeared in 1908, contained no less than 4,200 formulas and theorems, all completely stated and most of them proved. The *Formulario* greatly influenced Bertrand Russell and Alfred North Whitehead in their *Principia Mathematica* (1910–13). Vailati felt especially attracted to Peano's postulational approach, and to the logic of relations that had been developed earlier by Peirce and, partly in Peirce's footsteps, by the German logician Ernst Schröder.

In 1895, Vailati became an assistant to the projective geometer Vito Volterra. Having been promoted to honorary assistant the following year, Vailati initiated a course on the history of mechanics. Like Peirce, Vailati developed a great interest in the history of science, which set him apart from his positivist colleagues who dismissed the history of science as a menagerie of refuted theories, useful at best as a resource for lively anecdotes. It was also at this time that Vailati began to investigate the role of axioms and postulates in systems of geometry.

Vailati's academic career was short lived. In 1899, the same year in which he published two reviews of James's *The Will to Believe* (a third review was to follow the next year), he left academia to become a high school mathematics teacher. He remained actively engaged in pragmatism, however. In 1904 Vailati moved to Florence, where he met Papini and Prezzolini. It was also in Florence that he met Mario Calderoni, who soon became his main philosophical ally.

75

On Pragmatism

It was primarily Vailati's study of the history of mechanics as Volterra's assistant that led him to philosophy. Vailati quickly discovered that the sequence of scientific theories is not a fortuitous product of accidental circumstances (chance discoveries, practical demands, private inclinations, etc.), but that the history of science has its own inner logic. Hence, the history of science should not be approached as an accumulation of isolated theories and problems, but one should, Vailati writes, "analyze and consider from a general point of view the various methods of scientific investigation and the part each of them has effectively had in augmentation of the various realms of knowledge."[82] According to Vailati, it is by studying the *history* of science that one discovers the *logic* of science. Especially from the seventeenth century onward, scientists have dismissed the importance of the history of science, emphasizing that good science should always be a direct product of careful empirical observations. In their hostility toward the history of science, the early modern scientists were reacting particularly against the schoolmen, who they thought put too much faith in the ideas found in the books of the ancient philosophers. Galileo, for instance, firmly declares through the central character of his *Dialogue on the Two World Systems* that only the sensible world mattered and not, what he disparagingly termed, the "world of paper" (*mondo di carta*).

Vailati, living in an age that had gained a new appreciation for this "world of paper," argues that science is cumulative. Today's science contains the successful parts of the science of yesterday. This is most evident in mathematics and mechanics, but it is equally true for the basic concepts in physics, chemistry, psychology, etc. The symbols and formulas that have become second nature for today's mathematicians embody the work of countless generations of scholars. Their work, Vailati remarks, has been "concentrated and stored in those symbols and formulas which through habit we handle with great facility and rapidity."[83] Our faith in these symbols and formulas—which is evident, say, in the confidence with which we use logarithms or imaginary numbers—has become so great that we trust these formulas even more than our senses. In taking up the cause of the "world of paper," which Galileo had so firmly rejected, Vailati sided with the eighteenth-century mathematician Leonard Euler, who boldly declared that "our pencil is more to be trusted than our judgments." At the same time, Vailati was careful to warn against an overly exaggerated respect for formalisms.

Vailati's discovery that one cannot separate the "world of paper" from the science of mechanics directed his attention to the role of concepts, axioms, and arguments in science. Following partly in the

76

footsteps of the physicist Ernst Mach, Vailati developed an instrumentalist view of science. Concepts, mathematical symbols, hypotheses, etc., are not meant to represent anything, nor are they intended to be true. They are tools, or instruments, for organizing observational data. In Vailati's words, "The concepts of which mechanics makes use, and the suppositions upon which mechanics is based, clearly come to assume the character of instruments whose value depends solely on the service they render for attaining some proposed end."[84]

Vailati's instrumentalist approach is further confirmed by his rejection of the two dominant schools of thought on the nature of science: empiricism and rationalism. The empiricists rejected all theorizing and hypothesis formation on the ground that science should build directly upon observations. From our observations we subsequently derive through induction by enumeration general truths such as the laws of nature. Newton, with his famous dictum *hypotheses non fingo* (I do not invent any hypotheses), belonged to this school.

The rationalists, in contrast, saw science as built upon unshakable foundations (or axioms), which were often thought to be self-evident and which were connected with our observations through irrefutable deductive chains of arguments. Vailati objects to this second view that even in a science so well-ordered and developed as mechanics, there are no unshakable axioms. As he later explained in *Leonardo,* vaguely anticipating Haack's *foundherentism* (see section 11.1),

> Notwithstanding contrary suggestions, arising from images
> representing premises as "pillars" or "pegs" by which
> conclusions are "upheld," . . . the opposite case, in which the
> truth or certainty of conclusions, deducible from given
> premises, is apt to increase and consolidate the certainty of the
> premises themselves, is no less frequent nor less important to
> be kept in view. . . . There is hardly any branch of knowledge
> in which the premises are so indubitably secure that they
> cannot receive further plausibility from their leading to
> conclusions which are immediately verifiable.[85]

Vailati further denies that the relation between premises and conclusions is as one-directional as the rationalists make it out to be. Not only do premises support conclusions, but conclusions also support—and modify—their premises. For Vailati, deduction is a reciprocal control that propositions exert upon another. In a process of successive approximation, Vailati explains, the premises gain in precision and generality, while simultaneously "correcting those crude interpretations of experience from which they originally were suggested."[86] Like Peirce, Vailati saw science as a dynamic, self-correcting enterprise.

Instead of founding science on indubitable self-evident axioms, Vailati sought to ground it in its ability to control the world in which we live and act. For Vailati, scientific concepts, whether they represent zoological species, mathematical operations, or physical constants, must be interpreted, not as high-level abstractions from observational data, but as instruments that prove successful in bringing order to the manifold of sense impressions:

> Only with great effort and after long apprenticeship do we reach the point of seeing in such words as "force," "cause," "production," "agent," symbols useful for summarizing and classifying the results of our experience and which serve us to introduce order and discover analogies and laws among the congeries of data that we have before us. We do not even know, for example, whether the concept corresponding to the word "matter" and the distinction based on it are destined to acquire or lose importance with the progress of our knowledge.[87]

Vailati's interest in the role of concepts and his instrumentalist attitude made him particularly receptive to pragmatism, especially Peirce's maxim, which related the meaning of our conceptions expressly with their conceivable practical consequences. Vailati firmly rejects, however, the tendency of some pragmatists to mingle the question of meaning with that of truth. For Vailati, the question of meaning must be clearly separated from, and also precede, the question of truth: "The question of determining what it is we *want to say* when we enunciate a given proposition, not only is an entirely distinct problem from that of deciding *whether it is true or false;* it is a question that, in one way or another, must be decided before the treatment of the other can be initiated."[88]

Vailati sharply distinguishes concepts from sensory representations, arguing that "while sensations or representations are something purely passive or receptive, concepts are essentially a product of our selective or constructive activity."[89] Concepts are not derived from experience but are created by the mind in its purposive and interpretive activity, and then we impose them on our experience. As Vailati explains, "All 'facts' or 'things' in general to which we address our thoughts or attention are 'created' or 'constructed' by ourselves by processes which are in a certain measure arbitrary and partial."[90]

Though one can hear in this a faint echo of Schiller's conception of the making of reality, Vailati carefully cautions that "one must not restrict the world to the narrowness of the intellect, but it is the intellect which must expand and enlarge itself in order to be able to contain the image of the world as is."[91] Moreover, the arbitrariness Vailati allows in the formation of concepts does not extend to the truth or falsity of the assertions that are formed with them. Our concept of a leg may be a product of our understanding, but once we have created this concept, the question of how many legs we have is not.

Although concepts are products of our own making, it is not through an analysis of how they were formed that we come to understand what they mean. Concepts are justified by their use and we can say that we know what a concept means only when we know how to use it:

> The not knowing how to use a concept, the not knowing how
> to apply it, the not being in the position to recognize the facts
> included in the concept from other contrasting facts, finally,
> the not being able to connect to the eventual particular cases
> the consequences indicated in the general statements in which
> the concept figures as a term (deduction and prediction), is
> equivalent to not possessing the concept and to not having
> acquired it, whatever be the ability that one has to repeat the
> words that claim to define it.[92]

Vailati rejects the idea that concepts can have meaning in isolation. To determine the meaning of a concept, one must see the concept in action. That is to say, one must see the concept used in assertions, and it is through that use that concepts accrue meaning. Vailati even goes further. Even assertions, or propositions, have no meaning in isolation, that is, independent from the context within which they appear. This because it is the context that determines what the practical consequences of a proposition will be. Different contexts will give different consequences. The result is a sort of meaning holism that well antedates Quine's:

> A proposition is always more or less a member, a part of a
> theoretical organism, just as a word is a part of a sentence or
> proposition. To determine the meaning or to judge the truth of
> a proposition without attaching it, explicitly or implicitly to a
> system of other propositions, constitutes a problem as
> insoluble and absurd as that of determining the position of a
> body without referring to other bodies or guide marks. But this
> does not prevent one's asking what is the meaning of a

79

proposition given *by reference to other propositions,* and one can find answers to this question by the examination of consequences that can be drawn from a given system of propositions when one adds the proposition which is in question.[93]

Hence, with regard to meaning, Vailati's pragmatism involves the choice of a conceptual system. As with the concept, the meaning of a proposition is a function of the "logical medium" within which it plays its role, rather than of the principles through which it was construed. This can be said even of something as fundamental as the laws of logic. The laws of logic are not true or false depending on whether they conform to the "reality of things," but they are "opportune or not opportune to follow, according to the purpose for which they are proposed."[94] For Vailati there can be alternative logics, just as there can be alternative geometries, and those logics can depart as dramatically from our logical intuitions, as non-Euclidian geometries have departed from our intuitions of space. Moreover, we can choose between those alternative logics just as we can choose between different systems of measurement, and for both we make our choice on pragmatic grounds.

In his theory of truth Vailati also remains close to Peirce, rejecting the Jamesian idea that the truth of a proposition is determined by its practical consequences. According to Vailati, James, Schiller, and the magical pragmatists Papini and Prezzolini, have been too cavalier in their dismissal of the positivists' correspondence theory of truth, which resulted in an alternative that is itself too easy a target for criticism. Vailati denies that the notion of correspondence requires a passive and detached attitude, as James and his close allies seemed to assume. Rather, Vailati claims that

> to represent, for example, the properties that a given body *has,* is not to represent some present facts, but rather some facts that it *will have,* or *would have,* if the body in question were placed in such and such circumstances.[95]

Thus, to discover the truth goes beyond a mere gathering of facts. It involves, Vailati argues, "the exercise of those organizing and elaborating activities of experience, which, while artificially simplifying, impoverishing and schematizing reality, have no other purpose than that of making possible the representation and more perfect mastery of it."[96] To represent reality is to *grasp* it, not to copy it. Consequently, for Vailati, the divide between the pragmatic and the correspondence conception of truth is more apparent than real.

According to Vailati, pragmatism is often misinterpreted as a justification for the subject's believing anything she wants to believe. This he calls the pragmatism of the will-to-believists. In contrast, Vailati argues that pragmatism ought to go in the opposite direction. Far from suggesting a subjective turn, pragmatism embodies a quest for more objectivity by its unrelenting insistence on experiments and hard facts. The pragmatic maxim is not a personal criterion but a *public* criterion, in which meaning and truth are interpreted in terms of the scientific method.

In summary, Vailati seeks a middle way between the hot-tempered will-to-believists who found in pragmatism the Midas touch that could transform any desire into truth, and the cool detachment of the positivists, for whom our ideas, whether they are true or false, ideally do not interact with the world. Vailati agrees with the will-to-believists that our passions and interests play a role in the acquisition of knowledge, and even an important one, but emphasizes that their role is a restricted one. With his views on how the "world of paper" shapes our knowledge, Vailati comes close to the conceptual pragmatism that was developed later by Lewis (chapter 8), and Vailati's emphasis on the reciprocal support of premises and conclusions brings him in close vicinity to Susan Haack's foundherentism.

5.4 The Prezzolini – Calderoni Debate

When James visited Rome in 1905 and met with the Florentine pragmatists, the debate between the magical and the logical pragmatists had just reached its apex. The two main voices in this debate were those of Giuseppe Prezzolini and Mario Calderoni. Like Papini, Prezzolini directs most of his attacks against the positivists, finding much of his inspiration in Bergson and in the voluntarism of Croce. Prezzolini, who quickly became an enthusiastic disciple of Schiller, was the first to maintain that through the free exercise of our creative power we attain a state of divinity, a view he expands in the essay *"L'Uomo Dio"* (The God man).[97] This essay anticipates both Papini's "Death and Resurrection of Philosophy," which appeared later that same year, and "From Man to God," which appeared three years later.

Not surprisingly, Prezzolini sides with Schiller in his hostility to formal logic, and he does so on the ground that logic unnecessarily confines our thought. In *"La miseria dei logici"* (the logicians' misery), Prezzolini calls logic the greatest idol of contemporary philosophy and one that desperately needs to be smashed. Far from being the epitome of thought, formal logic is forced upon us because of the limitations of our

81

thought and our lack of imagination.[98] According to Prezzolini, the assumption that consciousness is inherently logical and that we generally act from rational motives is wholly mistaken, and he rejects the idea that there is a single universal logical system. "All our rational expressions," Prezzolini contends, "are nothing but expressions of sentimental states, signs of moral tendencies, manifestations of personal character and temperament."[99] Formal logic, which ignores all of this, is thus an impoverishment of our thought. It is something we need (often for practical purposes), but it is hardly something to be proud of, and we should avoid using it whenever we can.

Having thus dispensed with the philosophical establishment, Prezzolini outlines his own view while calling himself a sophist. (Recall that Schiller calls the sophist Protagoras the first pragmatist.) Against the positivist—whom Prezzolini sees as restricting our thought within the narrow limits of reason—the sophist stresses that we should follow our imagination and our dreams. Against the skeptic, the sophist urges us to embrace everything with a youthful enthusiasm: *"Everything is true, because I desire it. Man is able to be the creator of his truth."*[100]

Prezzolini's sophism is largely James's will-to-believe argument run amok. Later, in his book *L'Arte di persuadere* (the art of persuasion), Prezzolini goes as far as to claim that since we make truth, we can make others believe whatever we want them to believe, as long as we possess the art of persuasion. The aim of language, Prezzolini contends, is not to convey truth, but to excite the will of another, and for this a beautiful parable often works better than a perfect syllogism. Vailati dismisses the book as a "manual for liars."[101]

It is Calderoni, however, and not Vailati, who takes up the challenge posed by Prezzolini's polemic essays in *Leonardo*. Whereas Papini and Prezzolini saw pragmatism as a radical break with positivism and all that it stood for, Vailati and Calderoni saw pragmatism as both an extension and an improvement of positivism. Like Vailati, Calderoni had come to pragmatism primarily through Peirce, and it is from his Peircean background that he opposes the Prezzolini-Papini flavor of pragmatism. Prezzolini, and the will-to-believevists in general, Calderoni complains, have distorted pragmatism by giving the will far too much power over our beliefs.

In his criticism of Prezzolini, Calderoni seeks to remain close to the pragmatism of Peirce. According to Calderoni, Peirce's pragmatism is "only a request, expressed in a particularly suggestive form, to introduce experimentalism not only in the solution of questions but also in the choice of the questions to be treated."[102] What is more, Calderoni continues, the central idea behind Peirce's pragmatism is precisely to discourage the kind of intellectual practices that are seemingly allowed by James's will-to-belief argument, and which now are taken to new heights by Papini and Prezzolini. It is important to add the qualifier "seemingly," since James, in contrast to Papini and Prezzolini, explicitly restricts the application of the will-to-believe argument to pressing and momentous choices that cannot wait or do not allow for a scientific solution (section 3.2).

Prezzolini replies to Calderoni's criticisms by distinguishing two varieties of pragmatism. The first variety is the Peircean kind, which Prezzolini seeks to confine strictly to the realm of science and logic. The second variety, which is proposed by James and Schiller, focuses instead on the realm of morality. It is this second variety that Prezzolini adhered to, therefore, Calderoni's criticisms are misdirected.

In his rejoinder, Calderoni rejects Prezzolini's twofold division, which he sees as being based on a mere caricature of positivism. In its stead, Calderoni distinguished *three* varieties of pragmatism. The first is a straightforward application of Peirce's principle. On this first view, the purpose of pragmatism is to eliminate useless philosophical questions, which is an aim it shares with positivism. The second variety is the doctrine of the will to believe, taken in the radical sense where the will exercises some sort of supreme power over our beliefs. The *Uomo-Dio* doctrine of Papini and Prezzolini falls under this second variety. The third variety of pragmatism Calderoni distinguishes is a methodological pragmatism in which the will has some power over how inquiry will proceed, implying that it has some power over the progress of knowledge.

The pragmatism of Prezzolini, which falls under the second variety, Calderoni argues is antagonistic not only to positivism (Prezzolini's main target), but also to the first variety of pragmatism. In contrast, the third variety, to which both Calderoni and Vailati adhered, fits in nicely with the first and with positivism, while having at the same time distinct advantages over the positivism. Based on his triadic division, Calderoni concludes that the term "pragmatism" should be reserved either for the first and the third variety combined, or for the will-to-believe argument that is expressed in the second variety. By putting it this way, Calderoni's division becomes a methodological one, rather than one that is based, like Prezzolini's, on a prior distinction between two different and mutually exclusive realms: the scientific and the moral.

The debate between Prezzolini and Calderoni comes to an end with an essay entitled "*Il Pragmatismo messo in ordine*" (pragmatism put in order), which was signed by "The Florence Pragmatist Club."[103] This essay, which was actually written by Papini, opens with the claim that although no precise definition of pragmatism can be given, one can specify its main character which is that it "unstiffens" our theories and beliefs by recognizing their purely instrumental value, which makes them susceptible to change when the circumstances alter. Hence, pragmatism does not stand for a certain type of theory, but for a certain attitude toward theories. In Papini's view, pragmatism consolidates several recent tendencies in philosophy:[104]

> *Nominalism:* We should appeal to particular facts to determine the meaning of words.

> *Utilitarianism:* We should direct our intellectual activity to practical problems.

> *Positivism:* We should avoid verbal and useless questions, and acknowledge the provisional character of scientific theories.

> *Kantianism:* We should acknowledge the primacy of practical reason, which allows us to go beyond the mere empirically given, for instance, to seek moral perfection.

> *Voluntarism:* We should recognize the influence of the will and our sentiments on intelligence and science.

> *Fideism:* We should recognize the role of faith in the foundation and the development of our theories (recall the influence of Pascal's wager on James's "Will to Believe").

Within the context of the Prezzolini-Calderoni debate, Papini divides pragmatism into three areas that he regarded as complementary. The first area contains all those varieties of pragmatism that focus on the relation between the particular and the general. Papini distinguishes two subgroups in this area. The first is a pragmatism with respect to the formation of general propositions. Here pragmatism stands for the view that the meaning of a general proposition is determined by the particular consequences that someone who believes the proposition would expect. The second is a pragmatism with respect to the testing of general propositions. This is the view that general propositions must be verified in terms of their particular consequences. For the first subgroup, Papini mentiones Peirce and James by name, and for the second, one might think of Schiller.

Papini's second area involves those varieties of pragmatism that focus on the choice of representative conventions and ways of expression (definitions, classifications, abstractions, points of reference, units of measurement, etc.). The choices we make depend on the purposes we have set for ourselves, which in turn depend on our sentiments and our will. The principal purposes proposed in the sciences include practical applications, the economy of thought (Ernst Mach), mental peace, and the overcoming of fear. Although Papini does not mention him by name, one might classify Vailati in this second area.

The third area concerns those varieties of pragmatism that focus on the influence of faith and belief on truth and action. This includes, in particular, those varieties that study the *cause* of belief (such as James's will to believe), or the *effects* of belief on action or on its own verification. Papini considers this area to be of special importance, not only because it teaches us how to attain beliefs, but because it also teaches us how to transform reality through those beliefs. James's will-to-believe argument and the magical pragmatism of Papini and Prezzolini fall within this third area.

Papini sees the three areas not only as complementary, but also as intimately connected:

> It is easy to see what binds the three areas together: Their common aim is to act, that is, to strengthen our power of modifying things. But to act, you must also predict and to predict with confidence [*sicurezza*] you must have well-developed sciences, that is sciences that are at once expedient and verifiable.[105]

For Papini, the will to believe remains largely a prelude to the will to act. Although Papini does not mention Nietzsche by name at this point, he does use the phrase "will to power," suggesting that Nietzsche might have been close to Papini's mind when he was writing this.

In another essay, which appeared in English in 1907 under the title "What Pragmatism is Like," Papini uses Peirce's pragmatic maxim to define pragmatism. In this essay, Papini gives the following rendition of Peirce's principle:

> The meaning of theories consists entirely in the consequences which their followers may expect from them. To affirm anything actually means this: I foresee that certain things will follow, or that I shall do certain things.[106]

Application of this principle to the concept of pragmatism itself leads him to rephrase the question "What is pragmatism?" to "What actions or beliefs may be expected from a thinker who is a confessed pragmatist?"

Here is Papini's answer:

> His sympathies will be with the study of the particular
> instance; with the development of prediction; with precise and
> well-determined theories; with those which serve as the best
> instruments for the most important ends of life; with
> consciousness, with economy of thought, etc.[107]

In a phrase made famous by James, Papini called pragmatism a
corridor theory (*una teoria corridoio*). It is with this metaphor that Papini
closes his contribution to the Prezzolini-Calderoni debate. The entire
passage is worth quoting:

> Pragmatism is a collection of methods; from a certain point of
> view, it is the positive method made perfect, refined, and
> complete, and this is why one of its main features is its *armed
> neutrality*. This means that it does not decide upon questions,
> but it only says: given certain goals, I suggest you to use
> certain means rather than others. It is, thus, a *corridor
> theory*—a corridor of a large hotel where a hundred doors
> open into a hundred rooms. In one of those rooms there is a
> kneeler and a man who wants to reconquer the faith; in another
> there is a desk and a man who wants to kill all metaphysics; in
> a third there is a laboratory and a man who seeks new
> "handles" to grasp the future. . . . But the corridor belongs to
> all and everybody walks through it: if from time to time
> conversations start among the guests, no waiter will be so
> impolite as to break them up.[108]

For Papini, pragmatism is an attitude, or a collection of methods, but it is
distinctly not a philosophy. Its armed neutrality precludes that. In fact,
pragmatism is averse to philosophy. As Papini observes, "Pragmatism is
really *less a philosophy than a method of doing without philosophy*."[109]

5.5 The Demise of *Leonardo*

It was not long before Papini would realize that he could also do without
pragmatism. The magical pragmatism of Papini and Prezzolini quickly
proved untenable, even to its own proponents, because of its extreme
individualism. In the absence of an independent criterion of truth, the
solution to any intellectual or practical problem could only be a product
of caprice. *Leonardo* ceased publication in August of 1907. Guided by the

desire to bestow on the review "a death as beautiful and sudden as its birth," Papini and Prezzolini coauthored its obituary:

> For us *Leonardo* has always been something necessary, personal, sentimental—the voice that we could not quiet in ourselves, the diary of our spiritual voyages as Wandering Jews of culture. From the beginning it has always been an eruption of passion, and, precisely because it has been such an eruption, it could not last for long. When the lava that descends becomes calm and is reduced to a slow trickle, the volcano becomes an object of laughter.
>
> By this we do not mean that we are extinct volcanos. We will continue to act, to think, to search, and even to publish. But we do feel the need to rethink problems that we imagined to have been dissolved in the air, to reexamine all the opinions we expressed with such easy confidence, to search out new solutions to problems that appeared settled, to revisit and confirm our judgments about people and things, in short, to recommence once again our intellectual life.[110]

With the demise of *Leonardo,* pragmatism would quickly disappear as well. When recommencing their "intellectual lives," Papini fell into a religious crisis and converted to Catholicism, and Prezzolini embraced the idealism of Croce, who by that time had moved away from his earlier voluntarism. The demise of the Peircean strain in Italian pragmatism quickly followed suit as its two proponents both died prematurely. Vailati died in 1909 at the age of forty-six and Calderoni died five years later—he was only thirty-five.

6
Peirce Revisited: The Normative Turn

I know of no voyage of meditation from which, with any skill
in the navigation, a better profit is insured than from a quest
for the reasons for accepting or rejecting the maxim of
pragmaticism.

—Charles S. Peirce[111]

During the final fifteen years of his life, Peirce spent much time and effort
explaining, defending, and even proving pragmatism. In part this effort
came from a sincere belief that if one introduces a new concept one must
spell out what it stands for. Peirce strongly believed that the success of the
sciences was to a large extent due to the development of a technical
nomenclature in which each term had a single definite meaning that was
generally accepted. Even more so than had been the case for botany and
zoology, Peirce believed that philosophy was in desperate need of a proper
taxonomy. With views not easily checked by experience, if at all, precise
nomenclature for basic philosophical concepts, such as "reality," "self,"
"necessity," "universal," etc., is essential for molding the divergent
attempts of various philosophers into fruitful philosophical debate. Peirce
put this belief into action by uncovering the meaning of thousands of
philosophical terms for the twelve-volume *Century Dictionary,* thereby *de
facto* establishing the beginning of such a taxonomy.

Trained as a chemist, Peirce even envisioned a system of prefixes
and suffixes, as is common in chemistry. For example, the prefix "prope-"
could mark "a broad and rather indefinite extension of the meaning of the
term to which it was prefixed," and the suffix "-ism," which is already in
vogue to designate a doctrine, could be supplemented with the parallel
suffix "-icism," to mark, as Peirce phrased it, "a more strictly defined
acception of that doctrine" (EP2:334). Applying this newly developed

nomenclature to the doctrine of pragmatism, Peirce introduces the term "pragmaticism" to denote the more strictly defined acception of pragmatism, and characterized it as a form of prope-positivism. By this stricter definition, pragmatism—or *pragmaticism* as it is now called—is restricted to a maxim of logic:

> Pragmatism makes or ought to make no pretension to throwing positive light on any problem. It is merely a logical maxim for laying the dust of pseudoproblems, and thus enabling us to discern what pertinent facts the phenomena may present. But this is a good half of the task of philosophy. (CP 8.186)

Peirce thereby rejects the broadening of the doctrine conceived by James and Schiller. In Peirce's view, his fellow pragmatists had carried the doctrine too far by making it a speculative principle of philosophy. It is to this stricter definition of pragmatism that the present chapter is devoted. The attention will be focused largely on three sets of documents: Peirce's 1898 Cambridge Conference lectures, his 1903 Harvard lectures, and his 1905–6 *Monist* papers. In the *Monist* papers Peirce introduced the term pragmaticism.

Before engaging in this discussion it is good to recall that Peirce's rejection of pragmatism in favor of pragmaticism does not reflect a change of heart on Peirce's side, but rather a growing discontent with what others had made of pragmatism.

6.1 Peirce's Later Years

In 1878, when "How to Make Our Ideas Clear" (the paper that contains the pragmatic maxim) was published, Peirce was in the prime of his life and in the midst of a promising career. In 1879 he joined the newly established Johns Hopkins University, which was conceived primarily as a graduate school. Peirce actively participated in the academic community. He began a philosophical club and together with some of his students he published, in 1883, an influential book on logic: *Studies in Logic; By Members of the Johns Hopkins University*. John Dewey, who at the time took some courses with Peirce, later followed the same recipe with his *Studies in Logical Theory*. However, in the decade that followed Peirce lost his job at John Hopkins and was forced to resign from the US Coast Survey where he had worked for more than thirty years. In 1888, ten years after his influential 1878 article in *Popular Science Monthly,* Peirce had retreated to Milford, a small town in Eastern Pennsylvania, where he spent the rest of his life in growing isolation.

On Pragmatism

The premature demise of Peirce's academic career is due in part to his personality (as one of his students later put it, there was an air of irresponsibility about him), powerful enemies, and his second marriage to his mysterious mistress, Juliette Froissy Pourtalais, two days after he divorced his first wife, Zina Fay. In his defense, it should be said that Zina had left him six years before. Juliette's mysterious background added, no doubt, to the problem. She claimed that she was a daughter of European nobility, but there was a persistent rumor that she had been a French prostitute. Even today little is known about her. Shortly after their marriage, Peirce lost his job at Johns Hopkins University (the university president declared that he didn't want to be under the same roof with "so immoral a man"), and he never again held an academic position. In 1891, Peirce was forced to resign from the Coast Survey, in part because of troubles surrounding his gravity report, the result of swinging pendulums at different locations for many years . One of the problems with the report was that it was conceived by his peers to be set up in an illogical manner. As Simon Newcomb, then America's leading physicist, concludes in his peer evaluation,

> A remarkable feature of the presentation is the inversion of the logical order throughout the whole paper. The system of the author seems to be to give first concluded results, then the method by which these results were obtained, then the formulae and principles on which these methods rest, then the derivation of these formulae, then the data on which the derivation rests, and so on until the original observations are reached. The human mind cannot follow a course of reasoning in this way, and the first thing to be done with the paper is to reconstruct it in logical order. (W6:lxv)

Today, Peirce's mode of presentation is the standard.

By the time he resigned from the Coast Survey, the Peirces had already retreated to Milford, a few hours by train from New York City, where they had purchased a large property with a small farmhouse. Driven by grandiose but impractical plans, and stimulated by the booming economy, they quickly transformed the farmhouse into a mansion. Soon the economic depression set in. Nothing came of any of Peirce's plans and the property quickly became too expensive for them to maintain. Often going for days without food or firewood, the Peirces lived in poverty until Charles Peirce's death in 1914.

6.2 The Reaction to James's Will to Believe

William James dedicated *The Will to Believe* to "my old friend, Charles Sanders Peirce, to whose philosophic comradeship in old times and to whose writings in more recent years I owe more incitement and help than I can express or repay." Peirce was clearly touched by James's tribute, and he sent him a long letter of thanks. In this letter, Peirce also explains how his own views had shifted over the years. Commenting in particular on the essay that gave the book its title, Peirce writes,

> That everything is to be tested by its practical results was the great text of my early papers; so, as far as I get your general aim in so much of the book as I have looked at, I am quite with you in the main. In my later papers, I have seen more thoroughly than I used to do that it is not mere action as brute exercise of strength that is the purpose of all, but say generalization, such action as tends toward regularization, and the actualization of the thought which without action remains unthought.[112]

Peirce's comments reveal a sharp divide between the pragmatisms of Peirce and James—one that is of a metaphysical nature. Peirce is a realist and James a nominalist. For nominalists, only particulars are real. Consequently, a nominalistic interpretation of the pragmatic maxim, which is what James provides in *The Will to Believe,* relates the meaning of our conceptions to *particular* effects or concrete experiences. Peirce, on the other hand, holds that some generals are also real. Not only that, but on a realistic interpretation of the pragmatic maxim, the meaning of a conception can be, and often should be, connected with a general, not with particulars. Thus, although Peirce agrees with James that "the individual deed [is] the only real meaning there is in the Concept," he immediately adds that "it is not the mere arbitrary force in the deed but the life it gives to the idea that is valuable."[113] The emphasis is on the general, not the particular.

Thus, whereas James focuses on experiences, Peirce is thinking primarily in terms of what he called "habits." Habits are rules of action. They determine what our acts will be when we find ourselves in certain circumstances. Thus, in Peirce's reading of the pragmatic maxim, the meaning of the word "chair" is related, *not* to certain concrete sensory impressions, but to the circumstance that the object of this conception invokes in us the *habit* to sit in it. This should not be interpreted as a simple stimulus-response routine—if SEE CHAIR, then SIT—since situations are generally multifaceted. Sometimes seeing a chair will cause one to behave quite differently. When we see the chair in which Thomas Jefferson drafted the Declaration of Independence, we react differently than when we just need something to help us get a book from the top shelf. However, without some general tendency, without some regularization that puts the concept in context, any connection with brute experiential facts will be utterly devoid of meaning.

Shortly afterward, James invited Peirce to deliver a series of lectures in Cambridge. Peirce agreed enthusiastically and mailed James a proposal for a series of lectures called "On the Logic of Events." In these lectures, Peirce writes, he would discuss his system of logical graphs, the logic of relatives (Peirce's phrase for what we now call quantification theory), the theory of the categories, the law of the association of ideas, and the logic of abduction (or hypothesis formation), deduction, and induction.

James replies quickly, attempting to dissuade Peirce from the idea of devoting the lectures to logic:

> I am sorry you are sticking so to formal logic. . . . You can hardly conceive how little interest exists in the purely formal aspects of logic. Things on that subject ought to be printed for the scattered few. You are teeming with ideas—and the lectures need not by any means form a continuous whole. Separate topics of a vitally important character would do perfectly well.[114]

Peirce's reply is not without sarcasm. With a direct reference to James's letter, he proposes to name the lectures "Detached Ideas on Vitally Important Topics." The first lecture, he explains, "is about Vitally important topics, showing that where they are Vital there is little chance for philosophy in them."[115]

Having addressed James's insistence that the lectures deal with *vital* issues, Peirce moves to James's second comment, that the lectures "need not by any means form a continuous whole." Peirce explains,

> The second lecture is about detached thoughts & is intended to show that however little time people may have for connected thought outside their business, yet it is better to make it as connected as possible, not shunning detached ideas but seeking to assimilate them.[116]

For the third lecture, Peirce indicates that he would take James's will-to-believe argument directly by the horns: "My third lecture is to be upon the highest maxim of logic,—which is that the only strictly indispensable requisite is that the inquirer shall want to learn the truth."[117] Against James's "will to believe," Peirce argued for a "will to truth."

Soon Peirce sent drafts of the first four lectures to James for feedback. The result was a change of heart on James's part. In a letter dated 23 January 1898, James confesses that he would no longer object if Peirce were to reestablish his original title "The Logic of Events." The title Peirce eventually settled on was "Reasoning and the Logic of Things."[118] After the opening lecture, entitled "Philosophy and the Conduct of Life," there followed four lectures on logic, one on causation and force, one on habit, and one on the logic of continuity.

It is clear from the lectures that James's "Will to Believe" article remains close to Peirce's mind. What James had called genuine options (options that are living, forced, and momentous), Peirce here calls "matters of vital importance." And, like James, Peirce separates these matters from scientific questions. However, whereas James focuses most of his attention on genuine options, Peirce outright rejects the idea that philosophy is of any use when we are confronted with genuine options, that is, with matters of vital importance. Philosophy, at least in its present state, is too ill-equipped to help us. He even went so far as to state that practical applications of philosophy to religion and conduct, precisely what James believed to be most important, are "exceedingly dangerous" (EP2:29). Peirce is especially skeptical of our ability to use reason in resolving practical issues that we believe to be of great importance, because we are just too skillful in rationalizing what we do or want. As Peirce puts it,

> Men many times fancy that they act from reason when, in point of fact, the reasons they attribute to themselves are nothing but excuses which unconscious instinct invents to satisfy the teasing "why's" of the ego. The extent of this self delusion is such as to render philosophical rationalism a farce. (EP2:32)

Since in the end reason appeals to sentiment, Peirce maintains, we better rely directly on our instinct which is fallible, yet less likely to lead us as easily and as far astray as does reasoning. Because of this, Peirce argues that a philosophy that is too heavily dominated by practical affairs is corrupting:

> In philosophy, touching as it does upon matters which are, and ought to be, sacred to us, the investigator who does not stand aloof from all intent to make practical applications, will not only obstruct the advance of the pure science, but what is

> infinitely worse, he will endanger his own moral integrity and
> that of his readers. (EP2:29)

This is not to say that Peirce thinks reasoning useless. Quite the contrary, reasoning is very helpful, even indispensable, in those cases where we are not directed by practical motives. Logic may be of little help when trying to decide whether to marry someone (surely a genuine option in James's sense), but logic is certainly essential for anyone who is developing a metaphysical system or for someone who is engaged in scientific inquiry.

An important feature of reasoning is that when given enough time and left to run its own course (two conditions unlikely to be met in matters of vital importance), reasoning will eventually correct itself. Reasoning not only corrects its conclusions, it also corrects its premises; it even gives us a more solid basis for empirical data than observation:

> Every astronomer . . . is familiar with the fact that the
> catalogue place of a fundamental star, which is the result of
> elaborate reasoning, is far more accurate than any of the
> observations from which it is deduced. (EP2:43)

From the circumstance that inquiry has the vital powers of self-correction and growth, Peirce draws the conclusion that "there is but one thing needful for learning the truth, and that is a hearty and active desire to learn what is true" (EP2:47). What we need, Peirce argues, is not a will to believe, but a will to learn.

Peirce's analysis of reason led him to the following important conclusion, which he calls the first rule of reason: "In order to learn you must desire to learn and in so desiring not be satisfied with what you already incline to think" (EP2:48). From this first rule of reason, Peirce derives the important corollary: "Do not block the way of inquiry" (EP2:47). Blocking the way of inquiry is, for Peirce, the worst sin one can commit in inquiry, as it obstructs the self-correctiveness of reasoning. Classical obstructions include the claim that certain facts can never be known, that certain facts are ultimate (meaning that they cannot be explained in terms of anything else), and that certain facts have already attained their final and perfect formulation.

Hence, Peirce does not see pragmatism as a device for solving practical problems, nor does he consider our ability to solve such problems the justification of pragmatism, or of philosophy in general. Peirce's views differ in this respect significantly from the pragmatisms of James and Schiller, and even more so from the magical pragmatism of Papini and Prezzolini. Peirce does not see the world as an obstacle that is to be overcome, as something we must mend and tinker with to make it conform to our goals, but as "something great, and beautiful, and sacred, and eternal, and real" (EP2:55). We must be willing to learn the lesson the world is trying to teach us.

Peirce's Cambridge Conference lectures were given in the winter of 1898. Half a year later, on 26 August, James delivered his Berkeley address in which he introduced "pragmatism," while at the same time insisting that it should really be called "practicalism."

6.3 The Harvard Lectures on Pragmatism

Five years after the Cambridge Conference lectures, in the Spring of 1903, Peirce returned to Cambridge to deliver two courses of lectures: the Harvard lectures on pragmatism and the Lowell lectures "Some Topics of Logic."[119] In the Harvard lectures, Peirce again spells out how his views differ from those of James, who had again organized the lectures. The lectures contain, as Peirce tells his audience, "an examination of the *pros* and *cons* of pragmatism" (EP2:133). Moreover, since Peirce sees pragmatism as a maxim of logic rather than as a handy instrument for obtaining desirable practical results, he finds it requisite that pragmatism be proved, and the development of a proof of pragmatism becomes a focal point of his lectures.[120] Peirce did not spare his audience, and James later famously characterizes the lectures as "flashes of brilliant light relieved against Cimmerian darkness."[121]

Again, Peirce takes the maxim of his 1878 "How to Make Our Ideas Clear" as his starting point. He rejects, however, the proof that is latent in that paper and in "The Fixation of Belief" that preceded it. In those early papers, Peirce begins by observing that we constantly seek belief, defining belief as "that upon which we are prepared to act." Once this definition is granted, a proposition believed is by definition a maxim of conduct, and pragmatism is all but proven. But Peirce now asks what justified him in defining belief that way. In "How to Make Our Ideas Clear" he came to his definition after an analysis of our psychological constitution. Our minds just happen to work like that.[122] By 1903, Peirce found this answer no longer tenable. What if human nature were different? What if a prolonged use of pesticides caused a chemical modification of the human brain so that we would feel euphoria and satisfaction every time we are in doubt, and bored and restless when in a state of belief? Would pragmatism no longer be true? And there is more. If pragmatism is derived from the principles of psychology, which is a descriptive science that studies how we think, how are we to distinguish how we *should* think from how we *do* think?

In his 1903 Harvard lectures, Peirce seeks to develop a proof of pragmatism that did not depend on the accidental circumstance that our minds happen to work in a particular way. Peirce begins with the observation that pragmatism contains a normative component: The pragmatic maxim tells us how we should define our terms for them to have meaning. The discovery that the pragmatic maxim is normative led Peirce to consider pragmatism as a special application of ethics.

Ethics, Peirce continues, presupposes a distinction between what is admirable and what is not. This presupposes, in turn, that we have determined what we are prepared to admire and what we are not. This led Peirce to an even more general science, namely esthetics, which studies what is admirable in itself without any reference to anything else. In short, ethics depends on esthetics, with ethics being a specialized subcategory of esthetics, namely, the one that confines itself solely to what is admirable in human conduct. As Peirce explains in a draft of one of the lectures,

> An ultimate end of action *deliberately* adopted,—that is to say,
> *reasonably* adopted,—must be a state of things that *reasonably*
> *recommends itself in itself,* aside from any ulterior
> consideration. It must be an *admirable ideal,* having the only
> kind of goodness that such an ideal *can* have, namely esthetic
> goodness. From this point of view, the morally good appears
> as a particular species of the esthetically good. (EP2:210)

Esthetics, in turn, depends upon a pre-normative science, that is, one that merely contemplates phenomena as they enter before consciousness without making any distinction about them being good or bad, beautiful or ugly, desirable or undesirable, real or unreal, etc. Peirce called this science *phenomenology* or *phaneroscopy.* According to Peirce, the phenomenologist just opens her eyes and describes what she sees.

For Peirce, phenomenology is the most basic of the positive sciences, i.e., those sciences that seek factual knowledge. The positive sciences differ in this respect from mathematics, which seeks knowledge that is expressed in conditional or hypothetical propositions. Mathematicians, Peirce explains, do not seek to discover how things are, but only how they might be supposed to be (EP2:144).

Peirce divides the positive sciences into philosophy and the special sciences (physics, psychology, chemistry, political science, etc.). Philosophy, he added, "contents itself with a more attentive scrutiny and comparison of the facts of everyday life, such as present themselves to every adult and sane person, and for the most part in every day and hour of his waking life" (EP2:146). In this sense philosophy differs from the special sciences, which actively seek out new experiences, often with the use of special instruments (electron microscopes, spectrometers, cyclotrons, etc.), or with specially developed techniques, such as statistics or psychoanalysis. Philosophy's main purpose, according to Peirce, is to give us a general conception of the universe, a *Weltanschauung*, which can form a basis for the special sciences. Philosophy consists of phenomenology, the three normative sciences (esthetics, ethics, and logic), and metaphysics. Next, and building on the insights of philosophy, follow the special sciences.

Division of the Sciences	
MATHEMATICS	Studies how things can be supposed to be
POSITIVE SCIENCES	Study how things are
Philosophy	Studies the most general facts of everyday life
phenomenology	Studies phenomena as they appear in their immediacy
normative sciences	Study phenomena in their relation to ends
esthetics	Studies phenomena whose ends are to embody qualities of feeling
ethics	Studies phenomena whose ends lie in action
logic	Studies phenomena whose end is to represent something
metaphysics	Seeks a general conception of the universe that can act as a basis for the special sciences
The Special Sciences	Study facts that are deliberately sought out and often removed from everyday life

6.4 In Search of a Proof

Peirce's insistence that pragmatism be proven, even though the method has already proved itself capable of resolving many difficult issues, stems from the fact, familiar to scientists and philosophers, that simple rules like

97

this one often "have had to be greatly complicated in the further progress of science" (EP2:139). Put differently, it is quite safe to say that, *as a rule of thumb,* our conception of the conceivable practical consequences of a concept is the meaning of that concept, but can we truly say that no concept whatsoever has any meaning *apart* from those consequences? Are there no strange cases that require that the rule be fine-tuned? Is it not true that our most dependable beliefs sometimes fail when applied to specialized fields such as astronomy or quantum physics? Since genuine doubt regarding the maxim can be raised, it is appropriate to demand a proof.

This demand for a proof fits in nicely with Peirce's critical common-sensism. Peirce agreed with Scottish common-sensists, such as Thomas Reid, that Hume's empiricism was too narrowly conceived, which caused it to lead to skepticism. According to the common-sensists, our knowledge of external objects is not a product of sensations alone (as Hume had argued), but of sensations in combination with intuitively known general principles that were thought to be indubitable. Peirce agrees, but has a quite different take on why these commonsense beliefs are indubitable. They are indubitable, not because they are the product of an infallible intuition, but because we so firmly believe in them that we cannot really make ourselves doubt them. For Peirce, pace Descartes, you cannot really doubt what you firmly believe is true. It is in this sense—which fully conforms with Peirce's views in "The Fixation of Belief"—that Peirce maintains that we have indubitable commonsense beliefs (see section 2.3). This is not to say that these beliefs are above criticism, and Peirce emphasized repeatedly that we must actively seek to criticize them whenever the opportunity arises. This is why Peirce's common-sensism, in contrast to his predecessors in this area, is very decidedly a *critical* common-sensism.

As the division of the sciences sketched in the previous section indicates, any proof of pragmatism should begin with phenomenology and then run through the normative sciences. This is precisely what Peirce sets out to do. The above division shows also that the truth of pragmatism cannot be derived from the laws of psychology (as he had tried to do in the 1870s), or from metaphysics. Given the position of pragmatism within Peirce's classification of the sciences, no metaphysical or psychological truth can be used to support pragmatism without falling into a vicious circularity.

Peirce's proof is not an argument in the old rationalist sense, where each proposition follows by necessity from those that precede it. Peirce rejects Descartes's division of facts into those that are self-evident and those that are not, and he accept Descartes's accompanying argument that the latter, as Descartes explains it in *Rules for the Direction of the Mind,* can be known with certainty when they are derived from the former "through a continuous and uninterrupted movement of thought in which each individual proposition is clearly intuited."[123] Descartes compares this movement of thought with a chain composed of many links on which the connection depends.[124] Peirce rejects this notion of reasoning, which he sees largely as a product of two fundamental mistakes that he ascribes to Descartes: his method of doubt, and his faith in the infallibility of reasoning (the latter being a product of Descartes's notion of clear and distinct ideas).

Having dismissed the Cartesian chain argument, Peirce turned his direction to the schoolmen whom Descartes had so fiercely rejected, and opted for what he calls "the multiform argumentation of the middle ages" (EP1:28). Peirce characterizes this type of argumentation as follows:

> Philosophy ought to imitate the successful sciences in its methods, so far as to proceed only from tangible premises which can be subjected to careful scrutiny, and to trust rather to the multitude and variety of its arguments than to the conclusiveness of any one. Its reasoning should not form a chain which is no stronger than its weakest link, but a cable whose fibers may be ever so slender, provided they are sufficiently numerous and intimately connected. (EP1:29)

For us humans, who are fallible but have an instinct for guessing right, this "rope reasoning" is far more secure than even the simplest chain argument. Whereas a single broken link will rupture the entire chain, a rope will hold even if several of its fibers were to snap.

The proof of pragmatism Peirce develops in the Harvard lectures is an example of rope reasoning. As Peirce explains roughly two years after the lectures,

> Just as a civil engineer, before erecting a bridge, a ship, or a house, will think of the different properties of all materials, and will use no iron, stone, or cement, that has not been subjected to tests; and will put them together in ways minutely considered, so, in constructing the doctrine of pragmatism the properties of all indecomposable concepts were examined and the ways in which they could be compounded. Then the purpose of the proposed doctrine having been analyzed, it was constructed out of the appropriate concepts so as to fulfill that purpose. In this way, the truth of it was proved. There are

99

subsidiary confirmations of its truth; but it is believed that there is no other independent way of strictly proving it. (CP 5.5)

In the Harvard lectures Peirce largely follows this recipe, entrenching pragmatism firmly within phenomenology and the normative sciences. The main fibers of Peirce's proof of pragmatism include his doctrine of the categories (the "indecomposable concepts"), his argument that logic is a normative science (establishing "the purpose of the doctrine"), his doctrine of perception, and his treatments of deduction, induction, and abduction. It would lead us far beyond the scope of this brief introduction to attempt to spell out Peirce's multifaceted and elaborate proof. Instead, I will limit myself to a few of its core elements as they will help us to gain a better understanding of what this pragmatism is that Peirce is trying to proof.

6.5 Phenomenology and the Normative Sciences

For Peirce, the phenomenologist's central task is to bring order to the manifold of her observations. One way she can do this is by determining whether there are any general characteristics that are found in all phenomena, no matter whether these phenomena are forced upon us by outward experience, highly abstract conclusions of theoretical physicists, or colorful products of the most vivid nightmares. Such characteristics, Peirce called *categories,* after Aristotle, Kant, and Hegel. Hence, for Peirce, it became the business of phenomenology "to draw u p a catalogue of categories and prove its sufficiency and freedom from redundancies, to make out the characteristics of each category, and to show the relations of each to the others" (EP2:148). The catalogue of categories Peirce ultimately arrived at is remarkably short. There are only three of them, and he calls them, in an effort to avoid any contamination with already existing metaphysical systems, firstness, secondness, and thirdness.

Firstness is the pure presentness of the phenomenon, i.e., without any reference to anything that it might be presented to. As Peirce puts it, it is the phenomenon "such as it is, utterly ignoring anything else," for instance, a simple, self-effacing, positive quality of feeling. *Secondness* is the category of resistance or struggle. For Peirce, this second characteristic is also found in all phenomena. It is, moreover, not reducible to firstness, as secondness always involves two phenomena, whereas firstness involves only one. This second category, however, concerns otherness only in its purest form, that is without any notion of a relation between the two as doing so unavoidably introduces a third element, namely the relation. The notion of a relation between two objects brings us to Peirce's third category, that of *thirdness* or mediation. It is the acceptance of this third category that separates the realists, among whom Peirce reckoned himself, from the nominalists, among whom he classified James. For the realist, relations are as real as the individual objects they relate.

The above account shows quite clearly that you cannot have thirdness without secondness and no secondness without firstness, as you need a first before you can relate it to a second and you need two before you can introduce a third. But, for Peirce, it also works the other way around. You cannot have a first *without* also having a second, and you cannot have two *without* also having a third. The three categories are all-pervasive; they are present in all we can possibly think of. For instance, when you conceive of something purely in isolation (i.e., as a first), you are already also conceiving something else, namely, that what it is not (which is a second to it) that stands in a particular relation to it, namely, that of negation, thereby bringing in a third. Peirce devotes two full lectures to an extensive defense of the categories, including a defense of why there are no more than three.

Although phenomenology is the most basic of the positive sciences, it can appeal to mathematics, which is not a positive science but only studies the results of hypothetical states of things. In fact, the above derivation of the categories does precisely that. It draws conclusions from *hypothetical* pure firsts, pure seconds, and pure thirds; hypothetical, because, for Peirce, all three categories are present in all phenomena.

One important conclusion that can be drawn from the above analysis is that generality (or thirdness) is a basic constituent of *all* phenomena. This is an important result for Peirce, because his pragmatism seeks to relate the meaning of terms, etc., not to *particular* effects, as with James, but to the habits they inspire. These habits, however, must be *real* habits, not mere products of our fancy, which is what the nominalists contend. The habits must be real because otherwise Peirce's pragmatism would only relate terms to mental constructs, which is precisely what the pragmatists seek to avoid. Since habits are generals, and not particulars, the pervasiveness of thirdness in the phenomena we encounter becomes an important argument in support of Peirce's version of pragmatism, while it is at the same time a strong argument against the nominalistic interpretation of pragmatism.

By itself, however, the discovery of real generals does not prove pragmatism. Peirce's pragmatic maxim is a *normative* principle; it tells us how we should define our terms, or what we should expect from our

101

beliefs for them to have meaning. Hence, the proof of pragmatism should continue with an investigation of the normative sciences.

Whereas phenomenology studies phenomena as they appear in their immediacy (that is, in their firstness), the normative sciences study phenomena in their relation to specific ends, or, as Peirce puts it elsewhere, "in so far we can act upon it and it upon us."[125] That is to say, the normative sciences study phenomena in their secondness.[126] Traditionally, these ends have been beauty, goodness, and truth. Interpreted this way, Peirce explains, "esthetics considers those things whose ends are to embody qualities of feeling, ethics those things whose ends lie in action, and logic those things whose end is to represent something" (EP2:200).

Peirce goes to great lengths in showing, not only that logic is a normative science, but also how deeply it is intertwined with and depends upon the two more basic normative sciences, esthetics and ethics.

Thomas Hobbes once famously characterized reason as that faculty that enables us, unlike the brutes, "to multiply one untruth by another."[127] Peirce was not as cynical as Hobbes, but he acknowledges that the instincts of the lower animals "answer their purposes much more unerringly than a discursive understanding could do" (R 969:3). For Peirce, the singular most important advantage of reasoning is that it can critically evaluate itself:

> Reason is inferior to Instinct in several respects. It is less
> subtle, less ready, less unerring. The one respect in which it is
> superior is in being controlled, checked, criticized. This
> supposes, or constitutes,—the existence of bad reasoning.
> There is no such thing as bad instinct, unless it be bad in the
> eyes of something else. But there is reasoning that reason itself
> condemns; and were it not so, reason would be without its
> solitary advantage. (R 832:2).

Reasoning is thus subject to self-control. It is precisely because of this that we can pronounce inferences as good or bad. Inferences that are unconscious, and thus uncontrollable, are not subject to normative evaluation, just as acts that occur outside of our control, like the knee-jerk reflex or the dilation of our pupils, are not subject to moral approbation or reprobation. To put it briefly, reasoning is essentially self-controlled thought in the same manner as moral conduct is essentially self-controlled action.

A year later, in a draft for a review of Herbert Nichol's *Treatise on Cosmology,* this emphasis on self-control explicitly entered the pragmatic maxim:

> The method prescribed in the maxim is to trace out in the imagination the conceivable practical consequences,—that is, the consequences for deliberate, self-controlled conduct,—of the affirmation or denial of the concept; and the assertion of the maxim is that herein lies the *whole* of the purport of the word, the *entire* concept. (CP 8.191)

In the 1903 Lowell lectures, Peirce explains the notion of self-control when applied to reasoning in terms of rule-following:

> A person who draws a rational conclusion, not only thinks it to be true, but thinks that similar reasoning would be just *in every analogous case.* If he fails to think this, the inference is not to be called reasoning. It is merely an idea suggested to his mind and which he cannot resist thinking is true. (CP 1.606; emphasis added)

Thus emerge general patterns of reasoning that come to act like norms against which our reasoning in new or complex situations is measured. In short, reasoning by its very nature involves the application of rules or norms so that for each particular inference we must ask ourselves whether it satisfies those rules or not. Peirce's argument is very Kantian. The individual act, in this case the act of assertion, involves (if only tacitly) a *commitment* to repeat the act when at some other time we find ourselves in the same situation, or one that is sufficiently like it, *even* if we have at that time an inclination to do otherwise (which is where self-control comes in). For example, when I decide to set my alarm at 4:00 A.M. because I want to catch an early flight to London, this decision extends beyond the particularities of the current situation in that it involves the general rule, or the habit, that in comparable situations I should set my alarm as well. The purpose of logic is to develop good habits of reasoning.

The next question to ask is, What is the aim of reasoning? What constitutes logical goodness? Identifying logic with the critic and classification of arguments, Peirce examines three answers to this question, each corresponding with one of the three categories. If we stick to the category of firstness, the end of argumentation would be pure esthetic satisfaction. Good arguments would be those that are esthetically pleasing. This is the attitude of the Platonic idealist. For Peirce, this option is unsatisfactory. It may be feasible for an all-powerful God, but for humans this is not the case. Our ideals are all too easily shattered by the brute force of experience.

Alternatively, we could center on secondness, and make the brute force of experience our ultimate aim and benchmark. Good arguments would be those that lead us to certain preordained brute experiences. This is the attitude of the nominalist. It is this view that lies behind the pragmatism of James and Schiller, and that of Papini and Prezzolini.

For Peirce, this second option is also unsatisfactory. When we rely solely on blind compulsion, we make ourselves utter strangers to the world. We would never be able to *know* anything. Because pure secondness leaves no residue, we would be caught entirely within a web of our own making of which we do not know how it relates to the world. Recall what Peirce writes to James after receiving his copy of James's *The Will to Believe:* "It is not the mere arbitrary force in the deed but the life it gives to the idea that is valuable" (CP 8.250).

The above two choices are the only options open to the nominalist. The realist, who accepts also the reality of relations, has a third option as well. This is to hold that there are real relations within nature—relations "to which we can train our own reason to conform more and more" (EP2:212). Put differently, the realist can hold that there is in experience itself an element of reasonableness.

Admittedly, the claim that the universe is organized in a manner that agrees with our reason is merely a postulate; it is a claim that we *hope* to be true. But that is all that is needed, Peirce argues, since our only hope of ever knowing anything *presupposes* that this postulate is true, as does the distinction between logical goodness and badness. Moreover, if we accept an evolutionary account of the human species, as does Peirce, this agreement can be explained quite adequately in terms of adaptation. Reasoning is not something that is *external* to the universe, but over the course of its development, the human organism (like any other organism) has *internalized,* however imperfectly, part of the dynamic order of the universe—a universe that is itself still evolving.

On the realist interpretation of pragmatism, the meaning of a concept is thus not some singular experience or act (this being only an intermediate phase), but how such practical effects contribute to the development of the reasonableness of the universe (CP 5.3). Understanding is not gained by gathering disconnected facts, but by getting in tune with the concrete reasonableness of the cosmos.

Whether James truly understands what Peirce is up to in the Harvard lectures is doubtful, as the following exchange of letters reveals. At issue is again a clash between James's nominalism and Peirce's realism. Not long after the lectures, James writes in "Humanism and Truth," "The serious meaning of a concept, says Mr. Peirce, lies in the concrete difference to someone which its being true will make" (MT:37). James sent Peirce a copy of the paper and Peirce writes back:

I do not think I have often spoken of the "meaning of a concept" whether serious or not. I have said that the concept itself "is" *nothing more* than the concept, not of any concrete difference that *will* be made to someone, but, is nothing more than the *concept* of the *conceivable* practical applications of it."[128]

James replies instantaneously and not without some irritation about what he sees as Peirce making a lot of fuss about a minor point: "I am very sorry that the brief paraphrase by which I summed up what seemed to be the essential practical outcome of your view should seem so to belie it."[129] For Peirce, however, it is not a minor point at all, it is the main message of his Harvard lectures, which leads Peirce to reply to James with no less irritation: "My Harvard lectures were chiefly bringing out the point which you seem surprised I should attach any importance to."[130]

6.6 From Pragmatism to Pragmaticism

The Harvard Lectures were not published, but in 1905–6 Peirce published three articles in the journal *Monist:* "What Pragmatism Is," "Issues of Pragmaticism," and "Prolegomena to an Apology for Pragmaticism." As in the Harvard lectures, Peirce is again developing his own branch of pragmatism while distancing himself from the other pragmatists. Again the development of a proof of pragmatism is central, albeit that it is now called an apology.

In the third paper, the prolegomena to his proof of pragmatism, Peirce goes into great detail discussing his graphical logic—a geometric rather than an algebraic approach to logic—which he subsequently set out to use in his proof. The proof itself, however, was never fully completed and did not make it into print. Many manuscripts related to Peirce's proof have survived, but it would lead us too far astray to try to find our way through this enormous mass of material, much of which remains unpublished. Instead, we will concentrate on Peirce's general account of pragmatism in "What Pragmatism Is" and Peirce's later reflections on the doctrine.

Disappointed with what had become of pragmatism, Peirce renames his own view pragmaticism. Recall that the suffix "-icism" indicates that the doctrine is a more strictly defined reading of pragmatism. It is important to realize, however, that Peirce does not embrace the new term in order to mark a departure from his earlier work, but because he seeks to distance himself from the now fashionable use of the term. The term "pragmaticism," Peirce famously declares, "is ugly enough to be safe from kidnappers" (EP2:335). He proves right. Few have felt any inclination to use the term, and even Peirce failed to stick with it.

The centerpiece of pragmaticism remains the 1878 pragmatic maxim (section 2.4). Continuing in the course he set out in the Harvard lectures, Peirce spends much time and effort ensuring that the maxim be interpreted in realist terms. Recall the original maxim:

> Consider what effects, that might conceivably have practical bearings, we conceive the object of our conception to have. Then, our conception of these effects is the whole of our conception of the object. (EP1:132)

Peirce now interjects brief clauses that spell out what he had in mind with these "conceivable practical consequences." They are "consequences for deliberate, self-controlled conduct" (CP 8.191), or, as in a letter to F. W. Frankland, "consequences for rational conduct."[131] In a draft for a letter to Schiller, dated 10 September 1906, Peirce similarly elaborates on his choice of "practical" by explaining, "By 'practical' I mean apt to affect conduct; and by conduct, voluntary action that is self-controlled; i.e., controlled by adequate deliberation" (CP 8.322). A few years later Peirce writes Howes Norris Jr. that when he christened pragmatism he derived its name from πρᾶγμα (behavior), to show that it refers to the view "that the only real significance of a general term lies *in the general behavior which it implies.*"[132]

For Peirce, what constitutes meaning is thus not the "effects" qua sensory impressions, nor the singular act of bringing these effects about, but the deliberate, self-controlled conduct elicited by the concept. To make meaning consist exclusively in the concrete acts which the conception brings about would make brute force the *summum bonum* of pragmatism (R 284:3). For Peirce, such an interpretation is absurd. Drawing an analogy to music, Peirce observes, "Nobody conceives that the few bars at the end of a musical movement are the purpose of the movement" (CP 5.402n3). To give another analogy of his, one might as well contend that "the artist-painter's living art is applied to dabbing paint upon canvas, and . . . that art-life consists in dabbing paint, or that its ultimate aim is dabbing paint" (ibid.).

Peirce's general model is still that of the experimenter or laboratory man. The experimenter has a tendency to interpret the meaning of an assertion as a prescription for an experiment that, if carried out correctly, will result in an experience of a given description. As Peirce puts it,

When you have found, or ideally constructed upon a basis of
observation, the typical experimentalist, you will find that
whatever assertion you may make to him, he will either
understand as meaning that if a given prescription for an
experiment ever can be and ever is carried out in act, an
experience of a given description will result, or else he will see
no sense at all in what you say. (EP2:332)

Now one could object, as Peirce's imaginary opponent does
(EP2:339), that this is a nominalistic view because an experiment always
concerns a *particular* operation upon a *particular* object, leading to a
particular result, thereby reducing meaning to particulars. To take such a
position, Peirce counters, betrays a serious misunderstanding of what
experiments are all about. The meaning of an experiment lies not in any
of these particulars, nor in all of them together, but in the *phenomenon* that
this particular event exemplifies, which is not a particular at all:

> Indeed, it is not in an experiment, but in *experimental
> phenomena,* that rational meaning is said to consist. When an
> experimentalist speaks of a *phenomenon,* such as "Hall's
> phenomenon," "Zeemann's phenomenon" and its
> modification, "Michelson's phenomenon," or "the chessboard
> phenomenon," he does not mean any particular event that did
> happen to somebody in the dead past, but what *surely will*
> happen to everybody in the living future who shall fulfill
> certain conditions. (EP2:340)

Now, "what *surely will* happen to everybody in the living future who shall
fulfill certain conditions" is certainly something quite different from
singular experiences or discrete sensory data. The scientist, Peirce argues,
is always tacitly a realist; she cannot be otherwise, as without it the entire
enterprise of empirical science becomes void. Why experiment if all that
matters is the particular effects the experiment brings about?

What makes experiments valuable is that they are recipes for action.
For Peirce, the meaning of a proposition is always another proposition.
That is to say, it is a translation. Now there are countless ways in which
a proposition can be translated. So which of these would we call "its
meaning"? The pragmatist has an answer. It is, Peirce observes,

> that form in which the proposition becomes applicable to
> human conduct, not in these or those special circumstances,
> nor when one entertains this or that special design, but *that
> form which is most directly applicable to self-control under*

107

> *every situation, and to every purpose.* (EP2:340, emphasis added).

Recall that pragmatism, for Peirce, is a maxim of logic, and that logic studies how we should act.

Having thus explained what pragmatism stands for in his eyes, Peirce presents the following rendition of the maxim—cast in terms of his semiotics, or his doctrine of signs—which he believed to be equivalent to his original maxim of 1878:

> The entire intellectual purport of any symbol consists in the total of all general modes of rational conduct which, conditionally upon all the possible different circumstances and desires, would ensue upon the acceptance of the symbol. (EP2:346)

Recall that, for Peirce, we can only think in signs (section 2.1). By casting the maxim in semiotic terms, Peirce avoids one problem that has plagued modern philosophy. When we speak of meaning, are we talking about ideas, words, sentences, statements, beliefs, theories, etc.? For Peirce the maxim applies to anything that can become a symbol; a symbol being a sign "whose special significance or fitness to represent just what it does represent lies in nothing but the very fact of there being a habit, disposition, or other effective general rule that it will be so interpreted," whether this general rule may be natural or acquired (CP 4.447).

In this new rendition, Peirce goes to great lengths to ensure a reading of the maxim that is non-sensationalist, non-emotivist, and realist. It is non-sensationalist in that the meaning of a symbol is not cast in terms of sensations to expect. It is non-emotivist, in that it explicitly focuses on the *intellectual* purport of the symbol and links the meaning of the symbol to *rational* conduct. Finally, it is realist, in that it locates meaning not in particulars but in something general; and it does so in such a way that it impedes all attempts to reduce the general to the particular, as no set of particulars could possibly cover "all the possible different circumstances and desires."

7

Dewey's Engaged Instrumentalism

Philosophy recovers itself when it ceases to be a device for dealing with the problems of philosophers and becomes a method, cultivated by philosophers, for dealing with the problems of men.

—John Dewey[133]

Due to his deep concern for social and political issues, and his strong belief in the human capacity for working things out, John Dewey came to pragmatism from a quite different angle than either Peirce or James. Dewey was born in 1859 in Burlington, Vermont, to a family that was deeply affected by the Civil War. He studied at the University of Vermont, then taught high school for a few years before entering graduate school at Johns Hopkins University. Although Dewey took some courses with Peirce, it was not until half a century later, when he read Peirce's *Collected Papers,* that he began to appreciate Peirce. However, Dewey was deeply influenced by James especially by his *Principles of Psychology.* After his graduation, Dewey taught at the University of Michigan, where he met George Herbert Mead, before coming to the newly established University of Chicago, in 1894.

In Chicago, Dewey became actively involved in Hull House, a social settlement that was founded to improve the social conditions of the impoverished industrial working class. The settlement had been established a few years before by Jane Addams and Ellen Gates Starr for the purpose of emancipating working class people by offering them the advantages of a college education.[134] Initially, Hull House offered classes in academic subjects such as geometry, Shakespeare, and Greek art, but soon the curriculum shifted to address more directly the basic needs of the people who came to the settlement. Because of the active interest of Addams and other Hull House residents in social issues and the effects of industrial urbanization, the settlement quickly became a pioneer in progressive education, while developing in the process a new style of sociology. In 1895, Hull House residents coauthored *Hull-House Maps and Papers,* which established the mode of inquiry that would set the Chicago sociologists apart.[135] Writing in 1902, Dewey describes the settlement as "a place where ideas and beliefs may be exchanged, not merely in the arena of formal discussion—for argument alone breeds misunderstanding and fixes prejudice—but in ways where ideas are incarnated in human form and clothed with the winning grace of personal life" (MW 2:91). Dewey felt particularly attracted to the notion of the school as a social center and a clearing house of ideas.

In 1896, Dewey helped found the Laboratory School at the University of Chicago. The school, which was quickly dubbed the Dewey School, was specifically intended as a laboratory for testing pedagogic and psychological theories. Three years later, Dewey published *The School and Society,* a book that was based in part on his experiences with Hull House and the Laboratory School. In it Dewey objects to the passive lecture-type format that dominated education, arguing that learning should be an active and collaborative enterprise that is firmly rooted in the students' personal life experiences. Dewey's philosophy of education, with its emphasis on inquiry rather than the regurgitation of facts, is an early expression of his pragmatism. In 1904, problems with the university administration regarding the Laboratory School caused Dewey to leave. He went to Columbia University, where he remained till his retirement in 1930.

After his retirement, Dewey remained active as a public intellectual. In 1937, he traveled to Mexico to head a commission to investigate the conspiracy charges made by the Soviets against Leon Trotsky who was at the time living in exile in Mexico. A few years later he came forward to defend his main philosophical adversary, Bertrand Russell, who had been invited by the City University of New York for a one-year professorship in logic and the foundations of mathematics. Because of Russell's outspoken views on religion, this caused strong opposition from local clergy who brought the issue to court. The presiding judge, who later said he had to take a bath after reading Russell's books, forced the university to rescind its offer.[136]

7.1 Logic: His First and Last Love

In 1934, Dewey writes in a letter to Albert C. Barnes that logic was his "first and last love" (LW 12:537). Dewey's logic, however, is an experimental logic and as such has more affinity with the philosophy of science (with a broad conception of science) than with the formal logic that comes out of the quarters of Russell and Whitehead, whose approach to logic in their monumental *Principia Mathematica* is the main competitor to Dewey's own. For Dewey, logic is, as he puts it succinctly in his 1938 *Logic,* the "inquiry into inquiry" (LW 12:12). It should be noted, however, that what Dewey has in mind here is an *empirical* inquiry into inquiry. Dewey strongly believes that most philosophers have lost touch with the actual methods of inquiry as they were used in the experimental sciences, and he advocated that the experimental method be used in philosophy, including even the study of logic. That is to say, he believes that one could derive norms, rules, and procedures conducive to future successful inquiry by studying past inquiries that paid off and the reasons for their success. Consequently, Dewey grounded philosophy, including logic and the theory of inquiry, firmly in psychology. Psychology, Dewey writes shortly after he graduated from Johns Hopkins, "is the ultimate science of reality, because it declares what experience in its totality is; it fixes the worth and meaning of its various elements by showing their development and place within this whole. It is, in short, *philosophic method"* (EW 1:144). This approach to logic put Dewey on a collision course not only with the traditional, a priori conception of logic, but also with Peirce's normative conception of logic discussed in chapter 6.

In this chapter the emphasis lies on Dewey's logic as the theory of inquiry, not only because this is a central thread that runs through Dewey's thought, but also because one cannot really understand Dewey's pragmatism—or as he preferred to call it, his instrumentalism—without having a good grasp of his logic.

7.2 *Studies in Logical Theory*

While in Chicago, Dewey gathered a group of sympathetic thinkers with whom he published *Studies in Logical Theory,* which appeared in 1903.[137] In addition to Dewey, who wrote four of the eleven essays and edited the volume, seven of his former students were contributors. In the preface, Dewey briefly summarizes five points on which all agree: judgment is the central problem for logic, logic cannot be separated from psychology, judgments are experienced (so that logic is at least in part an empirical science), reality can only be defined in experiential terms, and there is no universal standard of truth apart from what is required for "readjusting and expanding the means and ends of life" (MW 2:296).

In the *Studies,* Dewey is already rejecting the traditional way of philosophizing, which he sees as stuck in pre-scientific habits and modes of thought that draw a sharp but wholly artificial divide between knowing and acting. Dewey hopes to rid philosophy of many pseudo problems that are products of the presuppositions and vocabulary of philosophy rather than its subject matter. Dewey's alternative is that philosophers should embrace the methods used in the experimental sciences, even in traditionally a priori fields like logic, thereby arguing for a thoroughgoing reconstruction of philosophy.

Studies in Logical Theory is enthusiastically received by William James, who sees in it the establishment of a genuine school in philosophy which he dubs "The Chicago School," and which he predicts would be influential for years to come. Schiller also gives the book a warm welcome, calling it a "weighty contribution to current logical controversy."[138] Peirce is more critical. In a letter to Dewey, he accuses the Chicago pragmatists of neglecting the normative aspects of logic in favor of a purely historical account of problem-solving techniques. As Peirce explains, "I do not think anything like a natural history can answer the terrible need that I see of checking the awful waste of thought, of time, of energy, going on, in consequence of men's not understanding the theory of inference."[139] As Peirce sees it, one might as well study the moral practices of Borneo headhunters, Utah Mormons, Wall-Street stockbrokers, and Greek cabdrivers in an attempt to discover the best rules for moral conduct. At best, it is a very roundabout procedure.

James's prediction came true, as the "Chicago School" did indeed flourish for years to come. However, it would continue to do so without Dewey. Shortly after the book was published, Dewey left the University of Chicago because of the problems surrounding the Laboratory School and the underhanded way in which his wife Alice was removed as the school's principal. Nevertheless, much of Dewey's subsequent thought is shaped by his repeated attempts to clarify and defend the position he takes in *Studies in Logical Theory*. The four essays he contributed to that volume reappeared with only minor changes as the opening chapters of his 1916 *Essays in Experimental Logic*. It is to this that we now turn.

7.3 Experimental Logic

In *Essays in Experimental Logic,* Dewey further develops the theory of knowledge he had advocated in *Studies in Logical Theory.* Philosophers, Dewey lamented, have pretty much treated all our experiences as if they are mere objects of contemplation. But when we have the flu, are faced with an overfilled fridge, or when a stunningly beautiful young woman crosses our path, what we are dealing with is clearly something other than a mere object of contemplation. What is more, to *conceive* of it as a mere object of contemplation so much alters its nature that it becomes a wholly different experience. One consequence of the traditional practice of reducing all experience to objects of contemplation, Dewey argues, is that knowledge becomes so detached from experience that the question of how this knowledge relates to its objects becomes an inexplicable mystery.

It is worth noting that with the *Essays* Dewey was in particular attacking the new realists who had replaced idealism as pragmatism's main adversary. Not only had the new realists, or neorealists as they were also called, come to dominate the philosophical scene, but Columbia University, where Dewey was teaching, was also one of their strong-holds.[140]

The new realists were arguably guilty of what Dewey famously called the "spectator theory of knowledge"—a view of knowledge in which the role of the knower is reduced that of a mere onlooker. For instance, in the "Program and First Platform of Six Realists," E. G. Spaulding stakes out the realist position as follows:

> Realism, while admitting the tautology that every entity which
> is known is in relation to knowing or experience or
> consciousness, holds that this knowing, etc., is eliminable, so
> that the entity is known as it would be if the knowing were not
> taking place. Briefly, the entity is, in its being, behavior, and
> character, independent of the knowing.[141]

The new realist's ideal of the knowing subject thus boils down to that of a passive onlooker—someone who studies the world as a detective examines a crime scene—careful not to disturb anything or leave any traces. For Dewey, this ideal might be approximated on occasion, but cannot and should not be taken as a model for how we acquire knowledge or for explaining what knowledge is.

Central to the new realists' view is the firm conviction that the *process* of knowledge acquisition is wholly independent of the knowledge that is obtained. For the new realist, neither the truth nor the meaning of the statement, "There are nine planets in our solar system," depends in any way on how we arrived at this conclusion. Consequently, a study of the historical process through which the statement is reached—interesting as it might be as an exercise in the history or anthropology of science—is of no help in determining its meaning or truth. For the neorealist, inquiry can be treated as the ladder Jacob built when he tried to climb to heaven. You can safely throw it away once you have reached your destination.

Dewey is of an entirely different opinion. The paradigmatic case of knowledge acquisition is not that of the scientist or philosopher who is leisurely contemplating this or that subject in his brown study, but the emergence of a concrete problem that demands a concrete response. "Reflection," Dewey writes, "appears as the dominant trait of a situation when there is something seriously the matter, some trouble, due to active discordance, dissentiency, conflict among the factors of a prior non-intellectual experience" (MW 10:326). Dewey calls this an indeterminate situation. For Dewey, all reflection is ultimately a product of an indeterminate situation. In a world without trouble there would be no thought.

An indeterminate situation occurs when conflicting responses are elicited, and we can proceed only when this conflict is somehow resolved. For instance, when I see a hot-dog cart on the other side of a busy street this may elicit simultaneously the hunger-induced response of crossing the street and the life-preserving response of not crossing the street. A process of reflection ensues, which will either make me suppress one of the two responses or reconcile them through some plan of action. The moment the conflict is resolved, reflection ceases until we find ourselves within a new indeterminate situation.

By focusing on the indeterminate situation, Dewey follows Peirce's doubt-belief theory where inquiry is similarly the product of a distress of some kind and comes to conclusion when this distress is relieved. Like Peirce, Dewey rejected the notion of universal doubt. Doubt is always related to a specific indeterminate situation. Dewey used the example of a man who is lost in the woods. That the uncertainty confronting the man cannot be separated from the situation within which it arose quickly becomes evident when we imagine him remembering the uncertainty without remembering the situation. At best, the memory would be a vague, noncognitive feeling of distress (MW 4:83).

By recasting the doubt-belief relation in terms of an organism that seeks to maintain homoeostatic equilibrium, Dewey expresses the problem of knowledge—more explicitly than Peirce had done—in naturalistic terms. Human behavior, up to the most theoretical endeavors, is continuous with the behavior of the so-called "lower organisms." There is no difference in kind between Einstein working out his theory of relativity and a lobster trying to catch a small crayfish that continues to elude it.

Dewey prefers the phrase "indeterminate situation" above "problematic situation," as the latter already points to the existence of a problem. For Dewey, problems are already *products* of inquiry. As the saying goes, "A problem well put is a problem half solved." Furthermore, for Dewey, it is very distinctly the *situation* that is indeterminate. As he puts it later in his *Logic* of 1938, "*We* are doubtful because the situation is inherently doubtful." And he adds immediately that "personal states of doubt that are not evoked by and are not relative to some existential situation are pathological" (LW 12:109). Hence, like Peirce, Dewey rejects Descartes's method of universal doubt. Moreover, the doubt elicited by indeterminate situations is *not* a purely subjective affair that can be resolved by manipulating our personal mental states, but is an objective, public relation of means and ends.

Dewey thus empathically denies the accusation—made most prominently by Russell—that he had made personal satisfaction the benchmark of truth and the ultimate aim of inquiry. As Dewey puts it,

> Mr. Russell proceeds first by converting a doubtful *situation* into a personal doubt. . . . Then by changing doubt into private discomfort, truth is identified with removal of this discomfort . . . [but on my view] "Satisfaction" is satisfaction of the conditions prescribed by the problem. (LW 14:56)

Thus, for Dewey, inquiry relates to the attempt of resolving the objective conditions of an indeterminate or problematic situation. For instance, if the problem is how to evenly divide five pieces of birthday cake among eleven children, it is not the personal satisfaction of the children or the cake-cutter that determines whether the cake is cut evenly, but whether the eleven children all get the same amount of cake. The same is true for knowledge acquisition in general. There, too, the issue is not whether the inquirers feel satisfied with the answer, but whether the answer solves the problem. Of course, solving the problem will generally satisfy the inquirers.

Dewey's views on education are based on the same principle, and the often made claim that Dewey's philosophy of education is child-centered is thoroughly misguided. Dewey does not think that humans are naturally intelligent and rational and that the task of the educator should be limited to that of a facilitator whose sole task it is to bring out the child's natural development. In *The Child and the Curriculum*, Dewey

115

explicitly criticizes the child-orientated theory of education, which he believes could only be based on a "sentimental idealization of the child's naïve caprices and performances" (MW 2:281f.). Education should be problem-oriented, not child-oriented. The child must learn to creatively adapt to the problematic situations likely to be encountered in life and which set the boundaries of what can or is to be done.

For Dewey, the acquisition of knowledge is thus always a function of a concrete, indeterminate situation where it is sought for the specific purpose of resolving a particular problem. Hence, for Dewey, knowledge involves the reorganization of an indeterminate situation aimed specifically at resolving conflicting or inhibited responses. Moreover, since for Dewey reflection comes to conclusion only in a successful experimental act (mere contemplation of the problem is not enough), all knowledge is in the end experimental knowledge; there is no pure a priori knowledge.

The upshot of all of this is that, for Dewey, who thinks reflection emerges within an indeterminate situation that has been transformed into a specific problem and terminates when this problem is solved, knowledge cannot be seen as independent from the conditions in which it arises and the situation to which it applies. This means that, for Dewey, all knowledge is thoroughly contextual. It is perhaps good to add as an aside that saying that knowledge is always contextual does not commit one to hold that all knowledge is dependent on the inquiry of which it is a product. Different inquiries can lead to the same conclusion or give entirely different solutions that are equally satisfactory. Just as there is more than one way to Rome, there is more than one way out of an indeterminate situation.

7.4 Whether All Judgments Are Practical

In the concluding essay of *Essays in Experimental Logic,* "The Logic of Judgments of Practice," Dewey seeks to elaborate his instrumentalist view and to see where it will lead him. He began with the noncontroversial point that science, at least from one angle, is a mode of practice. Scientists do not sit back in their armchairs contemplating physics, sociology, or pre-Pleistocene life with their eyes closed, instead they do things—they act. As Dewey concludes, "To say that something is to be learned, is to be found out, is to be ascertained or proved or believed, is to say that something is to be done" (MW 8:65).

Now, in the process of doing things, Dewey continues, scientists make all sorts of practical judgments. Practical judgments differ from

116

theoretical judgments. Whereas a theoretical judgment purports to say how things are, a practical judgement asserts how we want things to be, and, derivatively, what we should do to make them happen. Questions such as "What should we eat tonight?" and "Where will we go on our next vacation?" are examples of questions that require practical judgments. They cannot be answered by a description of our stomach content, however accurate, or by scrutinizing a world atlas, however detailed it might be. Science abounds in practical judgments. They are clearly prominent in the applied sciences, where the purpose could be to cure an infectious disease, to develop a method for locating subterranean rivers, or to make cars less dependent on fossil fuel. But practical judgments abound also in the theoretical sciences, where the purpose could be to test an already existing theory, to explain a specific phenomenon, or to examine the implications of some new or established idea, like that of dropping Euclid's parallel postulate, which led to numerous non-Euclidean geometries.

Having established the practical component of science, Dewey asks himself the following daring question:

> Suppose that the propositions arising within the *practice* of knowing and functioning as agencies in its conduct could be shown to present all the distinctions and relations characteristic of the subject-matter of logic: what would be the conclusion? (MW 8:65)

In other words, what would be the situation if *all* scientific judgments had the nature of practical judgments, however far removed they might be from our daily lives and however abstract and theoretical they may sound?

If all judgments are practical ones, thinking would be an art, like boatbuilding or watercolor painting, and all knowledge would be a product of the art of thinking. Now when we build a boat, Dewey, explains, we take raw material such as wood or iron and give it a shape that it did not have before in such a manner that it will serve the purpose for which we set ourselves to work. For Dewey, the same is true for thinking. Just like boatbuilding, thinking takes certain raw materials (memories, sensory experiences, etc.) and shapes them so as to make them fit a certain purpose, which is, in this case, *the purpose of attaining knowledge.* For Dewey, the new realist's ideal of a passive observer is untenable, since even the detached observer has its own agenda, namely the acquisition of knowledge. The astronomer, for instance, is never just passively recording what she sees, but already in the very act of observation itself, what she sees is being actively molded into objects that further the process of attaining knowledge. And even when for some moment she allows her thoughts to wander aimlessly, what she sees is still shaped by past purposes, some of which she may have long since forgotten or never have been consciously aware of.

What gives an *observation*—the raw material we encounter in our dealings with the world—its value, Dewey continues, is not something inherent within it, antecedent and independent of any motive we might bring with us, but how it contributes to the purpose at hand. For instance, in the case of boatbuilding we will find that certain types of wood are good for boatbuilding, whereas others are not. That is to say, the antecedent properties of the wood enter into the process of boatbuilding as limiting conditions. You cannot make everything out of just anything. You cannot, for instance, build a steamship from jelly, or a kite from thick slabs of concrete.

The same is true when our purpose is not that of building a boat, but that of attaining knowledge. In that case, too, some observations will contribute to the *purpose* of attaining knowledge; whereas, others will not. The famous distinction between primary and secondary qualities, Dewey maintains, is a case in point. The primary qualities, such as extension, number, and motion have proven far more useful in extending our knowledge of physical objects than secondary qualities, such as colors, smells, and sounds, and hence they are favored by scientists and philosophers alike. It would be incorrect though, Dewey insists, to conclude from this, as many have done, that primary qualities *truly* depict reality, whereas secondary qualities do not. This would be to fully misunderstand how inquiry works and what its object is. The orchardist, the woodworker, the painter, and the philosopher all see an apple tree differently, and it makes no sense to ask which of these reflects the real apple tree, or whether there is something like "the true apple tree" of which the above are all partial and partisan impressions.

Dewey makes a similar argument for the laws of logic. These laws are also products of inquiry. As Dewey points out in the *Logic,* "All logical forms (with their characteristic properties) arise within the operation of inquiry and are concerned with control of inquiry so that it may yield warranted assertions" (LW 12:11). Dewey agrees with Peirce that the aim of inquiry is settled opinion. However, since Dewey focuses much less on the long run than does Peirce, while agreeing with Peirce's fallibilism, Dewey in effect trades the notion of truth for what he calls "warranted assertibility."

Good logical principles ensue when we discover that certain inferences, all other things being equal, give dependable conclusions, i.e., are successful. In this respect, the inquirer is no different than the potter who learns that a certain technique of spinning the potter's wheel leads to good pots. What makes such principles or techniques regulative, or 'normative,' is that they give better results. In a very Peircean manner, Dewey explains,

> It can hardly be denied that there are habits of inference and that they may be formulated as rules or principles. If there are such habits as are necessary to conduct every successful inferential inquiry, then the formulations that express them will be logical principles of all inquiries. In this statement "successful" means operative in a manner that tends in the long run, or in continuity of inquiry, to yield results that are either confirmed in further inquiry or that are corrected by use of the same procedures. (LW 12:21)

Although he remains skeptical as to whether a Peircean ultimate opinion is attainable (even in principle), Dewey firmly believes in the convergence of inquiry (at least for practical purposes).

For Dewey, the relationship between knowledge and its object is thus very different from the contention, made by new realists and others, that knowledge—the *product* of inquiry—must be a faithful copy of the objects that entered the inquiry as its raw material. True, we must take account of this raw material, just as when we build a boat we must take account of the wood grain, its buoyance, etc. However, Dewey argues, this is very different from demanding that our knowledge be a mental replica of what one finds in nature. The raw material we start with, Dewey contends, "are not objects but means, instrumentalities, of knowledge: things by which we know rather than things known" (MW 10:347). This is the core of Dewey's instrumentalism. To ignore what motivates the inquiry, how it is conducted, and what it is aimed at, leads inevitably to a misconstrual of what knowledge is.

The analogy with art also points at the fact, often ignored, that both the tools the inquirer uses and the products he creates are, though manmade, not subjective. As Dewey points out, "The tools and works of art are neither mental, subjective things, nor are they antecedent entities like crude or raw material. They are the latter shaped for a purpose" (MW 8:68). They are objective both in the sense that they contribute to the purpose at hand—which may be the purpose of gaining knowledge—and in the sense that they depend upon the traits of the objects as they are prior to, or independent of, the act of gaining knowledge. For Dewey, the principles of logic are as objective as the principle that teakwood is the best choice for ship decks (as it is durable, strong, non-absorbent, doesn't rot, etc.). It is a matter of means and consequences.

7.5 Pragmatism

What Dewey calls "pragmatism" is not all that easy to define, since it is, for Dewey, like any other intellectual undertaking, a product of concrete perplexities and conflicts that were faced by philosophers and their kind. Consequently, it cannot be defined *in abstracto,* nor should we expect it to be clean around the edges. For Dewey, what pragmatism stands for is very much the result of an empirical study of (mostly scientific) inquiry. Like Peirce, Dewey sees pragmatism primarily as a method.

For the pragmatist, knowledge is in an essential way the product of an indeterminate situation that requires resolution. As Dewey puts it in *How We Think* (1910),

> [Pragmatism] starts from acts, functions, as primary data, functions both biological and social in character; from organic responses, adjustments. It treats the knowledge standpoint, in all its patterns, structures, and purposes, as evolving out of, and operating in the interests of, the guidance and enrichment of these primary functions. (MW 6:88)

The main deficiency of traditional, intellectualistic philosophy (Dewey also described his own view as anti-intellectualism), is that it wrongly separates knowledge from its working context. The intellectualist deliberately detaches the acquisition of knowledge from all other human endeavors, declaring it an end in itself that is altogether unaffected by anything else, most particularly our practical interests and personal desires. What fuels this approach is that it takes the acquisition of knowledge to be a wholly rational affair, and one that depends heavily on the feats of formal logic (the tangible side of rationality), where this rationality itself is seen as something self-sufficient, hovering far above the forever changing world of experience. What Dewey objects to is this radical separation of knowledge acquisition from its original function, which is to resolve indeterminate situations (which *do* include practical interests, emotions, and desires). Dewey calls this the "intellectualistic fallacy" (MW 6:89). Much of Dewey's logic is aimed at debunking this old notion of an autonomous, self-sufficient rationality.

However, while pragmatism may be called anti-intellectual, it is not anti-intelligent. To make this point Dewey shifts the focus from reason (as a fixed faculty) to reasonableness:

What is reasonableness? You see a person doing something that is unreasonable. What do you mean? . . . Either he is setting up ends that he hasn't got the means for realizing, or he is using the means in such a way that they won't give him the result he is after. Or, on the other hand, here are these conditions which might be used as means and he isn't using them as means. He isn't forming an end consequently to be reached in terms of the means, the resources that he has got in connection with the obstacles and the obstructions that have got to be overcome. (LW 11:565f)

When the notion or reason is not set a priori as a fixed faculty, but derived from a notion of reasonableness like the one sketched above, pragmatists are rationalists, Dewey claims, and they are so in a more sophisticated way than intellectualists are.

Although pragmatism sees reason as purpose-directed and action-involved, Dewey denies that pragmatism seeks to subordinate knowledge to desired practical results: "My pragmatism affirms that action is involved in knowledge, not that knowledge is subordinated to action or 'practice'" (LW 14:13). Pragmatism simply seeks to reintegrate knowledge with the world wherein we live. As Dewey puts it, "Pragmatism regards both knowledge and truth as bridges which enable us to approach our purposes" (MW 12:213). Aiming for Elysian bliss, the intellectualist tradition has burned those bridges.

Dewey's *Essays in Experimental Logic* contains two essays on pragmatism. In it, he describes pragmatism as follows:

[Pragmatism] insists that general notions shall "cash in" as particular objects and qualities in experience; that "principles" are ultimately subsumed under facts, rather than the reverse; that the empirical consequence rather than the *a priori* basis is the sanctioning and warranting factor. But all of these ideas are colored and transformed by the dominant influence of experimental science: the method of treating conceptions, theories, etc., as working hypotheses, as directors for certain experiments and experimental observations. (MW 4:100)

Dewey agrees with Peirce that pragmatism represents the habit of mind we find in the laboratory. Pragmatism brings the method of the experimental sciences into philosophy. Dewey also agrees with James that the method of pragmatism "should be applied as widely as possible; and to things as diverse as controversies, beliefs, truths, ideas, and objects" (MW 4:101).

Pragmatism, Dewey writes in the syllabus for one of his courses at Columbia, "grows out of the development of experimental methods and of genetic and evolutionary conceptions in science" (MW 4:253). As Dewey puts it years later, it is nothing but "the systematic elaboration of the *logic and ethics of scientific inquiry*" (LW 15:24). And although the term is conspicuously absent in the 1938 *Logic*, Dewey calls the book "thoroughly pragmatic" (LW 12:4). In brief, Dewey's pragmatism is by and large his experimental logic. However, while Dewey's pragmatism is empirical, he avoids a reductionist materialism and keeps a realist stance by allowing for the reality of universals. Pragmatism, Dewey remarks, "gives to thought and thought relations (universals) a primary and constructive function" (MW 7:328).

In Dewey's view, pragmatism pans out differently, depending on what it is applied to. In cases where we start with an empirically given *object*, Dewey followed the German chemist Wilhelm Ostwald's rule, quoted in James's *Pragmatism*, that the meaning of an object is the effects it produces upon us. For instance, when a bee taxonomist discovers a new species of bees, and names it, the meaning of this name consists in the practical reactions these newly discovered animals elicit from us or impose upon us.

The situation is different when we begin with *ideas*, not yet knowing the object they are meant to refer to or whether there even are such objects. In Dewey's view, such an idea is in essence "a draft drawn upon existing things." When the draft is honored, Dewey continues, that is, when "existences, following upon the actions, rearrange or readjust themselves in the way the idea intends," then we could say that the idea is true. For instance, the notions of mutation in genetics and of neutrino in physics were introduced first as ideas, and it was only later that the "objects" were found that corresponded with them.

Dewey briefly summarizes the difference between the two situations as follows: "the meaning of an *object* is the changes it requires in our attitude, the meaning of an *idea* is the changes it, as our attitude, effects in objects" (MW 4:103; emphasis added). The first situation is closely related to Peirce's interpretation of pragmatism; the second resonates, however faintly, James's will-to-believe argument.

7.6 Truth and Warranted Assertibility

In the *Logic* of 1938, Dewey introduces the phrase "warranted assertibility" to replace "belief" and "knowledge" (LW 12:15). Dewey tries to stay away from "belief" because of its ambiguity, as it can refer either to the *object* of belief or to the *state* of belief. Confusing these two has led in the past to serious misunderstanding. The distinction between Peircean pragmatism, with its emphasis on the object of belief, and Jamesian pragmatism, with its emphasis on the state of belief, is at least at some level a product of this confusion. The term "knowledge" is similarly ambiguous, as it can refer to the outcome of an inquiry that satisfactorily came to an end or to the object to which inquiry gravitates. In the second case, "knowledge" has, as Dewey puts it, "a meaning of its own apart from connection with and reference to inquiry" (LW 12:15).

The phrase "warranted assertibility" also has the advantage of making a clear connection with *inquiry* as what warrants the assertion. What we should be on the lookout for, Dewey observes, are "the *conditions* under which we reach warranted assertibility about particular matters of fact" (LW 14:169). Dewey's prime inspiration came from judicial language and proceedings. As he remarks in the *Logic*, "When it is ruled that certain evidence is admissible and that certain rules of law (conceptual material) are applicable rather than others, *something* is settled," and the final settlement is in part a product of such intermediary and partial settlements (LW 12:125). Dewey notes further that "in resolution of problems that are of a looser quality than legal cases we call them opinions *to distinguish them from a warranted judgment or assertion*" (ibid.; emphasis added). Hence, the notion of warranted assertibility has much to do with having the (procedural) right to assert something (e.g., to propose something as true or false), where these rights are themselves an intrinsic part of the procedure in question.

As a consequence, Dewey rejects the idea that the truth or falsity of a belief is determined by the effects of having the belief on the believer, a view to which James and Schiller lean:

> The question of truth-falsity is *not*, on my view, a matter of the effects of *believing*, for my whole theory is determined by the attempt to state what conditions and operations of inquiry *warrant* a "believing," or justify its assertion as true. (LW 14:183)

For Dewey, the issue of truth and falsity is thus not related to whether a belief is good for us, or whether it satisfies our desires, but to the indeterminate situation that spurred the inquiry, and the rules and restrictions intrinsic to that inquiry. Whether a belief is warranted, Dewey observes, is determined by "their pertinency and efficacy in 'satisfying' conditions that are rigorously set by the problem they are employed to resolve" (LW 14:183f).

123

The result is a correspondence theory of truth, but one that is more sophisticated than the traditional variant that trades on the metaphor of the disinterested spectator. A better metaphor is that of a key that corresponds with a lock; it is a congruity, a fitting in. Hence, Dewey concludes, "In the sense of correspondence as operational and behavioral . . . I hold that my *type* of theory is the only one entitled to be called a correspondence theory of truth" (LW 14:180). The disinterested spectator, who is wholly detached from her subject, does not correspond with what she perceives, and neither do her beliefs.

An important motivation for preferring warranted assertibility above truth is Dewey's embracing of Peirce's fallibilism. As Dewey explains:

> The position which I take, namely, that all knowledge, or warranted assertion, depends upon inquiry and that inquiry is, truistically, connected with what is questionable (and questioned) involves a sceptical element, or what Peirce called "fallibilism." But it also provides for *probability,* and for determination of degrees of probability in rejecting all intrinsically dogmatic statements, where "dogmatic" applies to *any* statement asserted to possess inherent self-evident truth. That the only alternative to ascribing to some propositions self-sufficient, self-possessed, and self-evident truth is a theory which finds the test and mark of truth in consequences of some sort is, I hope, an acceptable view. (LW 14:171f)

Dewey relates this fallibilism in a fairly Peircean way to what may be called a probabilistic theory of truth. We can never be certain that something is true, but given the appropriate conditions, we can be warranted in holding it for true. Although Dewey hesitated to equate truth with warranted assertibility, he did maintain that there is no *practical* difference between the two.

8

The Conceptual Pragmatism of C. I. Lewis

> Knowledge—so the pragmatist conceives—is for the sake of action; and action is directed to realization of what is valuable. If there should be no valid judgments of value, then action would be pointless or merely capricious, and cognition would be altogether lacking in significance.
>
> —C. I. Lewis[142]

Clarence Irving Lewis (1883–1964) spent most of his philosophic career at Harvard, where he connected the Golden Age of James and Royce with the work of V. W. O. Quine and Nelson Goodman, both students of his. Lewis was a contemporary of Rudolph Carnap and actively sought to connect the pragmatist outlook with the logical positivism that was quickly gaining ground in the U.S. Lewis was deeply influenced by Kant and he was intimately familiar with Peirce's logical writings, including the mass of manuscripts acquired by Harvard shortly after Peirce's death. In fact, Lewis was invited back to Harvard partly with the expectation that he would take a leading role in the reorganization of the manuscripts, and he practically lived with them for two years.[143]

In his own philosophy, Lewis focused on one of the key problems of pragmatism, namely, how to reconcile the notion that our experience is malleable to our purposes with the notion that facts are "hard." Lewis found his answer in a pragmatic epistemology that brought together the given, the world of "hard fact" that is not subject to our will, and the a priori which, being a creation of ours, is subject to our will and malleable to our causes.

125

8.1 Logics and Pragmatism

Before engaging in a discussion of the views of Lewis, a few comments are in order on his main teacher Josiah Royce (1855–1916) and Royce's relation to pragmatism. Possibly the two main reasons Royce is not generally associated with pragmatism are his adherence to an absolute idealism and the historical circumstance that he was generally considered James's principal opponent at Harvard. However, when reflecting on his own student years, Lewis remarks,

> It . . . impressed me that James and Royce had more in common—particularly the voluntaristic strain—than either of them recognized: and I was later gratified by Royce's reference to what he called his "absolute pragmatism."[144]

For Royce, our experience of nature is "an interpretation rather than a portrayal or a prediction of the objective facts of nature, an adjustment of our conceptions of things to the internal needs of our intelligence (which Royce considered absolute), rather than a grasping of things as they are in themselves."[145] In this manner, Royce combines a pragmatism for empirical matters with the view that the fundamental axioms of logic are absolute. "Our constructive processes," Royce writes, "possess a certain absolute nature and conform to their own self-determined but, for that very reason, absolute laws . . . which are the fundamental and immanent laws of the will itself."[146] For Royce, if we try to deny the axioms of logic, we unavoidably end up confirming them through a *reductio ad absurdum*. As it is thus impossible to show that the fundamental principles of logic are wrong, Royce takes them to be absolute. And what is more, logic can be grounded in them.

Lewis's study of alternative modal logics made him realize that this method of grounding logic is untenable, because rival logical systems pass this test equally.[147] As Lewis observes, "there are several logics, markedly different, each self-consistent *in its own terms* and such that whoever, using it, avoids false premises, will never reach a false conclusion" (MWO:248). Hence, Lewis finds that for each of these alternative logics, when we seek to disprove its fundamental principles, we end up reaffirming it, making all of them irrefutable when gauged on their own terms. From this, Lewis concluded that the decision of which logic to choose could only be based on extra-logical considerations. Lewis's solution to this problem, to which he was led by his reading of Peirce in the early 1920s, is essentially pragmatic: We favor those conceptual structures and ways of categorizing and classifying objects that best fit our plans and purposes. This led Lewis to conclude that "the ultimate criteria

126

for the laws of logic are pragmatic" (CL:323). Lewis subsequently extended this idea to the area of epistemology.

8.2 The Nature of Knowledge

Lewis's excursions into logic, together with his study of contemporary mathematics, form the basis of his pragmatic notion of the a priori, resulting in a theory of knowledge that combines the free creation of alternative conceptual schemes for interpreting experience with a pragmatic method for determining which conceptual scheme to favor. For Lewis, empirical knowledge is in essence a triadic affair. Its three elements are what Lewis called "the given," a priori conceptual schemes, and something to connect the two together. What Lewis termed "the given" is that element in perception that "remains unaltered, no matter what our interests, no matter how we think or conceive" (MWO:52). It is wholly independent of any activity of thought. Lewis's a priori conceptual schemes furnish the other end of the spectrum. They are entirely products of the free activity of thought. Moreover, for Lewis, the a priori and the given are wholly independent of each other. Neither limits the other or adds anything to it (MWO:37).

Various answers have been suggested to explain how our conceptual schemes connect with the world of brute fact. They run from Plato's allegory of the cave to Descartes's pineal gland, to Leibniz's idea of a preestablished harmony, to Darwinian ideas of an evolutionary adaption of the human organism to its environment. Lewis's answer is decidedly pragmatic: what connects a priori conceptual schemes with the given are our human needs and interests. Along that line Lewis remarked that empirical knowledge is "an interpretation, instigated by need or interest and tested by its consequences in action, which individual minds put upon something confronting them or given to them" (CL:241). Put differently, "the primary and pervasive significance of knowledge lies in its guidance of action: knowing is for the sake of doing" (AKV:3). Application of concepts to the given yields empirical knowledge, but this application is not just a product of the given that confronts the reasoner, but also of her aims and interests. Hence, for Lewis, truth is neither wholly found nor wholly a product of the mind.

8.3 The Given

Lewis derived his notion of the given from the undeniable fact that there is "such a thing as experience, the content of which we do not invent and

127

cannot have as we will but merely find" (AKV:182). Lewis insists that without the given, all knowledge would be wholly without content and arbitrary (MWO:39). Even the idealists, Lewis observed, hardly mean to deny that "my seeing at this moment a sheet of paper instead of a green tree is a datum which it is beyond the power of my thought to alter" (MWO:45). "Indeed," Lewis writes a few pages later, "an unqualified denial of this element in ordinary cognition is sufficient to put any theory beyond the pale of plausibility" (MWO:48).

In *Mind and the World Order*, Lewis defines the given as "that which remains untouched and unaltered, however it is construed by thought" (MWO:53).[148] No matter what our interests are or how we look at it, the given remains unaffected. A scholar, a baby, a bushman, and a chimpanzee, all *interpret* C. I. Lewis's fountain pen differently (as a writing implement, a teething-tube, etc.), but at the level of the given, Lewis maintains, it is the same to all. Note, however, that the given is only part of what we experience: "Subtract, in what we say, or hear, or otherwise learn from direct experience, *all that conceivably could be mistaken;* the remainder is the given content of the experience inducing this belief" (AKV:182f).

Lewis further realizes that his use of the phrase "the given" is somewhat misleading, as it hints at a certain unity that can only be conceptual. This is not what Lewis intends by the phrase. What he has in mind is rather, "the *element* of givenness in what we may, for usual and commonplace reasons mark off as 'an experience' or 'an object'" (MWO:59). However, even though we can *isolate* the given in this abstract way, we cannot "describe any particular given *as such,* because in describing it, in whatever fashion, we qualify it by bringing it under some category or other, select from it, emphasize aspects of it, and relate it in particular and avoidable ways" (MWO:52). Consequently, Lewis rejects the idea that the given can be identified through philosophical analysis, as with John Locke's idea of analyzing all that comes before the mind into "simple ideas," or with the "sense data" philosophy of G. E. Moore and Bertrand Russell. Simple ideas and sense data are, for Lewis, not given but are already sophisticated products of elaborate (a priori) conceptual systems. Nobody has ever had a simple idea or a sense datum by itself.

Lewis's approach to the given is phenomenological (in Peirce's sense of the term, see section 6.5). On several occasions, Lewis compares it with the "buzzing, blooming confusion" (the phrase is James's) on which the infant first opens its eyes. It is the world as it is found before *any* a priori system has been formed through which it could be interpreted.

The purely given is, for Lewis, not even a possible object of knowledge. The given cannot be known because all our knowledge involves concepts, which is something that *we ourselves* bring to the given. As with Locke's *substratum*, we can only say *that* it is, but not *what* it is.[149] In Lewis's words, "The given is *in,* not before, experience" (MWO:55). The given can only be interpreted.

The given must be distinguished further from the *object* which is given. As Lewis explains in *Mind and the World Order,*

> The given is presentation of something real, in the normal case at least; *what* is given (given in part) is this real object. But the whatness of this object involves its categorical interpretation; the real object, as known, is a construction put upon this experience of it, and includes much which is not, at the moment, given in the presentation. (MWO:58)

Thus, the object that is presented to me when I see Lewis's fountain pen is given to me only partially, and is interpreted by me as a fountain pen by relating experiences to it that are not presented, but which I anticipate having, were I to perform certain acts, such as unscrewing its cap, putting the tip on a sheet of paper, comparing it with past experiences, etc. Still, the aspects thus introduced are not products of my imagination, but relate to what is given. The baby who uses the pen to sooth the discomforts of teething may just as well discover that there is ink in the pen as the scholar who gently puts the pen to paper.

The given should not to be confused with reality. As Lewis puts it, "experience as it comes to us contains not only the real but all the content of illusion, dream, hallucination, and mistake. The *given* contains both real and unreal, confusingly intermingled" (CL:236). By applying conceptual systems, (that is, by positioning what is directly experienced within a framework that is *not* thus experienced) we can say that something is real or unreal. Reality, for Lewis, is a conceptual construction created by the human mind to fit its aims within scientific reasoning and its need as a social animal for a "common world." For example, an oasis at the horizon that disappears when one approaches it is called unreal because it does not meet the criteria that we have found to be conducive to satisfying our interests. Nothing in the content of the experience itself—that is in the experience that is still unpolluted by *any* conceptual system—furnishes any ground for calling the oasis unreal. As Lewis puts it in "The Pragmatic Conception of the *A Priori*,"

> Failure to behave in certain categorical ways marks it as
> unreal. Uniformities of the type called "natural law" are the

129

> clues to reality and unreality. A mouse which disappears
> where no hole is, is no real mouse; a landscape which recedes
> as we approach is but illusion. . . . That the uniformities of
> natural law are the only reliable criteria of the real, is
> inescapable. But such a criterion is ipso facto *a priori*. No
> conceivable experience could dictate the alteration of a law so
> long as failure to obey that law marked the content of
> experience as unreal. (CL:236)

For Lewis, the determination of reality, the classification of phenomena, and the discovery of natural law are all three intimately intertwined. The distinction between the real and the unreal is moreover essential to the act of interpretation: "It is only because the mind is prepared to judge it real or unreal according as it bears or fails to bear certain marks, that interpretation of the given is possible at all, and that experience can be understood" (MWO:13).

8.4 The *A Priori*

The discussion of the given showed that we can have no knowledge of external reality unless we first add something ourselves. To be able to see a fountain pen on the desk, or to see a flock of geese fly over, we must connect what is directly presented to us as given with a certain structure within which what is given can be understood as a fountain pen or as a flock of geese. What we add ourselves, Lewis calls the "a priori." Lewis sees a sharp divide between the a priori and the given. Whereas the given is wholly unaffected by what we may think, the a priori is wholly a product of thought; to put it in more technical terms, the a priori is analytic. This division between the given and the a priori was later criticized, most prominently, by Lewis's student W. V. O. Quine (section 9.5). Having thus separated the a priori from the given, Lewis next sought to bridge this divide pragmatically through the interpretative act. For him, it is in the interpretative act that the a priori and the given are brought together.

Although Lewis accepts the received view that the a priori is both necessary and independent of experience, he comes to this position in a untraditional way, which results in a novel conception of the a priori. First, Lewis rejects the generally held opinion that the a priori is necessary because the mind is forced to accept it as true. According to Lewis, the situation is exactly the opposite. The a priori is necessary, not because the mind is *forced* to accept it no matter what experience will bring, but because it represents the free attitude of the mind so that it does not at all matter whether experience agrees with it or not. As Lewis explains,

> Definitions and their immediate consequence, analytic propositions generally, are necessarily true, true under all possible circumstances. Definition is legislative because in some sense arbitrary. . . . If experience were other than it is, the definition and its corresponding classification might be inconvenient, fantastic, or useless, but it could not be false. (CL:233)

For Lewis, it is not the a priori that the mind is forced to accept as true, but the given. Hence Lewis contrasted necessary truth with what is factually contingent, but not with what is voluntary in thought and action.

Regarding the independence of the a priori of experience, Lewis makes a similar observation. Traditionally, what made the a priori independent of experience was that it was regarded as a product of the "inner light" of a reason that is absolute, even if instilled imperfectly in men. Experience was either assumed to fit this product, or miraculously agreed with it, as with Leibniz's notion of a preestablished harmony. Lewis again takes almost the opposite view. The a priori is independent of experience precisely because it "prescribes *nothing* to experience" (MWO:197). The a priori does not anticipate the given, but our attitude to it. Far from being absolute, the a priori is pragmatically established, which means invariably that there are alternatives to it:

> The thought which both rationalism and empiricism have missed is that there are principles, representing the initiative of mind, which impose upon experience no limitations whatever, but that such conceptions are still subject to alteration on pragmatic grounds when the expanding boundaries of experience reveal their infelicity as intellectual instruments. (CL:239)

For Lewis, having alternatives becomes a trademark of the a priori. The a priori can be distinguished from the given precisely by recognizing that it *has* alternatives; or as Lewis puts it, "by the ordinary criteria of responsibility in general—that a different mode of acting is possible and makes a discoverable difference" (MWO:232).

It is important to note that Lewis does not think that the a priori preceded all experience, as with the rationalist's innate ideas, which we were assumed to carry within us from birth. Rather, the conceptual schemes through which we seek to interpret a *particular* experience must be formulated in advance of that experience.

Lewis sees the a priori as distinctly analytic, thereby rejecting the Kantian notion of the synthetic a priori (MWO:231). In contrast to Kant, Lewis holds that a priori knowledge cannot tell us anything about the given; it only gives us the means through which we can give, for ourselves, some order to the given. For instance, once we defined death as a stoppage of breathing, no empirical observation can show that this definition is false. What may happen, as it did in this case, is that the definition conflicts with some other deeply ingrained a priori principle (such as the notion that death is irreversible) or that it fails to serve us well. Both call for a revision of the definition. Historically, the above definition was indeed replaced, first, by a definition in terms of a total stoppage of the flow of blood, and later by a definition that makes the absence of brain activity the predominant sign of death. In both cases the new definition did not prove its predecessor wrong, but simply led to its abandonment.

Mathematics has shown that elaborate a priori systems can be developed, and Lewis makes this the basis for his more general comment that all our knowledge contains "an element of just such logical order which rise from our definitions" (CL:244). Like Peirce and Schiller, Lewis is keenly aware of the development within nineteenth-century mathematics to do away with axioms and replace them with postulates, and his own view of the a priori is in part inspired by it.

8.5 Interpretation

Interpretation involves the application of a priori conceptual systems to the given, thereby imposing an order upon it. For Lewis, interpretation is something that *we* bring to experience. We can do this because we confront the given with certain ready-made distinctions and systems of classification. In Lewis's view, knowledge, or understanding, commences precisely "when some conceptual pattern of relationships is imposed upon the given by interpretation" (CL:250). To know, Lewis explains in *Mind and the World Order,* "is to find what is presented significant of what is not, just now, so presented" (MWO:44). Lewis thereby rejects the copy-theory of knowledge. We do not attain knowledge when we somehow furnish ourselves with a copy of what is presented. Rather, we know something when we can proceed from what is given to something that is not. To know that there is an oasis at the horizon, or that the object on the desk is a fountain pen, is to know how to act toward it and with what results. Again, the aim of knowledge is not to copy the given, but to cope with it.

Within interpretation there are two directions in which what is immediately presented can be related to what isn't: it can be related to further actual and possible experiences, or it can be related to our own interests and actions. Errors occur when I relate what is presently given to a future experience that fails to occur, or when I predict that something will serve my interest when it doesn't.

Regarding the first direction, Lewis maintains that there is some structure inherent to the given. The given cannot be a "smooth undifferentiated flux," Lewis observes, because in such an undifferentiated field, attention would not be able to mark any boundaries (MWO:58). What the boundaries are, however, can only be learned from experience and only in a manner that is inseparably wound up with our aims and actions:

> That the rug is on the floor or the thunder follows the flash, is
> as much given as the color of the rug or the loudness of the
> crash. But that I find this disjunction of rug and floor
> possessed of a meaning which the wrinkles in the rug do not
> have, reflects my past experience to taking up and putting
> down rugs. (MWO:59)

Recall that the given itself cannot be known, at least not in any substantial sense. It is that buzzing and blooming confusion to which we seek to give some order by imposing a priori schemes upon it. Even to identify the rug as an object, to object-ify it, is already to impose a conceptual scheme on what is presented. The point is, however, that when we perceive what we have come to recognize as rugs, there is something to what is given that makes it natural for us to separate rugs from floors in a way that we cannot separate rugs from wrinkles or from colors.

This brings us to the second direction Lewis distinguishes, where the given is related not to future actual or possible experiences, but to our own aims and interests. Here, how we categorize the given is related to the question of whether the interpretation leads to the result we desire. As Lewis puts it, "What the mixed and troubled experience will be—that is beyond me. But what I shall do with it—that is my own question, when the character of experience is before me" (MWO:265). Faced with what is given, I am free to impose any category upon it that I want, Lewis argues, and I am likely to pick those categories that serve my purposes.

How we classify a certain experience is thus determined by a learned relation that connects this experience to other experiences and to action.

In the end, what determines whether a certain interpretation is successful is whether it accommodates to our bent and serves our interests. That is to say, the issue of interpretation is a thoroughly pragmatic one.

8.6 Pragmatism, Truth, and Valuation

Since, for Lewis, knowledge results from the successful application of a priori conceptual schemes to the given, knowledge is for him always relative to a conceptual system. For Lewis, scientific as well as everyday knowledge is a product of deeply rooted attitudes and interpretative habits of thought. Nothing succeeds like success, and it is the past success of conceptual schemes that guides us in how to understand the world in which we live. The result is a thoroughly pragmatic theory of truth:

> There can be no more fundamental ground than the pragmatic
> for a truth of any sort. Nothing—not even direct
> perception—can force the abandonment of an interpretative
> attitude . . . except some demand or purpose of the mind itself.
> (MWO:266f)

On this account, alchemy was not replaced by modern chemistry because alchemy proved to be false (being an a priori system it applies to all possible worlds, including ours), but because the alchemistic categories and principles have been found not (or no longer) to connect with the given in a manner that serves our purposes. Pragmatists have interpreted this in terms of new truths taking the place of old truths, but Lewis finds this an unfortunate way of putting it. It would be more accurate to say that an old *interpretation* was replaced by a new one. In this process the old interpretation was not discovered to be false, but simply abandoned.

Lewis voices severe criticism of the pragmatism of James and Dewey whom he accused of neglecting the a priori. Because of this, they "seem to put all truth at once at the mercy of experience and within the power of human decision" (MWO:266). For Lewis, one does not begin by being a pragmatist, but one begins by construing a priori systems in which one is guided by intellectual motives that go well beyond the practical and the expedient, such as consistency, simplicity, and completeness. Without a well-developed a priori, Lewis insisted, the acquisition of knowledge remains a random leap in the dark. Any pragmatism that ignores this aspect of knowledge acquisition, Lewis insists, is no more than "a cheerful form of skepticism" (MWO:271). For Lewis, it is not in the *construction* of a priori systems, but only *in their application to the given* that one is to be a pragmatist. "We must all be pragmatists," Lewis observes, "but pragmatists in the end, not in the beginning" (MWO:267).

Lewis's pragmatist answer to the question of how to connect a priori conceptual frameworks with the given bestows a central place to value judgments. A priori schemes are chosen with a concrete purpose in mind, or because they best serve our needs in general and in the long run. Both cases entail an appeal to what we value. As Lewis explains in the introduction to *An Analysis of Knowledge and Valuation,*

> Knowledge, action, and evaluation are essentially connected. The primary and pervasive significance of knowledge lies in its guidance of action: knowing is for the sake of doing. And action, obviously, is rooted in evaluation. For a being which did not assign comparative values, deliberate action would be pointless; and for one which did not know, it would be impossible. (AKV:3)

In deliberate action, I act from the belief that the situation wherein I find myself can be altered according to my will to satisfy a present desire. For instance, I can walk to the tree down the road to pick one of its large red apples. Seen from this angle, Lewis's pragmatism comes down to the doctrine,

> that all problems are at bottom problems of conduct, that all judgments are, implicitly, judgments of value, and that, as there can be ultimately no valid distinction of theoretical from practical, so there can be no final separation of questions of truth of any kind from questions of the justifiable ends of action. (CL:108)

A value-neutral pragmatism, and thus a value-neutral philosophy, is a contradiction in terms.

Since determining which a priori system to adhere to involves a judgment as to its value, the value judgment must be independent of the a priori system that is being judged, otherwise the whole exercise would beg the question. Lewis's way out of this predicament is to make value judgments a species of empirical judgments. In fact, the central thesis of *An Analysis of Knowledge and Valuation* is that value judgments are empirical judgments and hence capable of verification.[150]

8.7 Empirical Knowledge

To get a better sense of how Lewis understands empirical knowledge, it is useful to consider his division of empirical knowledge into expressive statements, terminating judgments, and non-terminating judgments. *Expressive statements* are mere articulations of what is immediately presented in experience, without any commitment as to whether their object is real, a phantasm, or a representation of something else. The claim "I see what *looks like* a marble staircase down the end of the hall," Lewis considers an example of an expressive statement, as I am restricting myself wholly to what is given in experience (AKV:179). The situation is different for the apparently similar statement "I see a marble staircase down the hall," since there I am distinctly making a judgment about how the world is. Roughly, the difference is the following: Discovering that the staircase is part of a *trompe l'oeil* falsifies the second statement but does not affect the first one, as the later discovery does not alter the initial impression I had. It still *looked* like a marble staircase. For Lewis, expressive statements are thus non-falsifiable. They cannot be proven wrong. What is more, they are also unverifiable. No corroboration with any other fact can add anything to the initial impression that is captured in the expressive statement. Getting close to the stairs and seeing that the steps are really there and made of solid stone does not strengthen the original impression that it looked like a marble staircase. Since expressive statements cannot be falsified or corroborated, Lewis denies that they can be properly classified as knowledge. However, they do allow us to refer to the basic facts of experience.

Besides expressive statements, Lewis distinguishes between terminating judgments and non-terminating judgments. *Terminating judgments* are typically of this form: Given that I have a direct experience *S,* then if I do *A,* I will have a direct experience *E;* where *S* and *E* are experiences that can be captured in expressive statements.

Terminating judgments find their cue in what is immediately given, but what determines their meaning and truth is not given. For Lewis, however, terminating judgments can be verified; they can even be verified conclusively. Moreover, they are verified not by putting them under closer scrutiny, but by performing the act that connects *S* with *E*.[151] Hence, in contrast to expressive statements, terminating judgments can be shown true or false. Lewis considers the verified terminating judgment the paradigm of empirical knowledge. Terminating judgments, he observes, admit of "decisive and complete verification or falsification" (AKV:181).

The second type of judgment Lewis called *non-terminating judgements* on the grounds that

> while there is nothing in the import of such objective statements which is intrinsically unverifiable, and hence nothing included

in them which is not expressible by some terminating
judgment, nevertheless no limited set of particular predictions
of empirical eventualities can completely exhaust the
significance of such an objective statement. (AKV:184)

The statement that there is a marble staircase down the hallway is for
Lewis a non-terminating judgment. Although nothing included in the
statement is intrinsically unverifiable, no finite set of terminating
judgments can fully capture its meaning. This because no finite number
of terminating judgments—if I do *A,* I will experience *E*—would be
sufficient to fully exhaust the empirical significance of a non-terminating
judgment, as the number of possible actions that bear upon the issue is
endless. In Lewis's view, the class of non-terminating judgments
comprises most of the empirical statements we habitually make
(AKV:185). "Jupiter has four moons," "Most Americans are overweight,"
and "Mario married Maria" are all examples of non-terminating
judgments.

Although no finite set of terminating judgments can fully capture the
empirical significance of a non-terminating judgement, non-terminating
judgments can be verified or confirmed in terms of the terminating
judgments they entail. That is to say, the knowledge conveyed by a non-
terminating judgment is always probable knowledge, its probability being
a function of the verification of the terminating judgments it entails. For
Lewis, non-terminating judgments can be said to be "practically certain"
when the degree of their verification is such that "no later confirmation
can render what is presently judged more certain than it is at the moment"
(AKV:181).

Lewis's discussion of empirical knowledge betrays his pragmatist
slant. His notion of terminating judgments clearly breathes the spirit of the
principle of pragmatism, on which the meaning of a judgment is a function
of its conceivable practical consequences. In contrast to some of the
earlier pragmatists, however, Lewis refuses to limit the class of
meaningful empirical judgments to this type only, adding also non-
terminating judgments where there is no such one-dimensional connection
between the statement and the experiences to which the statement refers.
The meaning of a non-terminating judgment is more fluid, as it depends
on what groups of terminating judgments entailed by it are taken to be
representative of it, and its truth cannot be determined with certainty, but
only with a certain probability. Therefore, Lewis is situated closer to
Peirce and Dewey than to James and Schiller.

9

Pragmatism and Analysis: Morris, Carnap, Quine

> The empiricist temper receives its most vigorous contemporary expression in the writings of the American Pragmatists and in the writings of those who have been stimulated by the influences which have spread out from Vienna as a centre.
>
> —Charles W. Morris[152]

There is a general sense that pragmatism all but disappeared from the scene in the 1930s when logical positivism came to dominate the American landscape, only to resurface much later with self-proclaimed neopragmatists such as Richard Rorty. Although there may be some truth to this, one finds in American-style logical positivism and in the American branch of the analytic tradition a continuous pragmatist undercurrent. Notwithstanding profound differences, there are deep affinities and close historical ties. Recall that Peirce and Vailati saw an intimate connection between pragmatism and positivism, and that Quine and Goodman were both students of Lewis. But there are other connections as well. Particularly noteworthy is Charles W. Morris, a student of Mead at Chicago who, like Lewis, actively sought to connect pragmatism with logical positivism. Morris was largely responsible for Rudolph Carnap's emigration to the United States in 1936 and played a central role in the Unity of Science movement. Together with Carnap and Otto Neurath, Morris edited a series of monographs under the umbrella of the *International Encyclopedia of Unified Science.*[153] The current chapter will give only a very rough sketch of this period and one that is confined mostly to the early years.[154]

9.1 Logical Positivism

Like pragmatism, logical positivism, or logical empiricism as it is also called, falls within the empiricist tradition.[155] The logical positivists subscribed to the central thesis of the empiricists that only statements about sensory phenomena are genuine, and took this as their guide when discussing meaning, truth, and inquiry. For the logical positivists, meaningful empirical statements come only in two flavors: (1) statements that are cast directly in observational language; and (2) statements that can be reduced to, or translated into, statements that are cast directly in observational language. Thus any statement containing a theoretical term such as "electron," "gravity," or "hardness" must be translatable into a set of statements that are equivalent to it containing only observational terms. In reply to the question of how to establish this translation, the logical positivists point to the program of Russell and Whitehead, who, in their *Principia Mathematica,* seek to reduce mathematics to logic and set theory, and to Wittgenstein's 1921 *Tractatus Logico-Philosophicus.* Put very briefly, the translation, or reduction, must abide by the formation and transformation rules of first order predicate logic (what counts as a well-formed sentence, how to derive one sentence from another while preserving truth, etc.).

Carnap's 1928 *Der logische Aufbau der Welt* is the most ambitious product of this approach. In the *Aufbau,* Carnap seeks to do for epistemology what the *Principia* tries to do for mathematics. The aim of the book, Carnap points out, is to reduce all claims about reality to claims about the given. For Carnap, this means showing how each meaningful statement is in effect a logical construction of so-called observation sentences, which are sentences that capture raw, unanalyzed perceptual data, purportedly without any conceptual pollution.

In light of this, the logical positivists' answer to the search for meaning is relatively straightforward. The meaning of any statement, word, etc., is the observation statements into which they can be translated, while giving particular attention to the *relations* between those observation statements (which is where *logical* positivism differs from earlier forms of positivism, such as Comte's). Modern logic, they think, gives us a perfect and transparent medium by which those relations could be expressed precisely and unambiguously. For the logical positivists, knowledge is a matter of grasping those relations. It is not concerned with the *content* of our experience—which is private and non-communicable—but with the *logical structure* of experience, which *can* be communicated. It is the logical structure that renders concepts intersubjective. Thus it is not someone's unique and private experience of a certain shade of orange that constitutes knowledge, but how this experience fits within a larger structure that is communicable (it enables one to distinguish tangerines from apples, recognize lead paint, identify the Dutch soccer team, signal danger, etc.).

For the linguistically oriented logical positivists, this comes down to the question of how to relate experience to a language (the medium in which we express and communicate our thought), where "language" is to be interpreted broadly as "a set of symbols which are to be combined in accordance with a definite logical syntax" with the purpose "to mirror or express facts."[156] For the logical positivists a statement *expresses* a fact, not by eliciting certain sensations, but through its *structural similarity* with the fact. A statement is true if its components correctly reflect the components of the fact it expresses; it is false if they don't. This idea of knowledge as a mirror of reality is radically rejected by the pragmatists. It is explicitly criticized by Dewey (who, incidentally, was a contributor to the first monograph of the *Encyclopedia*)[157] and later becomes the focal point of Richard Rorty's criticism of contemporary philosophy in *Philosophy and the Mirror of Nature*.

9.2 The 1934 International Congress

A session at the 1934 International Congress of Philosophy, devoted specifically to the importance of logical analysis for epistemology, brought the pragmatists Ferdinand Schiller and Charles Morris together with the logical positivists Otto Neurath and Rudolph Carnap.[158] The session had a profound influence. While Schiller remained more or less an outsider, Morris, Carnap, and Neurath clearly gravitated toward each other. Morris arranged for Carnap's move to the University of Chicago, where he was teaching at the time himself, and shortly thereafter the three would begin coediting the *International Encyclopedia of Unified Science*, while Neurath remained in Europe.

In his own contribution to the session, Morris aims to show that pragmatism and logical positivism are, as he puts it, "essentially complementary," adding that "much is to be expected from a conscious cross-fertilization of the two" (LPP:23). In fact, much of Morris's own efforts in subsequent years would be directed precisely to such a conscious cross-fertilization. According to Morris, the connection between the two tendencies is strongest where they address the issue of meaning. At face value, pragmatists and logical positivists appear seriously at odds on this issue. Whereas pragmatists seek to connect the meaning of, say, a proposition with the expectation of the person who uses it, logical positivists connect its meaning with the syntactical rules of the language that determine its (legitimate) usage. For the logical positivists, when studying the meaning of a proposition one must not look at those who use it and the mental states they connect with it, but one must study how the proposition fits within the language in which it is uttered. Hence, for the logical positivists, the meaning of a proposition "becomes the non-analytic propositions which logically follow from it, i.e., which the syntax of the language allows" (LPP:27).

According to Morris, the contrast between the two views is largely illusory. Far from being mutually exclusive, they are complementary formulations of two aspects of the meaning situation. Following Peirce's triadic approach, Morris observes,

> Symbols have three types of relation: to a person or persons, to other symbols, and to objects; meaning has three corresponding dimensions or meanings, namely the biological aspect (meaning as expectation), the formalist aspect (meaning as that expressible in a particular speech), and the empirical aspect (meaning as functional substitutability for objects). (LPP:27f)

Here we find the root of the famous distinction between pragmatics (the relation of symbols to persons), syntax (the relation of symbols to other symbols), and semantics (the relation of symbols to objects). Elaborating upon the complementarity of pragmatism and logical positivism, Morris continues,

> If we say that the meaning of a symbol is the expectation it arouses, this is practically equivalent to saying that the meaning of a symbol is its possible extension (i.e., all the objects to which it can be applied), and this in turn is similar to saying that the meaning of a symbol is determined by the specification of those characters which an object must have for the symbol to be applied. And then since these characters must in turn be specified by the use of other symbols, we find ourselves led to the formalistic position that the meaning of a symbol is determined by its syntactical connections with other symbols (i.e., by the grammatical rules of its usage). (LPP:28)

The first part, where the meaning of a symbol is related to the expectations of its users, is addressed by the pragmatists; whereas, the second part, where the meaning of the symbol is related to the grammatical structure of a language, is addressed by the logical positivists.

141

That Morris's reading is an apt description of the standpoint of the logical positivists is confirmed by Carnap's contribution to the same session. Carnap describes the logical analysis of an expression precisely in terms of positioning the expression within a linguistic framework.[159] Moreover, for Carnap and for the other logical positivists, the proper subject of philosophy is very decidedly "the syntactical analysis of scientific language."[160]

9.3 Pragmatism and Pragmatics

Carnap accepts Morris's triadic distinction between pragmatics, semantics, and syntax, adding, with an explicit reference to Peirce, that a complete theory of language must address all three.[161] As Carnap explains in his *Introduction to Semantics,*

> In *semiotic,* the general theory of signs, three fields are distinguished. An investigation of a language belongs to *pragmatics* if explicit reference to a speaker is made; it belongs to *semantics* if designata but not speakers are referred to; it belongs to *syntax* if neither speakers nor designata but only expressions are dealt with.[162]

In the *Encyclopedia,* Carnap, switching the order, and with the help of an example, distinguishes them as follows:

> (1) the action, state, and environment of a man who speaks or hears, say, the German word 'blau' [*pragmatics*]; (2) the word 'blau' as an element of the German language [*syntax*] . . . (3) a certain property of things, viz., the color blue, to which this man—and German-speaking people in general—intends to refer [*semantics*].[163]

Pragmatics, for Carnap, is thus that part of a theory of language that concerns the relation between language and speaker: "If in an investigation explicit reference is made to the speaker, or, to put it in more general terms, to the user of a language, then we assign it to the field of *pragmatics*."[164] About the relation to pragmatism, Carnap notes, "It seems to me there is agreement on the main points between the present views of the *Vienna Circle* . . . and those of *Pragmatism,* as interpreted e.g. by Lewis" (TM:427).

Carnap's main contribution to pragmatics (although the term itself is conspicuously absent) is in "Testability and Meaning," which appeared in the journal *Philosophy of Science* in 1936 and 1937, two years after he met Morris and shortly after his emigration to the U.S. In "Testability and Meaning," Carnap deals with the question, What makes a statement verifiable, confirmable, testable? According to Carnap this is an empirical question, not a logical one. It belongs to, as he puts it, "a biological or psychological theory of language as a kind of human behavior, and especially as a kind of reaction to observations" (TM:454). Rejecting the possibility of an absolute verification, Carnap considers the issue of confirmation and testing a practical one (TM:426). Hence, for Carnap the issue of verification or confirmation concerns the relation between speaker and language, and thus belongs to pragmatics.

There are other moves toward pragmatism in Carnap's thought. In the controversy on the analytic-synthetic distinction, Carnap makes a distinct shift toward Lewis's position where the analytic-synthetic distinction is drawn along pragmatic lines.[165] Whether the sentence "All ravens are black" is analytic or synthetic depends on what we have *decided* the meaning of our terms to be—in this case, whether we have decided to make "being black" part of the meaning of "raven." Carnap holds a pragmatic view of explicit definitions, contextual definitions, reduction sentences, and even of entire linguistic frameworks:

> The introduction of . . . new ways of speaking does not need
> any theoretical justification because it does not imply any
> assertion of reality. To be sure, we have to face at this point an
> important question; but it is a *practical,* not a theoretical
> question; it is the question of whether or not to accept the new
> linguistic forms. The acceptance cannot be judged as either
> true or false because it is not an assertion. It can only be
> judged as being more or less expedient, fruitful, conducive to
> the aim for which the language is intended.[166]

In his 1934 *Logical Syntax of Language,* Carnap captures this attitude in his famous "principle of tolerance," which states that in philosophical analysis one may opt for any linguistic framework one wishes. As Carnap puts it, quite in contrast to Peirce, "In logic there are no morals. Everyone is at liberty to build up his own, i.e., his own form of language, as he wishes."[167] In effect, for Carnap, the choice is a pragmatic one. One picks the framework that works best.

9.4 Verificationism

The logical positivists saw an intimate connection between meaning and verification that went much further than the classic observation that before you can verify a statement you must first know what it means. They maintained the much more radical thesis that questions of meaning and of verification come down to the same.[168] As Carnap puts it in "Testability and Meaning," to know the meaning of a sentence is to know what it would be for that sentence to be found true. This view entails that "if for two sentences the conditions under which we would have to take them as true are the same, then they have the same meaning" (TM:420). In brief, for the logical positivists, the meaning of a proposition is its method of verification. This view is known as *verificationism,* and the logical positivists' criterion of meaning is called the *verifiability principle* or the *verification principle.* This principle plays a role not unlike that of the pragmatic maxim in pragmatism.

The logical positivists first maintained a strong version of the principle on which a statement is meaningful if and only if it can be conclusively shown true or false by relating it to sensory experiences. To know the meaning of a statement is knowing how to translate it into observation sentences. For example, "This teacup is fragile" would mean "If this teacup is dropped on the floor, it will break."

This version of the verification principle quickly proved too restrictive. For one thing, it called all statements about the past and about the future meaningless because such statements cannot be conclusively verified. Even claims as mundane as "I was born" had to be rejected, as it is clearly impossible for me to put myself in the situation in which I was born, which alone would conclusively verify the claim that I was born and give it its meaning.

Later versions of the verification principle relaxed the requirement that for a statement to be meaningful we must be able to conclusively show it to be true or false. It is to this more moderate version of the principle that Carnap and Neurath subscribed. As Carnap puts it in "Testability and Meaning," "If by verification is meant a definitive and final establishment of truth, then no (synthetic) sentence is ever verifiable" (TM:420). According to Carnap we can only *confirm* a sentence more and more, thereby increasing our confidence that the sentence is true. For Carnap, a sentence is confirmable if we know what conditions would confirm the sentence. Besides confirmability, Carnap also introduced the stronger notion of testability. A sentence is testable if we can produce experiments at will that would lead to its confirmation or disconfirmation. The notion of confirmability is wider, as not all sentences that are confirmable are also testable. The claim that there is life on planets in other galaxies is confirmable, as we know what conditions would confirm it, but is not testable. Having examined the concepts of confirmability and testability, Carnap distinguishes four types of empiricism depending on whether we require that every synthetic sentence is testable, completely testable, confirmable, or completely confirmable. Carnap himself favors the third and most liberal type.

At what point a specific claim is confirmed sufficiently to be accepted, Carnap considers a pragmatic issue:

> Suppose a sentence *S* is given, some test-observations for it have been made, and *S* is confirmed by them in a certain degree. Then it is *a matter of practical decision* whether we will consider that degree as high enough for our acceptance of *S,* or as low enough for our rejection of *S,* or as intermediate between these so that we neither accept nor reject *S* until further evidence will be available. (TM:426; emphasis added)

This led Carnap to the view that the acceptance or rejection of a non-analytic sentence always includes a conventional element, while remaining acutely aware that there is also a nonconventional element that generally plays the dominant role. Carnap is also well aware that for most practical purposes, and even within scientific research, a sufficient level of certainty is reached already after a few positive instances, after which no additional experiments are needed.

The inability to conclusively verify sentences is, for Carnap, not a mere practical hindrance, but one that could be overcome given enough time and resources. Like Lewis, Carnap concedes that universal sentences—most markedly those expressing natural laws—can never be fully verified because the number of instances they refer to is open-ended.

9.5 Quine's "More Thorough" Pragmatism

Willard Van Orman Quine (1908–2000) was Lewis's student at Harvard, and while he was still in his early twenties he came in close contact with logical positivism. He met with the Vienna Circle and visited Carnap in Prague, two encounters that proved decisive for Quine's philosophic development. After absorbing many of the logical positivists' views, Quine came to reject the view he ascribed to Lewis and Carnap on which the pragmatic element is limited strictly to the choice of a language or conceptual system, and that once this choice is made everything can be treated non-pragmatically. For Quine this position hinges on two dogmas that he sought to dispel in his famous 1951 "Two Dogmas of Empiricism." The two dogmas are the dogma of reductionism and the dogma of the radical separation of the analytic and the synthetic.[169] One effect of abandoning these two dogmas, Quine observes, "is a shift toward pragmatism," one that, as he puts it, is "more thorough" than the pragmatism of Lewis or Carnap (LPV: 20, 46).

According to Quine, the notion of analytic statements stems from the simple observation that, in general, truths depend not only on facts about the world (sometimes referred to as extralinguistic facts), but also on facts about the language. To use Quine's example, the statement "Brutus killed Caesar" would be false not only had the world been different in certain respects, but also had the English word "killed" meant something altogether different, like "to marry" or "beget."

That there are these two radically different components, has led to the conviction that when analyzing a statement—e.g., to determine whether or why the statement is true—we can neatly separate them. This conviction then spurred the notion that there could be sentences for which the extralinguistic component is nil, resulting in statements for which no extralinguistic fact can have any effect on their truth value. These are the so-called "analytic statements." In "Two Dogmas," Quine denied that we can separate both components, and he denied that there are statements for which the extralinguistic component is nil.

Whether there are any analytic statements is, for Quine, an empirical issue and he examines several options. He begins by distinguishing two kinds of analytic statements. First, there are those that are *logically* true, which means that they are true solely because of their logical syntax. An example is "All unmarried men are unmarried," which is true no matter what meaning one ascribes to "unmarried" or to "men." Then there are statements that can be turned into the first, as Quine puts it, by a substitution of synonyms. The statement "All bachelors are unmarried" belongs to this second kind. It can be translated into the first one by substituting "unmarried men" for "bachelors." The truth of statements in this second class clearly depends on the meaning of the terms used, as it is the identity in meaning of "bachelor" and "unmarried man" that justifies the substitution. Though not logically true or false, statements of this second kind, like the first, are true or false independent of any extralinguistic facts.

Quine focuses on the second, more interesting kind and examines several ways in which this substitution has been justified. We will discuss only one of them, namely, the view that the substitution is justified because "bachelor" is explicitly *defined* as unmarried male. Quine observes that although it is relatively easy to justify the substitutability by reference to a definition, it is quite something else to derive the analyticity of a statement from the fact that the substitution is based on a definition.

In fact, Quine argues, one cannot do so without tacitly introducing the notion of analyticity, which makes the argument circular. The truth is, Quine observes, there are no pure definitions that are wholly devoid of empirical content. Definitions are not framed in a vacuum, but depend on preexisting relations of synonymity. Had those other relations been different, the definition might not have been phrased that way, or might not have been phrased at all. For Quine, the definitions we make are always framed in an empirical context within which they make sense. The other attempts at establishing analyticity that Quine discusses in "Two Dogmas" fail for similar reasons, showing "how stubbornly the distinction between analytic and synthetic has resisted any straightforward drawing" (LPV:41).

The second dogma Quine addressed is that of *reductionism*. In its radical form, this is the view that every meaningful statement can be translated into a statement about immediate experience. This radical form quickly proved untenable, but reductionism survived in the more moderate thesis that "each statement, taken in isolation from its fellows, can admit of confirmation or infirmation" (LPV:41). For Quine, this dogma builds on the first, as its adherents maintain that for each statement one can isolate the empirical from the analytic component, adding that the former eventually "boils down to a range of confirmatory experiences" (ibid.).

With his refutation of these two "dogmas," Quine dealt a serious blow to the project of the logical positivists, including its more moderate forms. In its stead, Quine offers a moderate holism where the emphasis shifted away from statements, or sentences, to theories:

> A whole sentence is ordinarily too short a text to serve as an independent vehicle of empirical meaning. It will not have its separable bundle of observable or testable consequences. A reasonably inclusive body of scientific theory, taken as a whole, will indeed have such consequences. (PPE:26)

These theories, or conceptual systems, however, are underdetermined; that is, the same set of experiences can support a whole array of explanations. Consequently, when faced with what Quine calls "recalcitrant experiences," one has recourse to a number of alternative readjustments in the interior of the theory. As Quine puts it metaphorically,

> Total science is like a field of force whose boundary conditions are experience. A conflict with experience at the periphery occasions readjustments in the interior of the field. Truth values have to be redistributed over some of our statements. Reëvaluation of some statements entails

147

reëvaluation of others, because of their logical
interconnections. . . . But the total field is so underdetermined
by its boundary conditions, experience, that there is much
latitude of choice as to what statements to reëvaluate in the
light of any single contrary experience.[170]

Consequently, Quine sees us "as largely the author rather than discoverer
of truth" (PPE:34). However, at the same time he maintains that the
physical objects we arrive at are real, "down to the most hypothetical of
particles," because "we are always talking within our going system when
we attribute truth" (PPE:33f). Recall that with the analytic-synthetic
distinction gone, we can no longer pretend that we can neatly separate
what is out there from what we add to it ourselves.

In contrast to the logical positivists who subscribed faithfully to the
standard logic of the *Principia Mathematica,* Quine holds that nothing is
exempt from revision. Even the most deeply ingrained laws of logic are
open for revision, and Quine cites as an example a proposal to revise the
law of excluded middle to simplify quantum mechanics.

Quine's approach is distinctly pragmatic. Theories are tools for
predicting future experience through past and present experience. This
aspect of theories tells us what to settle upon when a recalcitrant
experience allows for alternative readjustments, as they invariably do:
"The edge of the system must be kept squared with experience; the rest,
with all its elaborate myths or fictions, has as its objective the simplicity
of laws" (LPV:45). Science is normative, with simplicity as one of its core
values. Its aim is to help us cope with the world. Hence, Quine concludes
"Two Dogmas" as follows:

Each man is given a scientific heritage plus a continuing
barrage of sensory stimulation; and the considerations which
guide him in warping his scientific heritage to fit his
continuing sensory promptings are, where rational, pragmatic.
(LPV:46)

Quine proves to be a reluctant pragmatist, however, and in his
subsequent work, references to pragmatism become increasingly rare. In
"The Pragmatists' Place in Empiricism," written in part in reply to an
article in the *Times Literary Supplement* (in which Quine is portrayed as
"the last pragmatist"),[171] Quine depicts the pragmatists as empiricists, but
as followers rather than leaders, that have only a cursory relation to what
Quine identifies as the five milestones of modern empiricism (PPE:37).[172]
Although Quine concedes that pragmatism has its attractions, his largely
nominalistic interpretation of the pragmatic maxim causes him to consider

it as merely a version of the verification principle, which by that time was all but refuted.

Discomforted about the myriad of tendencies within pragmatism, Quine limits his adherence to what he called pragmatism's two best guesses: its behavioristic semantics, which equates the meaning of a sentence with the believer's disposition to act, and the doctrine that truth is man-made, at least to a high degree (PPE:37). In an earlier draft, Quine adds further that labeling him a pragmatist is the product of a misinterpretation of the final paragraphs of "Two Dogmas of Empiricism."[173] Quine explains there that he agrees with Carnap that the choice of a conceptual scheme is a pragmatic one, while denying that the conceptual contribution to science can be neatly separated as being analytic—something Quine thought Carnap got from Lewis. But, Quine continues, all that does not make him a pragmatist:

> In so saying, I was apparently out-pragmatizing both the
> logical positivist Carnap and the professing near-pragmatist
> Lewis. But I find here no more claim to the title of pragmatist
> than to that of positivist; I was echoing Mach. The logical
> positivist Carnap had borrowed the word 'pragmatic' and I
> bandied it back. (ibid.)

Reluctant pragmatist or not, soon afterwards Richard Rorty would make Quine one of the bridgeheads of his own neopragmatism.

10

Richard Rorty's Neo–Pragmatism

> I do not think that pragmatism has a True Self, any more than
> America does. Competing narratives about America are
> competing proposals for what America should become, and
> the same goes for competing narratives about pragmatism.[174]

> —Richard Rorty

Richard Rorty (1931–) grew up in a pragmatist milieu. In his autobiographical "Trotsky and the Wild Orchids," he writes that his parents were active socialists at a time when pragmatism had replaced dialectical materialism as the predominant outlook of the New York intelligentsia to which his parents belonged. Only when he went to the University of Chicago, where the tide had since turned against pragmatism, did Rorty come under the spell of more absolutistic creeds. At Chicago, Rorty writes, pragmatism was considered "vulgar, 'relativistic,' and self-refuting" (PSH:8). It was a school of thought that missed something important:

> They pointed out over and over again, Dewey had no
> absolutes. To say, as Dewey did, that 'growth itself is the only
> moral end,' left one without a criterion for growth, and thus
> with no way to refute Hitler's suggestion that Germany had
> 'grown' under his rule. . . . Only an appeal to something
> eternal, absolute, and good . . . would permit one to answer the
> Nazis, to justify one's choice of social democracy over
> fascism. (ibid.)

But Rorty's search for absolutes ended in disillusion, which led him back to pragmatism, and especially to Dewey. Having made his initial career in analytic philosophy, it was *Philosophy and the Mirror of Nature,* the book in which he returned to pragmatism, that put Rorty on the map. It is to this that we now turn.

10.1 The Idol of the Mirror

The absolute with which Rorty took issue in *The Mirror of Nature* is the representationalism that had already attracted much of the pragmatists' fire. This is the view that Dewey had dubbed the spectator theory of knowledge (section 7.3). Rorty phrases the issue as follows:

> The picture which holds traditional philosophy captive is that of the mind as a great mirror, containing various representations—some accurate, some not—and capable of being studied by pure, nonempirical methods. Without the notion of the mind as mirror, the notion of knowledge as accuracy of representation would not have suggested itself. (MN:12)

Note that the mirror metaphor goes further than the image of the spectator. Whereas a spectator can still interpret what is seen, a mirror is wholly dumb. This does not mean that mirrors can't distort, but if they do so, they do it along established principles (such as the laws of optics) that can be discovered, analyzed, and duly corrected for.[175] Rorty believes that our desire to give our knowledge secure footing is the source of the mirror metaphor, as it gives a sense of neutrality to our sense impressions. As Rorty sees it, however, this desire is wholly misguided:

> The desire for a theory of knowledge is a desire for constraint—a desire to find "foundations" to which one might cling, frameworks beyond which one must not stray, objects which impose themselves, representations which cannot be gainsaid. (MN:315)

Rorty rejects the quest for absolute foundations, claiming that such a quest is merely a product of old superstitions and human insecurities, and one that is best abandoned. Note that, interestingly, Rorty interprets such foundations decidedly as constraints instead of the means through which we can get a grip on the world wherein we live, as did Dewey.

Rorty's main objections to the mirror metaphor are similar to those voiced by the classical pragmatists. Most significantly, picturing reality is not really what we are after when we seek knowledge, and where knowledge matters, the metaphor is of little or no help. As Rorty observes,

151

> Nobody engages in epistemology or semantics because he
> wants to know how 'this is red' pictures the world. Rather we
> want to know in what sense Pasteur's views of disease picture
> the world accurately and Paracelsus' inaccurately. . . . But just
> here the vocabulary of 'picturing' fails us. (CP:162f)

As Rorty observes elsewhere, "The notion of 'accurate representation' is
simply an automatic and empty compliment which we pay to those beliefs
which are successful in helping us do what we want to do" (MN:10). In
its place Rorty proposes a shift "from metaphors of isomorphism,
symbolism, and mapping to talk of utility, convenience, and likelihood of
getting what we want" (CP:163). In effect this is a shift toward
pragmatism, as knowledge acquisition becomes itself a mode of acting.

Ridding philosophy from the idol of the mirror has deeper
ramifications. The mirror metaphor implies the possibility of a neutral
vantage point—one that is independent of our wishes and desires, our
preoccupations and our idiosyncracies—and makes that its standard. The
idea is that when we approach things from such a neutral vantage point we
see them as they truly are. The pragmatist Rorty denies that such a neutral
vantage point (assuming it can be attained) can be a guarantee for truth:
"The pragmatist tells us that it is useless to hope that objects will constrain
us to believe the truth about them, if only they are approached with an
unclouded mental eye, or a rigorous method, or a perspicuous language"
(CP:165).

10.2 The Impact of Sellars and Quine

Rorty doesn't derive his central criticism of the mirror metaphor from the
classical pragmatists, but from the analytic tradition in which he was
trained and which is the main target of his criticism in *The Mirror of
Nature*. In Rorty's eyes, this tradition, which so forcefully rejected
pragmatism, is now gradually transforming itself into a species of it. For
Rorty, Wilfrid Sellars's attack on the given and Quine's attack on
necessity caused some serious cracks in the mirror that are beyond repair
and cannot be masked.

Traditional philosophy, as it is understood by Rorty, presupposes
that within our knowledge we can separate what is given from what is
added by the mind. The realization that sense impressions cannot be
wrong—they are just what they are, that they are purely given—has led
many to believe that they can be made a secure foundation for knowledge.
Sellars objects to this, arguing that this belief is the result of a confusion

of sense impressions with so-called basic propositions; i.e., propositions the truth or falsity of which is wholly determined by the occurrence or nonoccurrence of the sense impressions to which they refer. As indicated in the previous chapter, the central aim of the logical positivists, and of analytic philosophy more in general, is to ground all knowledge claims in such basic propositions. Sellars agrees that sense impressions cannot be wrong, but denies that they can count as knowledge. Propositions *about* sense impressions can be counted as knowledge, but they lack the quality of indubitablity, or givenness, that sense impressions have. They can be wrong, even though up to now, as Rorty puts it, "nobody has given us any interesting alternatives which would lead us to question [them]" (MN:175).

Rorty doesn't deny that we have sense impressions. We see patches of red, have pains, experience hunger, feel content, etc. What he denies is that sense impressions count as beliefs, or that they can play a role in justifying our beliefs. They are mere stimuli. Those who seek to ground our beliefs in sense impressions, Rorty contends, confuse the *formation* of a belief with its *expression* or its *justification*. Although the formation of the belief may be due to something pre- or non-propositional, its expression (which allows it to be communicated to others or to one's own future self) and the justification of this expressed belief take place wholly within language. For Sellars, "Science is rational not because it has a foundation, but because it is a self-correcting enterprise which can put any claim in jeopardy, though not all at once."[176] Of course, this is precisely Peirce's scientific method (section 2.3).

A second blow to the mirror metaphor comes from Quine in his rejection of the analytic-synthetic distinction. According to Rorty, Quine has shown us that we cannot distinguish between the "necessary," which is entirely 'within' the mind and under its control, and the "contingent," which is in part a product of what is given (MN:169). Rorty's observation is the same as the one he makes about the claim that basic propositions cannot be wrong. As with basic propositions, "a necessary truth is just a statement such that nobody has given us any interesting alternatives which would lead us to question it" (MN:175).

Rorty draws a radical conclusion from the criticisms of Sellars and Quine, namely, that there is no neutral ground on which to stand, and that there is no other way to assess philosophical views but from a study of existing criticisms and defenses of those views. That is to say, for Rorty, the criteria for evaluating any belief become wholly conversational ones. In the absence of neutral ground—the given or the analytical—"the True and the Right are matters of social practice" (MN:178). Since the

153

justification of a belief—of *all* belief—takes place within language, which is a social practice, justification—*any* justification—is ultimately a matter of social practice as well. When entering a linguistic community, we submit ourselves to its epistemic rules; the rules through which its members frame questions, utter warnings, give orders, express emotions, form justifications, etc. In sum, for Rorty, the justification of belief is always a social affair that is guided by established practice.

10.3 The Aim of Inquiry

Rorty's rejection of representationalism influences his take on inquiry. For the representationalist, inquiry had a clearly defined purpose, which is to discover the truth. We attain the truth when our beliefs accurately represent their objects. This approach gives us a quite solid criterion on which to judge how well or badly a specific inquiry is conducted. Good inquiry causes our beliefs to adequately represent reality. Epistemic practices that do not lead to this are bad, or unsound, or unscientific.

For Rorty, the aim of inquiry is not to *represent* reality, but to *use* reality to get what we want; that is, to bring us what we set out to achieve when we began the inquiry. Having rejected representationalism, Rorty embraces a causal theory of knowledge, arguing that the world "causes us to hold beliefs, and we continue to hold the beliefs which prove to be reliable guides to getting what we want" (PSH:33).

What we want, however, is highly multifarious, so that it makes little sense to speak of "the aim of inquiry" as if inquiry has a single, clearly defined goal. Inquiry may have many aims, all with different ramifications, including moral, social, and political ones. For the pragmatist, Rorty explains, "the pattern of all inquiry—scientific as well as moral—is deliberation concerning the relative attractions of various concrete alternatives" (CP:164). Because of this, Rorty rejects the idea of a scientific method, if by this is meant a fixed recipe, or algorithm, that allows us to "avoid the need for conversation and deliberation and simply tick off the way things are" (ibid.). It is to this conversational aspect of inquiry, which plays such a pivotal role in Rorty's nonrepresentational epistemology, that we now turn.

10.4 From Correspondence to Conversation

For Rorty, the rejection of representationalism radically opens up the playing field, as we are no longer constrained by the requirement that we must adequately mirror reality. Rorty seeks to stretch this playing field as far as it will let him, arguing that the *only* constraints set upon inquiry are conversational ones, a view he identifies with pragmatism. Referring explicitly to Peirce, Rorty explains that "the only sense in which we are constrained to truth is that, as Peirce suggested, we can make no sense of the notion that the view which can survive all objections might be false" (CP 165). Since objections are always cast in language, Rorty interprets this to mean that all constraints upon inquiry are conversational. Earlier in *The Mirror of Nature*, Rorty had already remarked that justification is a matter of conversation: "Justification is not a matter of a special relation between ideas (or words) and objects, but of conversation, of social practice" (M:170). Successful inquiry is inquiry that keeps the conversation going and the search for truth makes way for a search for solidarity. In *Consequences of Pragmatism* Rorty characterizes pragmatism wholly in conversational terms, calling it,

> the doctrine that there are no constraints on inquiry save conversational ones—no wholesale constraints derived from the nature of the objects, or of the mind, or of language, but only those retail constraints provided by the remarks of our fellow-inquirers. (CP:165)

Rorty is correct in observing that there is some affinity between this view and that of the classical pragmatists, but it is hard to defend that it is anything more than that. True, Peirce maintains that truth is identical with the final opinion, but what makes this opinion final for Peirce is not that the inquirers agree, but that they all come to the same conclusion and that all future inquiries will again come to the same conclusion. In Peirce's view it is not *the search for agreement* that drives inquiry, but having competent peers agree with you is a sign, rather, and often a welcome one, that what you believe to be true might indeed be so. The agreement that Peirce has in mind, however, is distinctly not a product of mere conversation, but the result of a prolonged interaction with a world that is there and that does not budge. This connection with the world is absent, or at best well-disguised, in Rorty's rendition. In fact, with its sole focus on agreement and conversational constraints, Rorty's interpretation undercuts Peirce's crucial distinction between the a priori method and the scientific method in "The Fixation of Belief" (section 2.3).

The notion that something extralinguistic might influence the formation of our beliefs is again conspicuously absent in the following passage that comes from *Objectivity, Relativism, and Truth:*

155

> For pragmatists, the desire for objectivity is . . . simply the
> desire for as much intersubjective agreement as possible . . .
> Insofar as pragmatists make a distinction between knowledge
> and opinion, it is simply the distinction between topics on
> which such agreement is relatively easy to get and topics on
> which agreement is relatively hard to get. (PP 1:23)

For Rorty, the inquirer does not even aim for anything more than to have others approve of his beliefs, and philosophy comes down to "a study of the comparative advantages and disadvantages of the various ways of talking which our race has invented" (CP:xl).

Rorty thus shifts the attention away from a privileged scientific method that prescribes how people should conduct their inquiry no matter what the inquiry is about or from which motives it began, toward a study of the vocabularies people use to express their problems, their aims, and their findings. What makes Galileo's physics superior to Aristotle's, Rorty argues, is not that Galileo made a better use of the so-called "scientific method," but because "Galileo was using some terminology which helped, and Aristotle wasn't" (CP:193).

As for the question regarding how Galileo came to this new and successful terminology, Rorty's answer is as simple as it is disappointing: "He just lucked out." It just turned out that Galileo's vocabulary worked better in bringing us the things we want than did Aristotle's. As to the question of what makes it so, Rorty admits, pragmatists have no answer, but neither do they need one; they reject the question. The different vocabularies are not made true or false by "the world," but they are like different tools that have alternative uses. For a change of vocabulary, such as the switch from Aristotle's way of speaking to Galileo's, no more arguments are required than for choosing, say, a Phillips screwdriver above a flat one. All that matters is that it works better. Rorty denies, however, that the improvements of vocabularies, like the one of Galileo over Aristotle, mark an objective course of progress. All we can say is that the new vocabularies work better in giving *us* what we want.

Rejecting representationalism for a form of instrumentalism, Rorty argues that "one should stop worrying about whether what one believes is well grounded and start worrying about whether one has been imaginative enough to think up interesting alternatives to one's present beliefs" (PSH:34). What is needed in science and philosophy is the vision and drive of an entrepreneur, rather than the myopic precision of a forensic accountant. The attitude of the Rortyan scientist and philosopher is not that of submission to an immanent teleology, as with Peirce, but a desire for being astonished and exhilarated (PSH:28). If scientists and philosophers would become pragmatists, Rorty remarks, "there would be less talk about rigor and more about originality. The image of the great scientist would not be of somebody who got it right but of somebody who made it new" (PP 1:44).

At the same time, Rorty does not deny that there is something like an external world, but its role seems almost negligible and we always encounter it under a certain description. As Rorty puts it in *Philosophy and Social Hope:*

> We can never be more arbitrary than the world lets us be. So even if there is no Way the World Is, even if there is no such thing as "the intrinsic nature of reality," there are still causal pressures. These pressures will be described in different ways at different times and for different purposes, but they are pressures none the less. (PSH:33)

Rorty agrees with Peirce that such causal pressures cannot be seen as truth-makers, epistemic anchors, neutral foundations, etc., but he rejects Peirce's idea that we have little option but to postulate that the opinions we form of them, assuming we inquire into them long enough (where "long enough" might be trillions of years), gravitate to a shared and conclusive agreement. Since, for Rorty, all we encounter must be captured under a certain description before it can be counted as knowledge, and because theories are underdetermined by data so that there are numerous, incommensurable descriptions for any datum (including scientific, poetic, and religious descriptions), Rorty rejects the idea that any description can be privileged or seen as representative and be called the true one. Rorty, in good pragmatist fashion, thus rejects the idea that it is somehow our job to *represent* this world—assuming there is indeed "one Way the World Is." It is our job, rather, to cope with these causal pressures.

It is not wholly clear, though, how we should interpret Rorty's insistence that, with representationalism gone, the only constraints upon inquiry are conversational ones. If theories are tools, you must show them in action, but that is hardly a mere conversational affair. Surely, I could try to convince you through an aprioresque mathematical narrative, waxing eloquently about straight lines, planes, triangles, etc., that a Phillips screwdriver works better than a flat one, but nothing beats the simple practice of showing that one fits snugly in the screw and the other doesn't. And what to do about the experimental scientist who late at night struggles to identify strands of protein under her microscope? We would surely call this inquiry, but it is hard to cast this wholly in terms of conversational constraints. It is difficult to deny, it seems, that there is a microscope and that there is something under it that, at least in part, dictates what she sees and that predates any descriptions of it. As Jay Rosenberg once aptly put it, "There's something that counts as getting it wrong. . . . Finding out whether one has gotten a pudding recipe right does. The proof of the pudding is in the eating. . . . If it got lumps in it, then something nonlinguistic has gone wrong."[177]

Despite all his talk about Galileo, one gets the distinct impression that Rorty really sides with Francesco Sizzi, the Florentine astronomer who refused to look through Galileo's telescope because he already knew that what Galileo claimed he saw could not possibly be true. It did not fit in the conversation.

10.5 Against Truth

With representationalism out the window, the notion of truth as correspondence with reality must be abandoned as well and a new conception of truth, if any, is called for. For Rorty, the crucial issue is not whether a belief is true, but whether we are justified in believing something, which for him comes down to the question whether we can defend the belief against the objections of others. Once we have finished talking about the justification of our beliefs, Rorty contends, there is nothing of substance left to say about truth, because we have no way of talking about truth other than in terms of the justification of belief. Hence, in *The Mirror of Nature* Rorty boldly claims that truth is "what our peers will, *ceteris paribus,* let us get away with saying" (MN:176). That is to say, it is "what you can defend against all comers" (MN:308). Rorty thus follows Dewey, who abandoned truth for warranted assertibility, but he also pushes it further, associating truth "with the consensus of a community rather than a relation to a nonhuman reality" (PP 1:23). Note that Rorty speaks of *a* community rather than *the* community as did Peirce.

For the pragmatist, Rorty exclaims, "truth is not the sort of thing one should expect to have a philosophically interesting opinion about" (CP:xiii). True, it is a characteristic shared by all true statements, but as there is such a diversity among true statements it is unlikely that anything of value or interest can be said about this characteristic. Rorty holds the same view about moral goodness. There is a wide variety of good acts, so that the notion of goodness, as something all good acts have in common, is as good as empty. Pragmatists, Rorty argues, reject the traditional attempts at isolating the true and the good as if these were the two most

158

precious gems of philosophy. In their place, they do not propose a rival theory of truth. On the contrary, they declare the whole enterprise of seeking theories of truth as outdated. One might as well continue to insist that chemical compounds should be analyzed in terms of the four basic elements: earth, fire, air, and water. Pragmatists, Rorty contends, propose a more radical revision. Traditional philosophy, they argue, is as outmoded as alchemy. Its subject, its techniques, and its vocabulary need serious overhauling. As Rorty puts it in one of the essays that make up *Consequences of Pragmatism,* "As long as we see James or Dewey as having 'theories of knowledge' or 'theories of morality' we shall get them wrong" (CP:160). There is also no need for a theory of truth. As Rorty explains,

> Inquiry and justification have lots of mutual aims, but they do not have an overarching aim called truth. Inquiry and justification are activities we language-users cannot help engaging in; we do not need a goal called 'truth' to help us do so, any more than our digestive organs need a goal called health to set them to work. (PSH:37f)

This leads us quite far from Peirce's insistence that inquiry is a conscious activity that calls for self-discipline and, hence, for norms we should seek to live up to.

At the same time, Rorty admits that being justified in believing that *p* does not entail that *p* is true, but since justified belief is only as far as we can go, the gap between the two is, as Rorty sees it, "forever unbridgeable."[178] It is not clear whether an appeal to truth is actually needed here or whether it is even legitimate for a pragmatist to do so, as the implied notion of truth would not pass muster with the pragmatic maxim. A simpler way of saying this, but in a way that altogether avoids using the notion of truth, is by admitting that justified beliefs are still fallible, meaning that although I am justified in believing that *p,* that belief may turn out not to deliver the goods.

This being said, for the nonrepresentationalist Rorty, the notion of truth comes to play a different, and far more modest, role. He accepts Tarski's disquotational use, which allows us to make metalinguistic remarks such as: "The sentence *Snow is white* is true, if and only if snow is white." In addition, the word "truth" can be used in a cautionary sense, as in: "This belief is justified, but is it really true?" Or it can be used to praise a belief; for instance, Rorty interprets William James's famous comment that the true is only the expedient in our way of thinking, to mean that the word "true" is not used to explain what constitutes the difference between true and false ideas or claims, but to endorse an idea or claim by praising it. According to Rorty, to say that a statement is true, is merely to give the successful inquirer "a rhetorical pat on the back." To make anything more of it by trying to 'clarify' this philosophically in a *theory* of truth, Rorty argues, only leads to trouble. In its place Rorty maintains a sort of epistemological emotivism, which, given Rorty's democratic disposition, means in essence that he sees Peirce's a priori method as the proper way of fixing belief.

10.6 Solidarity, Ethnocentricity, and Irony

Having thus dismissed traditional theories of truth and the notion of inquiry as something that leads us toward the truth, the question becomes what is it that we are doing when we are claiming that we are acquiring knowledge? Rorty's answer is that we are engaged in a conversation that is aimed at generating agreement—or, at least, interesting disagreement—in a way that helps us cope with life. As Rorty puts it in *Consequences of Pragmatism,* "In the end, the pragmatists tell us, what matters is our loyalty to other human beings clinging together against the dark, not our hope of getting things right" (CP 166). The metaphor is revealing. The darkness against which we are clinging together is at once impenetrable and threatening. Since nothing external or extralinguistic can generate agreement—since all that we encounter can be adjusted for in innumerable ways—we can in the end only count on ourselves. Hence, what we need is solidarity.

The solidarity Rorty speaks of, however, is not that of the world citizen, but is limited to one's own culture. There is no supracultural vantage point. The best one can aim for is to compare and contrast alternative cultural traditions from the perspective of the tradition that one grew up in. Inquiry cannot be truly disinterested, and always takes place within and against the background of a particular culture, namely, our culture. Rorty denies, however, the charge of cultural relativism. As he writes in *Objectivity, Relativism, and Truth,* "The pragmatist, dominated by the desire for solidarity, can only be criticized for taking his own community too seriously. He can only be criticized for ethnocentrism, not for relativism" (PP 1:30). Thus, for instance,

> When we say that our ancestors believed, falsely, that the sun went around the earth, and we believe, truly, that the earth goes around the sun, we are saying that we have a better tool than our ancestors did. Our ancestors might rejoin that their

tool enabled them to believe in the literal truth of the Christian Scriptures, whereas ours does not. Our reply has to be, I think, that the benefits of modern astronomy and of space travel outweigh the advantages of Christian fundamentalism. The argument between us and our medieval ancestors should not be about which of us has the universe right. It should be about the point of holding views about the motion of heavenly bodies, the ends to be achieved by the use of certain tools. Confirming the truth of scripture is one such aim, space travel is another. (PSH:xxv)

Rorty is thus not a cultural relativist (in which case he would refuse to privilege one culture above the others), nor is he an objectivist (in which case he would admit of certain supracultural criteria of truth or purpose), but he is an ethnocentrist. He is aware of the relativity of our culture, while at the same time privileging it because doing so is our best, if not our only, option: "We must, in practice, privilege our own group, even though there can be no noncircular justification for doing so. We must insist that the fact that nothing is immune from criticism does not mean that we have a duty to justify everything" (PP 1:29). Rorty is not telling us to take our culture for granted or to declare it the golden standard with which to measure other cultures. The point is, rather, that we cannot really escape our own culture; we can only criticize it piecemeal. Philosophers, for Rorty, should become cultural critics, all-purpose intellectuals who address current problems, not from the aspect of eternity but in a historicist manner. Thus, whereas Peirce shies away from what he called "topics of vital importance" because philosophy is too ill-equipped to deal with them, Rorty sees them as all that philosophers should talk about. Ironically, Rorty's ethnocentrism allows him to speak of the external world in the same way as the objectivist does, as our current way of talking about this world runs largely in an objectivist vocabulary.

So how do we convince people from other cultures that we are right and they are wrong? Rorty's answer is that we do this by changing their vocabulary; by making them see things as we see them. We could, for instance, teach the alchemist about modern chemistry. This is more than telling the alchemist that his method is wrong. He must come to see the physical world in an entirely different way. Moreover, for Rorty, changing how one *sees* the world means changing how one *speaks* about it. Such a change of vocabulary is, furthermore, not a logical affair. Quite the opposite. Logic applies only within the confines of an already set vocabulary that determines what moves are permitted and what moves are not.

What then about our own vocabulary? Can we change that as well? We have seen that, for Rorty, we change the views of others by exposing them to our vocabulary. But this does not work in our own case. We cannot similarly try to change *our own* vocabulary—our own way of seeing things—by exposing ourselves to our own vocabulary (i.e., to how we see things). In an important sense, what Royce believed about logic (section 8.1), Rorty holds for our vocabulary as a whole: it is final and self-justifying. We cannot put our own vocabulary up for discussion because that same vocabulary will always remain the measuring rod and the benchmark for all we say or think, including the reflections upon our own vocabulary. Of course we can be made to change our mind by being exposed to the vocabularies of others, but that is another issue. The question here is whether we can be genuinely critical toward our own vocabulary and change it, as it were, from within. Rorty thinks we can, and the method he suggests is that of irony. Since our vocabulary is its own benchmark, Rorty maintains that we can only put it up for discussion when we knowingly and willingly violate some of its rules. That is to say, when we feign ignorance or consciously misapply it with the deliberate purpose to provoke and unmask. Rorty calls this the method of irony and those who practice it "ironists," adding that apart from the confrontation with a foreign vocabulary, it is only through irony that we can escape our ethnocentrism.

Ironists, Rorty explains, are "never quite able to take themselves seriously because [they are] always aware that the terms in which they describe themselves are subject to change, always aware of the contingency and fragility of their final vocabularies, and thus of their selves" (CIS:73f). There is a sense in which irony can be considered an alternative to Peirce's fallibilism, but one that keeps the nonlinguistic world (which was so important to Peirce), safely at bay. Finally, in his discussion of irony, Rorty's conversationalism can be discerned quite clearly in the background, as the ironist is playing very distinctly a linguistic game.

162

11

Susan Haack's Foundherentist Epistemology

> Somehow classical pragmatism, in the form of Peirce's
> aspiration to renew philosophy by making it more scientific,
> has been transmuted into the vulgar pragmatism fashionable
> today.
>
> —Susan Haack[179]

Some call her the intellectual granddaughter of Peirce, which is an apt description, as she is in many respects a direct descendant of him. The key elements of Peirce's thought, such as his extreme scholastic realism, his critical common-sensism, his theory of perception, and his fallibilism are all prominent in Haack, as are his care for terminology, his focus on inquiry, and his insistence on "the will to learn." Sometimes Peirce's views return with a twist (for instance, his extreme scholastic realism resonates in Haack's innocent realism); sometimes his views are developed further and updated for our time (like the addition of fake reasoning as a special form of pseudo inquiry). Whereas Rorty represents the Schilleresque side of pragmatism, Haack solidly represents the Peircean strand.

The title of Haack's third book, *Evidence and Inquiry,* concisely captures the central tenet of her thought, which is to examine what makes evidence stronger or weaker and inquiry better or worse conducted. The issue of evidence and inquiry is also central to her later books: *Manifesto of a Passionate Moderate* and *Defending Science—Within Reason.*

It is important to keep in mind from the outset that the question, what makes *inquiry* better or worse conducted, is very different from the

163

question, what makes *evidence* better or worse. Though the two are often confused, they are, as Haack puts it, "as different as . . . criteria for judging roses are from instructions for growing them (unlike the former, the latter would, for example, inevitably mention horse manure)" (M:105). A common fallacy that follows from the failure to properly distinguish the two is to conclude from the observation that there is more than one way in which an inquiry can be conducted that there are different sets of criteria by which to evaluate the result. We might call this *the pluralist fallacy:* A pluralism of legitimate methods of inquiry is taken to entail a pluralism of standards of evidence. Pragmatists, who see a close connection between inquiry and truth, must be particularly attentive to this fallacy. Siding with Peirce, Haack admits a pluralism of good methods of inquiry, while rejecting a pluralism of criteria of good evidence.

11.1 The Empirical Justification of Beliefs

In *Evidence and Inquiry,* Haack addresses two classic questions of epistemology: "What counts as good, strong, supportive evidence for a belief?"; and "What is the connection between a belief being well-supported by good evidence, and the likelihood that it is true?" The first leads to what she calls the project of explication, and the second to the project of ratification (EI:1).

The two classic theories that deal with the first project are foundationalism and coherentism. *Foundationalists* make a distinction between basic and derived beliefs, adding that basic beliefs are those that can be justified independently of any other beliefs. Descartes's clear and distinct ideas are examples of such basic beliefs, as are beliefs expressed in Lewis's expressive statements and in Carnap's observation sentences. *Basic beliefs* are not justified by being related to other beliefs, but by the subject's direct experience or intuition, by being self-justifying, etc. *Derived beliefs* are justified subsequently in terms of these basic beliefs. On this view, the belief that there are rhinos in Nepal would be justified by relating it to a set of observation sentences about rhino sightings in Nepal.

For *coherentists,* beliefs are not justified by relating them to so-called "basic beliefs," as no beliefs can be said to be basic, except by being part of a coherent set of beliefs. This means that for the coherentist, justification is wholly a matter of relations among beliefs. Beliefs are justified by being supported by other beliefs; they mutually support each other. Foundationalists allow for nonbelief input in the justification of beliefs (as this is how basic beliefs are justified), but they also hold that justification is one-directional. Basic beliefs justify derived beliefs, but derived beliefs cannot justify basic beliefs, or even contribute to their justification. This one-directionality follows at once from how foundationalists distinguished (and defined) basic beliefs, namely, as beliefs that are justified *independently* of their relations with other beliefs.

According to Haack, coherentism and foundationalism do not exhaust the options. One could conceive, for instance, of a theory that, as she puts it, "allows the relevance of experience to justification, but requires no class of privileged beliefs justified exclusively by experience with no support from other beliefs" (EI:19). And it is along these lines that Haack develops her own view, which she names "foundherentism," and which can be captured roughly in the following two theses (EI:19):

> (FH1) A subject's experience is relevant to the justification of his empirical beliefs, but there need be no privileged class of empirical beliefs justified exclusively by the support of experience, independently of the support of other beliefs.

> (FH2) Justification is not exclusively one-directional, but involves pervasive relations of mutual support.

As its name indicates, foundherentism combines elements of *found-*ationalism and co-*herentism.*

Since, for Haack, the subject's experience does play a distinctive part in empirical justification, she shifts the focus deliberately to the process of inquiry, construing knowledge as a product of it. For Haack, justification is not merely a matter of *what* you believe, making justification wholly a matter of analyzing the belief content, but also of *why* you believe it, which is in turn related to *how* you came to believe it. The social nature of inquiry then ensures that in the long run individual biases are overcome. As to *how* we come to believe something, Haack further differentiates between the initiating causes (i.e., those that historically first led to the belief) and the causes that are operative when the question of justification comes up (EI:75). The latter may differ from those that initially caused the belief. To use Haack's example, you may be first convinced of the innocence of the accused because he has an honest face and later because you found out that he has a watertight alibi. In this case the justification will *not* be in terms of what initially caused the belief (seeing his honest face), but the watertight alibi learned of later.

For Haack, justification is, moreover, a gradual affair. It comes in degrees, running from a rough first approximation (like an educated guess) to deeply entrenched beliefs, and proceeding generally through what Haack calls a method of "successive approximation," which is neither

165

wholly logical nor wholly empirical. Haack's foundherentism is not the only alternative to foundationalism and coherentism. Examples of other "third options" are reliabilism, contextualism, and Rorty's ethnocentrism (for the last see section 10.6).

11.2 The Analogy of the Crossword Puzzle

For Haack, the crossword puzzle is an analogy aimed at representing the structure of relations of evidential support. The traditional analogy used in this context is that of a mathematical proof. Mathematical proofs reveal how complicated theorems can be derived from a few simple axioms, and it is also the proof that justifies the theorem. Euclid's *Elements,* the standard mathematics textbook for about two millennia, has in effect become the paradigm for how to justify knowledge claims. According to Haack, those who make mathematical proof the model for empirical justification have a mistaken view of the aim of inquiry. The aim of inquiry is not an isolated conclusion, as with a mathematical proof, but rather having the important parts of one's puzzle filled in.

The analogy of the crossword puzzle, Haack argues, gives a more apt representation of what knowledge is and how it is acquired than the traditional analogy of the mathematical proof. As she explains,

> How reasonable a crossword entry is depends on how well it is supported by its clue and already intersecting entries; on how reasonable those entries are, independent of the entry in question; and on how much of the crossword has been completed. Similarly, what makes evidence stronger or weaker, a claim more or less warranted, depends on how supportive the evidence is; on how secure it is, independent of the claim in question, and on how much of the relevant evidence it includes. (DS:24)

In contrast to a mathematical proof, which is one-directional, a crossword puzzle allows for a pervasive mutual support among beliefs, and shows how this is possible without lapsing into a vicious circularity.

As mentioned before, though rejecting a pluralism for criteria of justification, Haack maintains a pluralism for the conduct of inquiry; a view that returns in the crossword analogy:

> There can no more be rules for when a theory should be accepted and when rejected than there could be rules for when to ink in a crossword entry and when to rub it out; "the" best

procedure is for different scientists, some bolder, some more cautious, to proceed differently. (DS:25)

Haack's crossword analogy extends Peirce's rope analogy in an interesting and important way (see section 6.4). Recall that Peirce rejected the Cartesian notion of chain reasoning (a classic representation of the mathematical proof), in which every step is deductively linked with those before and after it in such a way that were a single link to snap the whole chain would break. In its stead, Peirce gave the analogy of a rope: an argument is like a multitude of thin and fragile strands that, twined together, become a strong and durable rope. In contrast to a chain, which breaks with its weakest link, a good rope retains its strength were one of its strands to pop.

Haack's crossword analogy has a far richer texture than the analogy of the rope. For instance, it shows why and where a particular strand may be woven into the rope; it reveals the fundamental interconnectedness of facts; and, as solving a crossword puzzle involves inquiry, which rope making does not, it better exemplifies inquiry. The crossword analogy also shows the interplay of the two theses of foundherentism. FH1 is represented by the relation of the entry to its clue, while FH2 is represented by the relation of the entry to other entries, some of which are already filled in, while others are still blank.

The analogy even allows for Kuhnian-type paradigm shifts, and does so in a manner that combines the possibility of wide-scale scientific revolutions with a robust and more continuous notion of evidential support. When it becomes increasingly difficult to fill in the smaller peripheral entries of the puzzle, this may cause us to erase a larger and more central entry and replace it with another, causing a ripple effect throughout the puzzle.

11.3 Standards of Inquiry

Inquiry is the focal point of Haack's thought. Siding with Peirce and against Rorty, she maintains that there are certain core standards of well-conducted inquiry. Although the sciences are exemplary in maintaining such standards, and people often speak with reverence of the "scientific method," the standards are by no means special to the sciences but apply to any sort of empirical inquiry. As Haack observes,

> As far as it is a method, it is what historians or detectives or
> investigative journalists or the rest of us do when we really
> want to find something out: make an informed conjecture

about the possible explanation of a puzzling phenomenon, check how it stands up to the best evidence we can get, and then use our judgment whether to accept it, more or less tentatively, or modify, refine, or replace it. (DS:24)

As to what makes inquiry good, Haack sides with Peirce, who remarked that science "does not so much consist in knowing, not even in 'organized knowledge,' as it does in diligent inquiry into truth for truth's sake, without any sort of axe to grind, . . . from an impulse to penetrate into the reason of things."[180] Good inquiry is not just a matter of using the right methods, but first and foremost a matter of having the right attitude. In well-conducted inquiry, the researcher is genuinely interested to discover how things really are, i.e., in discovering what is true. As Haack puts it,

> The genuine inquirer is not a collector of true propositions, nor is he a worshiper of an intellectual ideal. But he does want the true answer to his question: If he is inquiring into whether smoking causes cancer, he wants to end up believing that cigarette smoking causes cancer if cigarette smoking causes cancer, and that it doesn't if it doesn't . . . (M:9)

Inquiry is not always conducted with this aim in mind, and being well aware of this, Haack distinguishes two types of pseudo inquiry: sham reasoning, which she takes from Peirce, and fake reasoning. In *sham reasoning,* the inquirer does not seek to discover how things truly are, no matter where the search will lead him, but seeks to support a proposition he is already deeply committed to and that is nonnegotiable. The sham reasoner can be a creationist who seeks to square empirical findings with a literal interpretation of the book of Genesis, or a molecular biologist whose research is guided by the expectations of the commercial interests funding the research. The characteristic feature of sham reasoning is, Haack explains, "the 'inquirer's' *prior and unbudgeable commitment* to the proposition for which he tries to make a case" (M:8f).

Fake reasoning goes even a step further. The *fake reasoner* is driven neither by a genuine desire for truth, nor by a desire to show that certain cherished beliefs are true, but is wholly indifferent to truth. The fake reasoner is driven by quite different considerations, such as a wish for promotion, money, fame, or even notoriety. As Haack observes, "In some areas of contemporary academic life a clever defense of a startlingly false or impressively obscure idea can be a good route to reputation and advancement" (M:9). What Peirce calls dismissively "studying in a literary spirit" also falls under this second type. The aim is not to find or

168

to convey true answers, but to write a clever and esthetically pleasing book or paper.

But why should one not be a sham or fake reasoner? Why is intellectual integrity important? Certain pragmatists, and others also, have argued that inquiry should be subservient to our direct needs; that one should not care too much about such abstract and detached notions as "truth" and "getting it right." Haack's answer is a pragmatic one:

> There is instrumental value in intellectual integrity, because in the long run and on the whole it advances inquiry, and successful inquiry is, by and large, instrumentally valuable. Compared with other animals, we humans are not especially fleet or strong; our forte is a capacity to figure things out, and hence to anticipate and avoid danger. (M:13)

This is not to say that our capacity for figuring things out is infallible, nor that in certain circumstances believing a falsehood may not be more advantageous or instrumentally valuable. Nonetheless, over-belief (believing more than is warranted by one's evidence), and under-belief (not believing when one's evidence warrants belief), are things for which one might be held morally culpable, as would be the case with the shipowner in Clifford's example (M:14; see also section 3.2).

11.4 Justification and Truth

In addition to the question of what counts as strong evidence for a belief (the project of explication), Haack addresses the issue of the connection between a belief being justified and it being true (the project of ratification). According to Haack, the genuine inquirer wants to know the true answer to the questions he asks. The goal of inquiry, she writes, "is substantial, significant, illuminating truth" (EI:203). Hence, in the search for criteria of good justification, we focus specifically on those that increase the likelihood that justified beliefs are true.

The notion of truth that Haack has in mind conforms to Aristotle's classic insight that to say of what is that it is, or of what is not that it is not, is true, and Peirce's insight that whether something is true is wholly independent of what you or I or anyone in particular may think about it. To say that a certain proposition is true must thus not be identified with the claim that people are justified in believing it, but with the claim that things really are as the proposition says they are. The two are not the same. There are truths that never become justified beliefs, and there are cases where one is justified in having beliefs that are not true. The young

169

child playing by itself in the park is better off believing wrongly that all toadstools are poisonous than believing rightly that some of them taste really good. The question then becomes whether there is any relationship between a belief being justified and that same belief being true, and if so, what that relationship is and under what circumstances we are entitled to say that certain justified beliefs are true.

There are those, like Rorty, who deny that there is such a relation, arguing that having justified beliefs is the highest we can ever aspire to. Calling a justified belief true does not really add anything, Rorty notes, as we can only talk about truth in terms of the justification of beliefs. From this, Rorty draws the conclusion that to call a justified belief true is only to give it a rhetorical pat on the back by ascribing to it a character that, though void, is of noble ancestry. It is like the atheist who calls an excellent bottle of wine "divine."

As Haack sees it, the problem is that many critics of the project of ratification, and this includes Rorty, set their standards for truth too high and then complain that truth is unattainable or that the entire notion of truth is misconceived. Haack, for her part, denies that we can do without truth, observing that even those who explicitly reject truth cannot avoid making frequent implicit appeals to it.

Haack's own approach to truth is a modest one. She does not seek to prove that some of our beliefs must be true, as the foundationalist does, but merely to give "reasons for thinking that, if any truth-indication is possible for us, the foundherentist criteria are truth-indicative" (EI:205). In broad outline, her argument is Peircean. She argues that within inquiry we can only proceed in the hope that there is a true answer to every question we ask; that is, we can only proceed in the hope that theories that are well-supported are truth-indicative

The question that remains is this: assuming it is possible to find truths, what makes evidence, as the foundherentist explains it, truth-indicative? Haack's answer is, in part, an empirical one. Relativists, neopragmatists, conventionalists, postmodernists, etc., all have made much ado about what they consider evidence for a plurality of standards of evidence. People at different times and in different cultures or subcultures, it is argued, count different things as evidence. A physician and an astrologer, for instance, may refer to very dissimilar facts when explaining someone's chronic fatigue, such as the growth of microscopic organisms in a blood culture for the first, and the constellation of the planets in relation to the subject's birth for the second. Their reliance on evidence so divergent is often taken to imply that they maintain different standards of evidence. Not so, says Haack. It is not that their *standards* of evidence are different, but their background beliefs diverge so much that they disagree on what facts to accept as evidence. However, when defending their respective views, the physician and the astrologer will engage in parallel explanations about observations, causal connections, commonsense intuitions, logical relations, analogous cases, etc., revealing that deep down they maintain the same type of standards. To put it very briefly, the wide variety of ways in which groups of people defend their views points to differences in background beliefs rather than a plurality in standards of evidence.

Rather than making her own culture the benchmark for good evidence, as Rorty does in his conversationalism and ethnocentrism, Haack makes human nature the benchmark of good evidence. As she phrases it herself,

> I would not say that 'all men by nature desire to know,' in the
> sense Aristotle intended; but a disposition to investigate, to
> inquire, to try to figure things out, *is* part of our makeup,
> though not, for many people, an overriding part. (EI:215)

For Haack, inquiry is a distinctly *human* affair, not a distinctly Western-European affair or a distinctly white-males-in-lab-coats affair. For Haack, concern for experiential anchoring and for explanatory integration is endemic to our species, and not, as she puts it, "a local quirk of 'our' criteria of evidence, in any parochial sense of 'our'" (EI:209). More concisely, dismissing Rorty's ethnocentric approach, Haack advocates for an anthropocentric epistemology:

> I see these standards—essentially, how well a belief is
> anchored in experience and how tightly it is woven into an
> explanatory mesh of beliefs—as rooted in human nature, in the
> cognitive capacities and limitations of all normal human
> beings.[181]

Foundherentism fits this bill. Regarding its truth-indicativeness, all it requires is that "our senses give us information about events around us and that introspection gives us information about our own mental goings-on" (EI:213). If we accept Haack's fallibilism (that we can be mistaken about anything, though not about everything), we can only assume this to be true whenever we engage in inquiry. Were we to believe that neither our senses, nor introspection would yield us any information—assuming we could even make sense of such an assumption—inquiry as we know it would be utterly pointless. And any theory that takes such a position puts itself, to use Lewis's phrase, beyond the pale of plausibility.

11.5 Against Vulgar Pragmatism

What Haack calls "vulgar pragmatism" is a particularly vocal branch of pragmatism that of late has received a wide following, especially among nonphilosophers. The vulgar pragmatists, of whom Haack considers Rorty the main spokesperson, maintain that the justification of our beliefs has nothing to do with truth—a view that they seek to give extra weight by explicitly allying themselves with the classical pragmatists, most specifically James and Dewey (although they are in fact closer to Schiller and the magical pragmatists Papini and Prezzolini). She calls it a *vulgar* pragmatism because of its appeal to the common people, as opposed to philosophy professors; because of its preference for the vernacular, as opposed to philosophy's (and logic's) technical jargon; and because of its consequent lack of cultivation (it tills the soil only lightly) and refinement (as there is little interest in precision and exactness). Put briefly, the vulgar pragmatists stress the common association of pragmatism with expedience rather than principle. Note that it is precisely this association of pragmatism with expediency that made Peirce shy away from the word.

Haack argues that the conversationalist turn Rorty has set in motion is the product of a misreading of the classical pragmatists; a misreading that is made possible by raising what may justifiably be called a false dichotomy: either accept a mirrorlike correspondence view, or else a nonrepresentational conversationalism. On the latter view, inquiry is no longer aimed at discovering how things really are, but at ensuring that the conversation continues, preferably in new and exciting venues.

It is difficult to deny that this dichotomy is too coarse. It leaves no room, for instance, for Dewey's "more sophisticated" correspondence theory (section 7.6), or, for that matter, for Haack's foundherentism. We must either accept a rather simplistic copy theory of knowledge or give up altogether on the project of ratification. Either our knowledge mirrors reality, or there can be no standards of evidence other than the approval of our peers. Who these peers are is always historically determined, and in the absence of any independent standards, we have no other option but to treat all peers as equal. We have no ground to separate the inquirers from the inquisitors, or the lone voice of reason from the angry mob. What counts is the approval of the strongest, meaning those best situated to carry forward the conversation to which we contribute.

Once the dichotomy is drawn like this, pragmatism, which really belongs somewhere in the middle, easily tips in the direction of conversationalism. Consequently, the vulgar pragmatist rejects Haack's project of ratification, arguing that all there is to the justification of belief is the approval of our peers; i.e., people whom *we* believe are competent to judge our beliefs. If conversationalism is granted, ethnocentricity is hard, if not impossible to avoid.

Haack dismisses this approach as disingenuous and cynical, as the aim of inquiry is no longer guided by a genuine desire to have our questions answered, but to find answers that will be approved by our peers, where that approval itself is similarly contingent on our approval of it. As a result, justification becomes a matter of convention. It is like paper money. I accept your dollar bills because you accept mine and vice versa, and it is because of this that dollar bills accrue their value. For the vulgar pragmatist, it is thus that beliefs get justified. The justification of belief, like the value of paper currency, is wholly a social institution that is maintained by convention. It also makes the justification of belief wholly a product of our choices, not something that is dictated by things on which we have at best only a limited control. The vulgar pragmatist's approach is cynical because the inquirer inquires *knowing* that the questions she asks cannot be answered and that the best to be hoped for is some consensus on how the fill the silence that follows the question. It is cynical, because the vulgar pragmatist seeks to rub out precisely what spurred the question.

11.6 Critical Common-Sensism

One way to further situate the above is by noting that Haack seeks to wedge a more reasonable option between two more extreme views that have become fashionable. The first, which she calls the old deferentialism, is the view that is found among many logical positivists and the scientistically inclined. Its focus is on "the logic of science," rationality, and objectivity. The second view, which she names the new cynicism and which includes the vulgar pragmatists, focuses on very different aspects, such as power, politics, and rhetoric. Whereas the old deferentialists revere science, the new cynics are deeply suspicious of it. To them all this talk about objectivity and scientific method is only a disguise for a policy of exclusion. For instance, in *Rethinking History,* Keith Jenkins writes, "History is a discourse, a language game; within it 'truth' and similar expressions are devices to open, regulate and shut down interpretations. Such truths are really 'useful fictions' that are in discourse by virtue of power."[182] There are no objective standards, but only power games.

For Haack, Peirce's critical common-sensism provides a *via media* between the old deferentialism and the new cynicism. Like the old deferentialist, the critical common-sensist maintains that there are

173

objective standards of better and worse evidence and of better and worse conducted inquiry. However, as the above account of Haack's views testifies, it sees those standards as more flexible and less formal than the old deferentialist does. Simultaneously, critical common-sensism meets the concerns of the new cynics halfway by acknowledging that science is a human enterprise in which inquirers have all sorts of motivations and in which observation is always already theory-laden. However, in contrast to the new cynics, the critical common-sensist does not see these aspects of inquiry as an impediment to the process of understanding how things truly are. Quite the contrary, the social nature of inquiry and the stubbornness of the world of facts tend to filter out personal idiosyncracies and group biases. Hence, pragmatists should be common-sensists that are driven by the will to learn while keenly aware of their fallibility.

12

The Prospects of Pragmatism

> For whatever else pragmatism is or is not, the pragmatic spirit is primarily a revolt against that habit of mind which disposes of anything whatever—even so humble an affair as a new method in Philosophy—by tucking it away . . . in the pigeon holes of a filing cabinet.
>
> —John Dewey[183]

Pragmatism is a restless doctrine. Peirce calls it "a house at war against itself concerning not inconsiderable questions," and there is much truth in that.[184] From the contemporary debate between Susan Haack and Richard Rorty, described in the last two chapters, it is moreover clear that this war is far from over. This perpetual conflict within pragmatism is often seen as a bad sign, making some, especially those who are desperate for certainty, ill at ease. Sometimes this restlessness and inner conflict is also taken as an indication that pragmatism has no inner core, that it is a mere agglomeration of loose strands that are historically related, but that never grew into a systematic whole. The preceding chapters show, however, that pragmatism is a well developed and well-thought-out philosophical position, or if one prefers a more conservative stance, that there is no reason to assume that pragmatism is any more disjointed than its competitors.

It is perhaps also good to reemphasize at this point that pragmatism is first of all (and most of all) a *method* for doing philosophy, and not a collection of set viewpoints on specific issues. At the same time, it is a method that strikes philosophy at its very core. As a doctrine of meaning, it forces us to rethink key philosophic notions, such as "truth," "mind," "identity," and "reality," so that a consistent application of this method

175

leads to a thoroughly pragmatized (or, if one prefers, pragmaticized) philosophy.

12.1 A Philosophy for Frontier Towns

Now, why be a pragmatist? In the first chapter I quoted Michael Novak who, in *American Philosophy and the Future,* attributes pragmatism's distinctive edge to the pioneer mentality that had crept into America's intellectual circles. Faced with the challenges of the new continent, the old rules and the closed universe they implied no longer worked. The pragmatism that grew out of this is a philosophy that is particularly suited for frontier towns; it is well-adapted to meet new challenges as well as traditional ones.

The Western frontier of the North American continent may have closed, but countless new ones have opened up, expanding our horizons in unexpected venues. Technological and social innovations have radically reshaped our world, and they will most likely continue to do so in dramatic ways. For example, one frontier that has opened up and that is widening itself rapidly is the increasing symbiosis of man and machine, from artificial knees and pacemakers to bionic eyes. Instead of using technology merely to replace biological functions, new innovations could be used to enhance or modify human capabilities. If bionic eyes are possible, why not widen the spectrum of our vision, for instance, to include infrared, which would give us night vision? If we can repair nerves running to the tactile receptors on our skin, why not put those receptors elsewhere or replace them altogether with electronic sensors? And by using radio transmission, touch would not even need to be continuous with our body. If technology progresses in such areas we might see radical changes in what we now call the human body, and our mind might become an altogether different beast.

Pragmatism is in important respects an outgrowth of the same modern scientific development that is opening up these new frontiers. Recall, for example, the influence of Darwin on the early pragmatists. And with its close link between knowledge and action, its future-directedness with its focus on practical consequences, and its conceptual flexibility without losing sight of reality, pragmatism seems of all the existing philosophical approaches best adapted to the challenges of our time.

12.2 Realistic Worldmaking

The focus on changing times should not be taken as an apology for relativism in whatever guise it may come (and I am including Rorty's ethnocentrism here). Yes, we *make* our world, but, to use Schiller's distinction, we don't *create* it. We have to be realistic. There is no escape from the fact that part of our world is as it is independent of what we may think about it, and even of what we may think about anything. Even though we may make ourselves doubt this in our brain (especially while doing professional philosophy), we cannot really doubt it in our heart. In fact, any genuine inquiry—that is any inquiry into a question with the belief that there is a right answer to it *and one that we might find*—presupposes this belief. This is true not only for the scientist, but also for the jury member who must decide a verdict in a trial and for the patient who wants her doctor to determine whether a lump in her breast is a malignant tumor, or not. This is not to imply that one can be absolutely certain of the answers one finds, not even when they happen to be true, for a proposition being true and the proposition being believed are altogether different issues. As has been shown, pragmatists found a third way out between dogmatism and skepticism. They are fallibilists. That is to say, they maintain that though we can be sure that many of our ideas are true, we cannot be absolutely certain of any single one of them. Our knowledge does not rest on poles, like the houses in Amsterdam, but it floats.

To be sure, there is always a human contribution to any knowledge claim. In fact, pragmatists passionately deny that we can be mere spectators and they make the circumstance that at all levels we are actual players in the world a central tenet in their thought. For the pragmatist there is no difference in kind between knowing and acting. Knowing is a species of acting and comes with all the subject-centeredness that accompanies acting. However, from the circumstance that the object inquired into cannot be disentangled from what the inquirer brings in—for instance in the form of a conceptual scheme or personal interests—it does not follow that what the object is depends wholly on the inquirer or does so even to any significant degree. In "The Will to Believe," James is very careful to note at the end that even though we are ultimately free to choose what to believe, we make that choice at our own peril, and we will have to face its consequences. As James puts it, "Each must act as he thinks best; and if he is wrong, so much the worse for him" (WJ:735).

Still, it is the frontier town with all its excitement, risks, rowdiness, and challenges that is paradigmatic for today's world, and not the quiet limestone cathedral with its solemn appeal to established tradition. The pragmatic maxim, Peirce's insistence on the scientific method and intellectual integrity, James's notion that pragmatism "unstiffens" our theories, the close connection between knowledge and action, and Dewey's focus on the indeterminate situation, make pragmatism particularly well-positioned as a philosophy to help us cope with the challenges of today, whether they are in pure mathematics, political theory, medical ethics, or philosophy itself.

Selective Bibliography

Abel, Reuben. *The Pragmatic Humanism of F. C. S. Schiller* (New York, 1955).

Aune, Bruce. *Rationalism, Empiricism, and Pragmatism* (New York, 1970).

Burke, F. Thomas, D. Micah Hester, and Robert B. Talisse (eds.). *Dewey's Logical Theory: New Studies and Interpretations* (Nashville, 2002).

TM Carnap, Rudolph. "Testability and Meaning." *Philosophy of Science* 3 (1936): 419–71; 4 (1937): 1–40.

Colella, Paul E. "Two Faces of Italian Pragmatism: The Prezzolini-Calderoni Debate, 1904–1905." *Transactions of the Charles S. Peirce Society* 30 (1994): 861–96.

Conkin, Paul K. *Puritans and Pragmatists* (New York, 1968).

Cooper, Wesley. *The Unity of William James's Thought* (Nashville, 2002).

Debrock, Guy. *Process Pragmatism: Essays on a Quiet Philosophical Revolution* (Amsterdam, 2003).

De Waal, Cornelis. *Susan Haack: The Philosopher Responds to Critics* (Amherst, forthcoming).

———. *On Peirce* (Belmont, 2001).

EW Dewey, John. *The Early Works, 1882–1898.* 5 vols. (Carbondale, 1967–72).

MW ———. *The Middle Works, 1899–1924.* 15 vols. (Carbondale, 1976–83).

LW ———. *The Later Works, 1925–1953.* 17 vols. (Carbondale, 1981–90).

———. *The Essential Dewey.* 2 vols. Edited by Larry Hickman and Thomas Alexander (Bloomington, 1998).

Dickstein, Morris (ed.). *The Revival of Pragmatism. New Essays on Social Thought, Law, and Culture* (Durham, 1998).

Diggins, John Patrick. *The Promise of Pragmatism: Modernism and the Crisis of Knowledge and Authority* (Chicago, 1994).

Fisch, Max H. *Peirce, Semeiotic, and Pragmatism* (Bloomington, 1986).

Gale, Richard. *The Divided Self of William James* (Cambridge, 1999).

Golino, Carlo L. "Giovanni Papini and American Pragmatism." *Italica* 32.1 (1955): 38–48.

Gunn, Giles B. *Beyond Solidarity: Pragmatism and Difference in a Globalized World* (Chicago, 2001).

DS Haack, Susan. *Evidence and Inquiry: Towards Reconstruction in Epistemology* (Oxford, 1993).

EI ———. *Manifesto of a Passionate Moderate* (Chicago, 1998).

M ———. *Defending Science—Within Reason* (Amherst, 2003).

Hall, David L. *Richard Rorty: Prophet and Poet of the New Pragmatism* (Albany, 1994).

Hausman, Carl R. *Charles S. Peirce's Evolutionary Philosophy* (Cambridge, 1993).

Hester, D. Micah and Robert B. Talisse. *On James* (Belmont, 2003).

On Pragmatism

Hickman, Larry. *Philosophical Tools for a Technological Culture: Putting Pragmatism to Work* (Bloomington, 2001).

Hook, Sidney. *Pragmatism, Democracy, and Freedom* (Amherst, 2002).

Hookway, Christopher. *Peirce* (London, 1985).

———. *Quine* (Stanford, 1988).

Innis, Robert E., *Pragmatism and the Forms of Sense: Language, Perception, Technics* (University Park, 2002).

MT James, William. *The Meaning of Truth* (Cambridge, Mass., 1975).

———. *Pragmatism* (Cambridge, Mass., 1975).

WJ ———. *The Writings of William James: A Comprehensive Edition.* Edited by John J. McDermott (Chicago, 1977).

EPh ———. *Essays in Philosophy* (Cambridge, Mass., 1978).

WB ———. *The Will to Believe and Other Essays in Popular Philosophy* (Cambridge, Mass., 1979).

———. *The Principles of Psychology.* 3 vols. (Carmbridge, Mass., 1981).

Ketner, Kenneth L. *A Comprehensive Bibliography of the Published Works of Charles Sanders Peirce.* 2nd ed. (Bowling Green, 1986).

Kuklick, Bruce. *The Rise of American Philosophy* (New Haven, 1977).

MWO Lewis, C. I. *Mind and the World Order: Outline of a Theory of Knowledge* (New York, 1929).

AKV ———. *An Analysis of Knowledge and Valuation* (La Salle, 1946).

CL ———. *Collected Papers of Clarence Irving Lewis* (Stanford, 1970).

Margolis, Joseph. *Reinventing Pragmatism: American Philosophy at the End of the Twentieth Century* (Ithaca, 2002).

Menand, Louis. *The Metaphysical Club: A Story of Ideas in America* (New York, 2001).

Misak, C. J. *Verificationism: Its History and Prospects* (New York, 1995).

———. *Pragmatism* (Calgary, 1999).

———. *Truth, Politics, Morality: Pragmatism and Deliberation* (London, 2000).

Misak, C. J. (ed.). *The Cambridge Companion to Peirce* (Cambridge, forthcoming).

LPP Morris, Charles W. *Logical Positivism, Pragmatism, and Scientific Empiricism* (Paris, 1937).

———. *The Pragmatic Movement in American Philosophy* (New York, 1970).

Mounce, H. O. *The Two Pragmatisms: From Peirce to Rorty* (New York, 1997).

Mulvaney, Robert J. and Philip M. Zeltner. *Pragmatism: Its Sources and Prospects* (Columbia, 1981).

Murphy, John. P. *Pragmatism: From Peirce to Davidson* (Boulder, 1990).

Novak, Michael (ed.). *American Philosophy and the Future* (New York, 1968).

Papini, Giovanni. "What Pragmatism is Like." *Popular Science Monthly* 71.10 (1907): 351–58.

———. *Four and Twenty Minds* (New York, 1971).

F ———. *The Failure.* (Westport, 1972). Published in Britain as *A Man–Finished.*

Parker, Kelly A. *The Continuity of Peirce's Thought* (Nashville, 1998).

CP   Peirce, Charles S. *The Collected Papers of Charles S. Peirce*. 8 vols. (Cambridge, Mass. 1931–35, 1958).

————. *Charles Sanders Peirce: Contributions to "The Nation"* (Lubbock, 1975).

W   ————. *The Writings of Charles S. Peirce: A Chronological Edition.* 30 vols. projected (1982–).

EP   ————. *The Essential Peirce.* 2 vols. (Bloomington, 1992, 1998).

Perry, Ralph B. *The Thought and Character of William James.* 2 vols. (Boston, 1935).

Posner, Richard A. *Law, Pragmatism, and Democracy* (Cambridge, Mass., 2003).

Pratt, Scott L. *Native Pragmatism: Rethinking the Roots of American Philosophy* (Bloomington, 2002).

Putnam, Hilary. *Pragmatism: An Open Question* (Oxford, 1995).

Putnam, Ruth Anna. *The Cambridge Companion to William James* (Cambridge, 1997).

TT   Quine, W. V. O. *Theories and Things* (Cambridge, Mass., 1981).

LPV   ————. *From a Logical Point of View* (Cambridge, Mass., 1953).

PPE   ————. "The Pragmatists' Place in Empiricism." In Mulvaney and Zeltner, pp. 21–39.

Rescher, Nicholas. *Realistic Pragmatism: An Introduction to Pragmatic Philosophy* (Albany, 2000).

Riccio, Peter M. *On the Threshold of Fascism* (New York, 1929).

R   Robin, Richard. *Annotated Catalogue of the Papers of Charles S. Peirce.* (Amherst, 1964).

MN   Rorty, Richard. *Philosophy and the Mirror of Nature* (Oxford, 1980).

CP   ————. *Consequences of Pragmatism* (Minneapolis, 1982).

CIS   ————. *Contingency, Irony, and Solidarity* (Cambridge, 1989).

PP   ————. *Philosophical Papers*. 3 vols. (Cambidge, 1991–1998).

PSH   ————. *Philosophy and Social Hope* (London, 1999).

Rosenberg, Jay. "Raiders of the Lost Distinction: Richard Rorty and the Search for the Last Dichotomy." *Philosophy and Phenomenological Research* 53 (1993): 195–214.

Rosenthal, Sandra B. *The Pragmatic a Priori: A Study in the Epistemology of C. I. Lewis* (St. Louis, 1976).

————. *Classical American Pragmatism: Its Contemporary Vitality* (Urbana, 1999).

Rumana, Richard. *Richard Rorty: An Annotated Bibliography of Secondary Literature* (Amsterdam, 2002).

Saatkamp Jr., Herman J. (ed.). *Rorty and Pragmatism: The Philosopher Responds to His Critics* (Nashville, 1995).

Schiller, F. C. S. *Riddles of the Sphinx: A Study in the Philosophy of Evolution* (London, 1891).

AP   ————. "Axioms as Postulates" in *Personal Idealism.* Edited by Henry C. Sturt (London, 1902), pp. 47–133.

On Pragmatism

————. *Humanism: Philosophical Essays* (London, 1903).

EB ————. "Pragmatism," *Encyclopaedia Britannica* 11th ed. (1911): 246–48.

————. *Formal Logic: A Scientific and Social Problem* (London, 1912).

————. *Studies in Humanism* (London, 1912).

HP ————. *Humanistic Pragmatism: The Philosophy of F. C. S. Schiller.* Edited by Reuben Abel (New York, 1966).

Schilpp, Paul Arthur (ed.). *The Philosophy of C. I. Lewis* (La Salle, 1968).

————. *The Philosophy of John Dewey* (La Salle, 1989).

Schneider, Herbert W. *A History of American Philosophy.* 2nd ed. (New York, 1963).

Searles, Herbert L., and Allan Shields. *A Bibliography of the Works of F. C. S. Schiller* (San Diego, 1969).

Seigfried, Charlene Haddock. *Pragmatism and Feminism: Reweaving the Social Fabric* (Chicago, 1996).

Shook, John R. *Pragmatism: An Annotated Bibliography, 1898–1940* (Amsterdam, 1998).

Sleeper, R. W. *The Necessity of Pragmatism: John Dewey's Conception of Philosophy* (New Haven, 1986).

Smyth, Richard A. *Reading Peirce Reading* (Lanham, 1997).

Talisse, Robert B. *On Dewey* (Belmont, 2000).

Thayer, H. S. *Meaning and Action: A Critical History of Pragmatism.* 2nd edition (Indianapolis, 1968).

Thompson Paul B. and Thomas C. Hilde. *The Agrarian Roots of Pragmatism* (Nashville, 2000).

Vailati, Giovanni. "A Study of Platonic Terminology." *Mind* 15 (1906): 473–85.

————. "Pragmatism and Mathematical Logic." *Monist* 16 (1906): 481–91.

West, Cornel. *The American Evasion of Philosophy: A Genealogy of Pragmatism* (Madison, 1989).

White, Morton. *Pragmatism and the American Mind* (London, 1973).

Wilshire, Bruce W. *The Primal Roots of American Philosophy: Pragmatism, Phenomenology, and Native American Thought* (University Park, 2000).

Winetrout, Kenneth. *F. C. S. Schiller and the Dimensions of Pragmatism* (Columbus, 1967).

Zanoni, Candido P. "Logical Pragmatism: The Philosophy of G. Vailati." Dissertation (University of Minnesota, 1968).

Endnotes

1. Peirce (Lubbock, 1975), 3:234.
2. WJ:86.
3. Max Weber, *The Protestant Ethic and the Spirit of Capitalism* (New York, 1958), p. 232; first published (in German) in 1904–5.
4. Novak (New York, 1968), p. 87. See also Waldo Frank, *Our America* (New York, 1919), p. 26–29.
5. Menand (New York, 2001), p. x.
6. Such as Albert Schinz's *Anti-Pragmatism* (Boston, 1909).
7. Bertrand Russell, *Philosophical Essays* (New York, 1966), p. 110; originally published in *Edinburgh Review,* April 1909.
8. Ibid.
9. G. K. Chesterton, *Orthodoxy* (London, 1908), p. 64.
10. Max Horkheimer, *Eclipse of Reason* (New York, 1974), p. 50.
11. Leon Kass, *Toward a More Natural Science* (New York, 1985), p. 98. For a more nuanced view, see Glenn McGee, *The Perfect Baby: A Pragmatic Approach to Genetics* (Lanham, 1997) and *Pragmatic Bioethics* (Nashville, 1999), edited also by McGee.
12. In a letter to Francis C. Russell, 17 August 1892. Unless stated otherwise, all references to correspondence are to the Peirce papers held at Harvard. See Robin (1964) for details.
13. René Descartes, *Meditations on First Philosophy,* Third Meditation.
14. The original thesis is present in Euclid's *Elements*, and was first refuted by Georg Cantor in the nineteenth century.
15. For a more extensive discussion, see Cornelis de Waal, "The Real Issue Between Nominalism and Realism, Peirce and Berkeley Reconsidered," *Transactions of the Charles S. Peirce Society* 32 (1996): 425–42.
16. J. J. Rousseau, *Emile* (London, 1911), par. 387.
17. René Descartes, *Principles of Philosophy,* Part 1, art. 45; G. W. Leibniz, "Reflections on Knowledge, Truth, and Ideas" in Philip Wiener (ed.), *Leibniz Selections* (New York, 1951): 283–90.
18. René Descartes, *Meditations on First Philosophy,* First Meditation.
19. A similar argument is given later by O. K. Bouwsma, "Descartes' Evil Genius," *Philosophical Review* 58 (1949): 26–36.
20. Also in the "Fixation of Belief" Peirce leaned in this direction, as can be seen from the example of the rotating disk of copper (EP1:112).
21. Aristotle's classic definition of truth as saying of what is that it is and of what is not that it is not (*Metaphysics*, 1077b26), would be an example of a conception of truth that reaches the second grade of

clearness.

22. See W 3.271f, 1878.

23. For some of these criticisms, see Cornelis de Waal, "Eleven Challenges to the Pragmatic Theory of Truth," *Transactions of the Charles S. Peirce Society* 35 (1999): 748–66.

24. WJ:387.

25. James (1981), p 23; original in italic.

26. Up to 1904 this text had only a limited circulation and for many James's *Varieties of Religious Experience* (New York, 1902) provided the first introduction into James's brand of pragmatism.

27. Arthur O. Lovejoy, "The Thirteen Pragmatisms," *Journal of Philosophy* 5 [1908]: 5–12, 29–39): 6–7.

28. An English translation of the essay is found in EPh. Both essays were products of the discussions held much earlier in the 1870s within the Metaphysical Club. See chapter 2.

29. Perry (1935), 2:409.

30. See e.g. Louis Menand, *The Metaphysical Club* (New York, 2001).

31. In 1905, James lamented: "I once wrote an essay on our right to believe, which I unluckily called the *Will* to Believe" (WJ:457).

32. W. K. Clifford, *Lectures and Essays* (New York, 1901), p. 175; first published in the *Contemporary Review* of January 1877, the same year Peirce's "The Fixation of Belief" appeared. Along the same vein, though not commented upon by Clifford, it would be wrong not to believe in cases where the evidence does warrant the belief.

33. Op. cit., p. 164f.

34. In "The Fixation of Belief," Peirce had paid little attention to the moral aspects of belief, focusing instead on the different ways in which belief can be fixed. It is clear, however, that Clifford would accept only Peirce's fourth method of fixing belief. As for Peirce himself, he would agree with James that this is too demanding.

35. WJ:353. The quotation is from Arthur James Balfour's *The Foundations of Belief* (London, 1894). Fifteen years earlier, in *A Defense of Philosophic Doubt* (London, 1879), Balfour had already tried to show that scientific knowledge depends just as much on an act of faith as does theology.

36. In a 26 March 1907 letter to Théodore Flournoy, James explains that Papini and Schiller had given him "great confidence and courage. I shall dedicate my book, however, to the memory of J. S. Mill."

37. Letter of 13 September 1907, included in Perry 2:480.

38. *The Meaning of Truth,* p. 50.

39. On James's theory of truth see, e.g., Hilary Putnam's "James's Theory of Truth" in (Putnam, 1997), H. S. Thayer's introduction to *The Meaning of Truth,* and Harvey Cormier's *The Truth is What Works: William James, Pragmatism, and the Seed of Death* (Landham, 2001).

40. It is worth mentioning that this "bundle theory of experiences" does have its precursors in both Locke and Berkeley. Locke and Berkeley quickly came to reject such a theory, however, and it might be objected, with James, that in the process of this they slipped back into old presuppositions on what lies beyond the "veil of ideas."

41. Locke, *Essay* (Oxford, 1975), IV.iv.8.

42. HP:70.

43. Protagoras's main argument is found in Plato's *Theaetetus* 166A–168B.

44. Review of *The Will to Believe* (*Mind* 6.24 [1897]: 547–54), p. 548.

45. Ibid.

46. "William James and the Making of Pragmatism" (*The Personalist* 8.2 [1927]:81–93), pp. 89–92.

47. "Humanism and Humanisms" *(The Personalist* 18.4 [1937]: 352–69): 363–67. The same comment is found in "William James and the Making of Pragmatism," pp. 89f.

48. "The Definition of 'Pragmatism' and 'Humanism'" (*Mind* 14.54 [1905]: 235–40), 239. This essay returns in a revised version in *Studies in Humanism.*

49. "Pragmatism and Pseudo-Pragmatism" *(Mind* 15.59 [1906]: 375–90), 377.

50. "Peirce and Pragmatism" *(The Personalist* 16.2 [1935]:169–73): 171.

51. "The Definition of 'Pragmatism' and 'Humanism'," p. 237f.

52. "Why Humanism?" in J. H. Muirhead (ed.) *Contemporary British Philosophy* (New York, 1924): 385–410, p. 397.

53. *Studies in Humanism,* p. 53.

54. Review of *The Will to Believe,* p. 548.

55. Op. cit., p. 551.

56. "The Definition of 'Pragmatism' and 'Humanism'," p. 236f.

57. "Peirce and Pragmatism" *(The Personalist* 16.2 [1935]:169–73), 170, 173.

58. "The Definition of 'Pragmatism' and 'Humanism'," p. 236f.

59. Included in MT.

60. "The Definition of 'Pragmatism' and 'Humanism'," p. 236f.

61. Ibid., p. 237.

185

62. In Wallace Nethery, "Schiller in the Library" *(The Personalist* 45.3 [1964]: 326–28), p. 327.

63. See his "The Objective Reality of Perspectives" in *The Philosophy of the Present* (Chicago, 1932), pp. 161–75.

64. From the program statement, *Leonardo* I.1 (1903): 1; tr. Riccio (1929), p. 48.

65. Georges Sorel, *De l'utilité du pragmatisme* (Paris, 1921), 21f.

66. On the German reaction to pragmatism, see Hans Joas, "American Pragmatism and German Thought: A History of Misunderstandings," in his *Pragmatism and Social Theory* (Chicago, 1993), pp. 94–121. See also Perry (1935), 2:579–82.

67. Interview with André Révesz, *Sunday Times,* 11 April 1926 (Late London Edition), 15–16; p. 15, col. 2.

68. H. W. Schneider, *Making the Fascist State* (New York, 1928), 310.

69. Cited in Riccio (1929), p. 33.

70. Henry James (ed.), *The Letters of William James* (Boston, 1920), 2:227.

71. Papini (1907), 354.

72. On the *Leonardo* period, see Walter L. Adamson, *Avant-Garde Florence: From Modernism to Fascism* (Cambridge, 1993), esp. ch. 2.

73. *Florence, Flower of the World* (New York, 1951), p. 135. See also Papini's essay on Da Vinci in *Four and Twenty Minds* (New York, 1971 [1922–1]), pp. 15–25. In this essay, Papini found the historical Leonardo too much of a positivist and replaced him with his own perception of Leonardo, shaped in way that better satisfied Papini's own needs and desires (what he called the "living Leonardo," as opposed to the "historical Leonardo").

74. From the program statement, *Leonardo* I.1 (1903): 1; tr. Riccio (1929), p. 48.

75. *"Campagna per il forzato risveglio"* (campaign for a forced awakening) *(Leonardo* [August 1906]: 193–99), p. 194.

76. *"Morte e resurrezione della filosofia,"* *Leonardo* 1.11/12 (December 1903): 1–7.

77. Schneider called Papini and Prezzolini "pre-fascists" (op. cit., 244).

78. Letter of 27 April 1906, reprinted in Giorgio Luti, *Firenze corpo 8: Scrittori, riviste, editori del '900* (Florence, 1983), p. 39; quoted, with omissions, in Perry (1935), 2:572.

79. *Sunday Times* interview with Révesz, p. 15, col. 1; emphasis added. On Mussolini's relation to pragmatism, see e.g., Thayer, p. 321–23; W. Y. Elliott, *The Pragmatic Revolt in Politics: Syndicalism, Fascism, and the Constitutional State* (New York, 1968), esp. pp. 313–50; H. W.

Schneider (op. cit.), esp. pp. 230–42; Horace Kallen, "Mussolini, William James, and the Rationalists," *Frontiers of Democracy* 4.35 (May 1938).

80. See e.g., Adamson (op. cit.), esp. pp. 79–94; E. Paul Colella "Philosophy in the Piazza: Giovanni Papini's Pragmatism and Italian Politics" *Journal of Speculative Philosophy* 11 (1997): 125–42.

81. *Il Popolo d'Italia,* 28 November 1914.

82. *Scritti* 66; translation, Zanoni (1968), 47.

83. *Scritti* 72; translation, Zanoni (1968), 50.

84. *Scritti* 75f; translation, Zanoni (1968), 51.

85. Vailati, "On Material Representations of Deductive Processes," *Journal of Philosophy* 5 (1908): 309–16, 311.

86. "L' 'arbitrario' nel funzionamento della vita psichica" (the 'arbitrary' in the functioning of psychic life), *Rivista di Psicologia Applicata* 6 (1910): 166–83; 234–48; 385–416), 403; tr. Zanoni (1968), 185. The "L'arbitrario," was published posthumously by Calderoni, based on notes he and Vailati had made before Vailati's death, and combined with passages from Vailati's earlier writings. It is not included in the *Scritti.*

87. *Scritti* 61; translation, Zanoni (1968), 35.

88. *Scritti* 923; translation, Zanoni (1968), 77.

89. "L'arbitrario" 245; translation, Zanoni (1968), 175.

90. "L'arbitrario" 247; translation, Zanoni (1968), 175.

91. *Scritti* 53; translation, Zanoni (1968), 194.

92. *Scritti* 573; translation, Zanoni (1968), 176.

93. *Scritti* 758; translation, Zanoni (1968), 149.

94. *Scritti* 152; translation, Zanoni (1968), 172.

95. *Scritti* 578; translation, Zanoni (1968), 154.

96. *Scritti* 578; translation, Zanoni (1968), 155.

97. *Leonardo* I.3 (January 1903), 3–4.

98. Giuseppe Prezzolini, *"La miseria dei logici I & II,"* *Leonardo* 1.4 (8 February 1903): 5–7; I.6 (8 March 1903): 7–8.

99. Prezzolini, cited in Colella (1994), 870f.

100. Prezzolini, cited in Colella (1994), 872.

101. Vailati "Un Manuale per i bugiardi: Prezzolini, *L'Arte di persuadere," Rivista de Psicologia Applicata* 2 (1907); *Scritti,* p. 770–76.

102. Calderoni, quoted in Colella (1994), 878.

103. *Leonardo* III (April 1905): 45–8.

104. Ibid., pp. 45f.

105. Ibid., p. 46.

On Pragmatism

106. Papini (1907), p. 352.

107. Ibid., pp. 352f.

108. *Leonardo* III (April 1905): 47 (ellipsis in original).

109. Papini (1907), p. 354.

110. "La fine" (the end), *Leonardo* V (August 1907): 257–63; passage quoted from pp. 262f.

111. R 279.

112. Perry (1935), 2:222.

113. Ibid.

114. Letter of James to Peirce of 22 December 1897.

115. Letter of Peirce to James of 4 January 1898.

116. Ibid.

117. Ibid.

118. The lectures are published as *Reasoning and the Logic of Things: The Cambridge Conference Lectures of 1898,* edited by Kenneth Laine Ketner (Cambridge Mass., 1992).

119. The Harvard lectures are included in EP2 as selections 10–16; a separate edition of the lectures, with extensive commentary, is published as *Pragmatism as a Principle and Method of Right Thinking,* edited by Patricia Ann Turrisi (New York, 1997).

120. Not quite demanding a proof, as did Peirce, James nonetheless published the first two of his 1906 Lowell lectures (later reprinted in *Pragmatism*) in the *Popular Science Monthly,* under the umbrella title "A Defense of Pragmatism."

121. WJ:363. It seems James is confusing Peirce's 1903 Harvard lectures on pragmatism with the Lowell lectures on logic which Peirce gave later that year. It is quite clear that James had the Harvard lectures in mind.

122. Alternatively, in his 1880 "On the Algebra of Logic" Peirce presented a neurophysiological derivation of logic; see W4:163–65.

123. John Cottingham, Robert Stoothoff and Dugald Murdoch (eds.) *The Philosophical Writings of Descartes* (Cambridge, 1985), I.15.

124. Ibid., see also I.120.

125. Turrisi, op. cit., p. 66.

126. Metaphysics, the third and final branch of philosophy studies phenomena in their thirdness.

127. Thomas Hobbes, *Selections* (New York, 1930), p. 23.

128. Letter from Peirce to James, 6 December 1904.

129. Letter from James to Peirce, 7 December 1904.

130. Letter from Peirce to James, 17 December 1904.

131. Letter to F. W. Frankland, 25 February, 1907.

132. Letter to Howes Norris Jr., 28 May 1912; emphasis added.

133. MW 10:460.

134. See esp. Jane Addams, *Twenty Years at Hull-House* (New York, 1910); Mary Lynn McCree Bryan and Allen Davis (eds.), *Hundred Years at Hull House* (Bloomington, 1990); Shannon Jackson, *Lines of Activity: Performance, Historiography, Hull-House Domesticity* (Ann Arbor, 2000).

135. Jane Addams (ed.) *Hull-House Maps and Papers, by Residents of Hull House: A Social Settlement* (New York, 1895).

136. For a detailed account, see *The Bertrand Russell Case,* edited by John Dewey and Horace M. Kallen (New York, 1941). See also Betrand Russell, *Why I am Not a Christian* (New York, 1957) and the appendix on the Russell case added to it by Paul Edwards.

137. A useful edition is John Shook (ed.) *The Chicago School of Functionalism. Volume 2: Studies in Logical Theory* (Bristol, 2001), which contains as an appendix all reviews of the book, including those of James and Schiller, and relevant correspondence between Dewey and Peirce.

138. Shook (op. cit.), p. 3.

139. CP 8.239; also in Shook (op. cit.), p. 21. The surviving manuscript of this letter, which was found among the Peirce papers at Harvard, appears to be either draft or a letter which Peirce decided not to send. No reply by Dewey to this letter was found.

140. British new realism centered around G. E. Moore and Bertrand Russell; American new realism was driven in part by the "Platform of Six Realists," which appeared in 1910. For an overview of the American movement, including Dewey's role in it, see Cornelis de Waal, *American New Realism 1910–1920*, 3 vols. (Bristol, 2001).

141. De Waal (op. cit.), 1:57.

142. CL:112.

143. Schilpp (1968), p. 16.

144. Ibid., p. 5.

145. From Royce's introduction to Henri Poincaré's *The Foundations of Science* (Lancaster, 1946), p. 17.

146. Daniel Robinson (ed.), *Royce's Logical Essays* (Dubuque, 1951), p. 93f.

147. See especially Lewis's "The Structure of Logic and Its Relation to Other Systems" *Journal of Philosophy* 18 (1921): 505–16.

148. This definition of the given comes close to Peirce's definition for "existence," which he distinguished from "reality." See e.g. CP 8.12.

149. *Essay* (Oxford, 1975), II.xiii.19.

150. Lewis's account shows certain similarities with Dewey's approach in chapter 10 of *The Quest for Certainty.* See White (1973), ch. 11.
151. Note that, for Lewis, the truth of a conditional is independent of the truth of its antecedent, so its truth can be asserted even when the antecedent is false.
152. LPP:22.
153. The monographs were published by the University of Chicago Press. The 19 monographs that appeared were later compiled in two volumes entitled *Foundations of the Unity of Science,* edited by Otto Neurath, Rudolph Carnap, and Charles Morris (Chicago,1955, 1970).
154. For an excellent overview, see George A. Reisch "A History of the *International Encyclopedia of Unified Science*," Dissertation (University of Chicago, 1995).
155. For a good overview and a selection of key texts, see A. J. Ayer (ed.), *Logical Positivism* (New York, 1959). See also Bruce Aune, *Rationalism, Empiricism, and Pragmatism* (New York, 1970).
156. Albert E. Blumberg and Herbert Feigl "Logical Positivism: A New Movement in European Philosophy" *(Journal of Philosophy* 28 [1931]: 281–96), p. 287.
157. "The Unity of Science as a Social Problem," in *Foundations of the Unity of Science,* pp. 29–38.
158. The papers for this session, as well as a partial account of the discussion, appeared in *Actes du huitième congrès international de philosophie à Prague 2–7 Septembre 1934* (Prague, 1936), pp. 121–160; a fifth speaker was H. Mehlberg.
159. "Die Methode der logischen Analyse," in *Actes du huitième congrès,* pp. 142–45; see esp. p. 143.
160. Carnap, *Philosophy and Logical Syntax* (London, 1937), p. 7.
161. Carnap in *Foundations of the Unity of Science,* 1:146.
162. Carnap, *Introduction to Semantics and Formalization of Logic* (Cambridge, Mass., 1961), p. 8.
163. Carnap in *Foundations of the Unity of Science,* 1:146; terms in square brackets added.
164. *Introduction to Semantics,* p. 9.
165. See "Meaning Postulates," *Philosophical Studies* 3 (1952): 65–73.
166. Rudolph Carnap, "Empiricism, Semantics, and Ontology," *(Revue International de Philosophie* 11 [1950]: 20–40), 31f. emphasis added.
167. Rudolph Carnap, *Logical Syntax of Language* (London, 1937), p. 52.

168. On verificationism and its relation to pragmatism, see Lewis, 1970; W. P. Alston, "Pragmatism and the Verifiability Theory of Meaning" *(Philosophical Studies* 6 [1955]: 65–71); Misak, 1995.
169. "Two Dogmas of Empiricism," LPV, 20–46; originally published in 1951. See also Morton White, "The Analytic and the Synthetic: An Untenable Dualism," in *Pragmatism and the American Mind* (London, 1973), and Stanley Munsat, *The Analytic-Synthetic Distinction* (Belmont, 1971).
170. LPV:42.
171. Ernest Gellner "The Last Pragmatist: The Philosophy of W. V. Quine," *Times Literary Supplement* (25 July 1975): 848–53.
172. Discarding practically all references to pragmatism, Quine included the first half of "The pragmatists' Place in Empiricism," which deals strictly with the development of empiricism under the title "Five Milestones of Empiricism" (TT 67–72).
173. Draft dated 22 August 1975; copy preserved in the Max H. Fisch Papers at the Peirce Edition Project, Indiana University, Indianapolis.
174. In Saatkamp (1995), p. 68.
175. Dewey also used the mirror metaphor (e.g., MW 3:318); see also Francis Bacon *New Organon* 1.41.
176. Wilfrid Sellars, *Science, Perception, and Reality* (New York, 1963), p. 170.
177. Rosenberg (1993), p. 201.
178. In Saatkamp (1995), p. 149.
179. M:2.
180. CP 7.49, 1.44; cited in M:49.
181. "A Foundherentist Theory of Justification," in Ernest Sosa and Jaegwon Kim (eds.) *Epistemology: An Anthology* (Oxford, 2000), pp. 226–36, p. 233.
182. Keith Jenkins, *Re-thinking History* (London, 1991), p. 32.
183. LW 17:39f.
184. Peirce (Lubbock, 1975), 3:234; see also the preface to the current volume.

Index